S0-BMY-535

The
Elusive

Policy
ur II

DATE DUE			

The Elusive Enemy

American Foreign Policy
Since World War II

Simon Serfaty
University of California, Los Angeles

Little, Brown and Company
Boston

Library of Congress Catalog Card No. 70-184241

First Printing

Published simultaneously in Canada
by Little, Brown & Company (Canada) Limited

Printed in the United States of America

To Kathleen

Preface

We reappraise in the present the actions of the past in order to avoid repeating mistakes when facing the difficult problems of the future. Over the last few years the problem that has dominated American life is the war in Vietnam. The war, however, has been a belated "discovery," for, potentially at least, it has represented an integral part of American foreign policy in the post–World War II era.

With the war in Vietnam very much in the background, I have attempted in this short book to narrate and to interpret the growth of American interventionism after World War II. In so doing, I have also attempted to place the present in perspective and to treat, as Louis Halle put it, the cold war as history. It is a narration generally without heroes, and perhaps even without villains. The analyst of foreign policy questions, may well resemble Camus's judge-penitent: he makes judgments reluctantly because these judgments are usually made upon himself as well.

The purpose of this book is to examine some of the main events that have shaped American foreign policy in Europe and in Asia. These events include the beginnings of the cold war, the application of containment to Europe and its extension to Asia during and after the war in Korea, and the solidification of a globalist outlook during the years when John Foster Dulles was heading the State Department. These events and the policies related to them are examined in detail in Chapters 2 through 5. In the next three chapters, the situations that were particularly significant in the sixties, and continue to be significant, are discussed: the disarray in the Atlantic Alliance, the dilemmas of nuclear weapons, and the quagmire in Indochina. In Chapter 1, some major features of the Vietnam debate are placed within the historical framework of the isolationist-interventionist controversy. In the concluding chapter, Chapter 9, I have offered some preliminary observations on the way in which President Nixon's foreign policy relates to this debate.

This study is not intended to be a comprehensive one. In space it is essentially confined to Europe and Asia; it does not deal explicitly with such questions as the domestic determinants of foreign policy. In time it begins late and ends late. In theory, it does not attempt to set a specific conceptual framework. In practice, it flirts with many revisionist views without endorsing them, be it on the cold war, containment, or Indochina. Yet, the observations that can be made about American experience in Europe and Asia can be adequately extended to problems likely to emerge elsewhere. Foreign policy after World War II departed from tradition enough to justify it as the starting point of this study; and the information presently available on Nixon's foreign policy is sufficient to justify a nonpolemical evaluation of it. Theoretical books on international relations abound; it is time for academicians to make their writing more immediately and publicly relevant to policy questions. Foreign policy is unfortunately such that definite conclusions are all too often pretentious and inadequate.

I have often wondered whether it is not true, as A. J. P. Taylor once claimed, that the best diplomats are those who do

not know what they are doing. Events unfold, sometimes foreseen, sometimes unexpectedly. They make the best policies fail,
and they also make the worst policies succeed. Presidents Truman, Eisenhower, and Nixon all have had their "doctrines."
Presidents Kennedy and Johnson both had their "grand designs."
Yet, many of their diplomatic successes were achieved outside the
guidelines set by their respective doctrines and designs; many of
their failures were met on the basis of their doctrines and designs.
For, as George Kennan, who once headed the Policy Planning Staff
at the White House, put it: "One moves through life like someone
moving with a lantern in dark woods. A bit of the path ahead is
illuminated and a bit of the path behind. But the darkness
follows hard on one's footsteps, and envelops our trail as one
proceeds."

Acknowledgments

I am greatly indebted to those who helped me in writing this book. Special gratitude goes to Robert W. Tucker, whose influence on my own thinking is apparent in repeated instances throughout the following pages. Helpful criticisms and suggestions were provided by my colleagues Richard Baum and Bernard Brodie. William Gerberding and Robert E. Osgood also read parts of the manuscript in its initial form. Stephen Baker, a promising young scholar, provided me with invaluable research assistance on certain portions of this book, especially Chapter 8.

As always my sister Reinette has been of inestimable sustenance and help. I should like to thank her here. Finally, this book is dedicated to Kathleen, whose toleration and love comforted me at every stage of writing and editing.

Contents

The Elusive Enemy

*American Foreign Policy
Since World War II*

1

**The
Protracted
Debate**

The Formative Years

In the manner America conducts its foreign policy, there is
an open invitation to debate it and to struggle for the undisputed
privilege of directing it. This phenomenon must be explained by
the manner in which American foreign policy is presented to the
public, wrapped in a sweeping rhetoric that commits the country
to grandiose but often questionable policies. Frequently more
responsive to what needs to be stated domestically than to what
can be done internationally, official declarations and policies may
generate popular frustrations and ultimately lead to "great debates" as public opinion, when finally aroused, is polarized into
two camps, one favorable and the other hostile to the government's actions.

A national propensity to public debates is further related to

1

the constitutional ambiguity of who makes foreign policy. The president alone takes responsibility for any action at any one moment. But his decisions are made against a background that includes many individual and institutional actors who regard themselves qualified, in the words of a noted foreign analyst, "to declare policy, denounce it, influence it, correct it, or comment on it," thus making the United States "the most verbose democracy in history."[1] Finally, public debates are also promoted by the vacuum of information and, until recently, the lack of active participation by the general public. Long in the dark age of international ignorance, the American people have remained receptive to a Manichean and jingoistic description of the world, a description where national forces of good, justice, and freedom can easily be distinguished from foreign forces of evil, injustice, and tyranny.

That the American people should have become engaged, in the mid-sixties, in a major controversy over the nature, the objectives, and the instruments of their foreign policy is by itself not very startling. This controversy, inasmuch as it questioned America's role in the world, began even before the Republic was founded and has been pursued uninterruptedly ever since. Throughout the eighteenth century, the colonists resented the burdens inflicted upon them by wars waged in America for the sake of non-American interests. They felt that the colonies were used as expendable tools by the European Great Powers, then the primary if not the only actors in world politics. It was shocking, wrote Thomas Paine in 1776, that "America, without the right of asking why, must be brought into all the wars of another, whether the measure be right or wrong, or whether she will or not." The Republic about to be formed would equate its independence from external domination with independence from entanglement in other states' disputes. Noninvolvement in the "contests, broils, and wars of Europe," as Hamilton later put it, was therefore the ultimate objective. "England to Europe, America to itself," concluded Thomas Paine, who described as "common sense" his belief that the true interest of America was to steer clear of European contentions.[2] So convinced of this was Jefferson that he anticipated a day when "we may formally require a meridian of partition through the ocean which separates the two hemispheres, on the hither side of which no European gun shall ever be heard, nor an American on the other . . ." [3]

The search for isolation from the political ills that plagued the European continent was prudent and necessary, based as it was on the intrinsic weakness of the new American state and its need to provide more substance and cohesion to its territorial skeleton. "Young as we are," wrote Jefferson at the turn of the nineteenth century, "and with such a country before us to fill with people and with happiness, we should point in that direction the whole generative force of nature." [4] A seed time was required to absorb the continuous flow of immigrants, reconcile regional and national interests, and explore, exploit, and develop all available resources. America's isolationist impulse thus emerged as a tactical approach to foreign policy, a means toward national goals of internal expansion and external preservation. But in order to be secured such an impulse might occasionally require American intervention in European affairs: in his Farewell Address, George Washington pointedly recommended that the principle of non-entanglement be occasionally discarded in "extraordinary emergencies" and in order to keep America's defensive posture "respectable."

In dealing with interventionism, President Washington was already experiencing the inherent difficulty of determining when to intervene and when not to intervene. Clearly, he preferred the latter. But in not overlooking the former option the retiring president was laying down rules so general that they depended almost entirely upon the circumstances that would surround some specific situation in the future. When were emergencies truly extraordinary and when did America's defensive posture cease to be respectable? In other words, when should the ordinary policy of isolation give way to an extraordinary policy of intervention and how long ought such a shift last? Clearly extraordinary was the situation in 1778, when the colonists concluded an alliance with the king of France to secure their independence from England. But to what extent was America's national interest threatened in 1812 when, in the midst of the Napoleonic wars then being waged in Europe, the United States declared war on Great Britain — a war that became, in the words of an eminent American historian, "the most unpopular war that this country has ever waged, not even excepting the Vietnam conflict?" [5] At the time, many deplored President Madison's action as a destructive policy by which national felicity had been converted into insecurity and humiliation. These early dissenters rightly believed that America did not have the resources needed to fulfill its objectives in entering the war. Already they derided overbearing commitments to national self-abnegation: "The United States," Madison had proclaimed in 1804, "owes it to the world as well as to themselves to let the example of one government at least, protest against the corruption which prevails." [6] But these early dissenters also denied that any part of America was endangered by England or any of its land-locked allies: "Happy in its local relations; removed from the bloody theater of Europe . . . with territorial possessions exceeding every real want . . . from invasion nothing to fear; from acquisition nothing to hope," America had little to gain from such a conflict.[7] Conversely it was feared that the country had much to lose being on the side of France and against the rest of Europe, because in the aftermath of the war it would be exposed either to retaliation from the other European powers (now free to join hands against the diplomatically isolated United States) or to the vassalage of the victorious French emperor.

Yet intervention appeared to be required because in 1812, as at any other time, isolation remained possible only through intervention. Intervention indicated America's resolve to prevent, actively when necessary, the conditions in Europe that might lead any nation or group of nations to contemplate a direct attack upon the United States. As Jefferson put it at the time, "We especially ought to pray that the powers of Europe may be so poised and counterpoised among themselves that their own security may require the presence of all their forces at home leaving the other parts of the world in undisturbed tranquility." [8] Thus, intervention and nonintervention complemented each other within the continued balance of power in Europe, and the American position varied according to the shifts of the balance. On the side of England's ascendancy on the ocean in 1806, the United States was wishing success to Napoleon in 1807 when, after the *Chesapeake* affair in June of that year, war with Great Britain appeared probable. But in the summer of 1808, with

Napoleon invading Spain, Jefferson turned again toward Great Britain because he feared that Napoleon's victory in Spain might spell America's misfortune even more directly by forcing Spain to concede the Floridas to the French. As Alexander Hamilton frankly put it, the "coolest calculations of interest" prevented America from becoming the instrument of, or allied to, the ambitions of any single European nation. The threat was thought to be self-evident: such a nation, "aggrandized by new acquisitions and her enemies reduced by dismemberments," might then become "the mistress of Europe, and consequently, in a great measure, of America." [9]

As the nineteenth century wore on, however, isolation took the appearance of a divine privilege, the perceived outcome of American national wisdom and superior virtue. Yet, still unanswered, some earlier questions continued to be argued in a protracted debate. What was the content of America's national interest? Was it confined to the Western Hemisphere, or did it extend beyond physical bounds and necessitate the support of any group throughout the world fighting for similar democratic ideas? And if the latter, what form should American support of such groups take?

These questions had all been raised and argued during the Napoleonic wars. But throughout the nineteenth century they gained new intensity as the prudent and sober calculation of the early years of the Republic yielded to a growing confidence in the nation's capacity to defend its interests and to uphold justice for all. In the 1820's, for example, public enthusiasm for Greece's resistance against Turkey was placed in its true perspective by John Quincy Adam's portrayal of the United States as "the well wisher to the freedom and independence of all, [but] . . . the champion and vindicator only of her own." [10] In opposing President Monroe's temptation to intervene in Greece, John Quincy Adams, then secretary of state, also needed to question America's relationship with Europe and the conservative Holy Alliance, which had been formed following the defeat of France in 1815. Did such an alliance affect the security of the United States, either territorially or spiritually, by undermining the humanistic foundation upon which the new Republic rested?

Speaking, however ambiguously, in favor of intervention,

Daniel Webster, then at the beginning of his political career, advocated that as one of the nations of the world "a part we must take, honorable or dishonorable, in all that is done in the civilized world." And Webster asked that the American people actively oppose "the doctrines . . . [that] prostrate the liberties of the entire civilized world." [11] Those against intervention, on the other hand, wanted the United States to continue emphasizing domestic matters over international questions and to limit its objectives to the prosperity and security of its own citizens. Americans had enough to do at home, they suggested, without adding the problems of other nations whose relevance to America's safety and well being was, to say the least, dubious. They saw America's resources as too scarce to implement a policy of active opposition to more powerful European nations. "Because the world is full of oppression," wondered Representative Silas Wood of New York, "is this government the Hercules that is to free it from the monsters of tyranny and slavery? And are we bound to emulate the chivalrous achievements of the renowned Knight of La Mancha, by engaging in conflict with every windmill that we may in the delirium of our frenzy, imagine to be a tyrant?" [12]

Later on, in 1851, public support for Hungary reached its peak when Louis Kossuth, the Magyar leader, visited the United States. Kossuth was one of the first revolutionary leaders to experience America's verbal recklessness and moderate actions. So, Daniel Webster, by then secretary of state, warmly applauded "Hungarian independence, Hungarian self-government, Hungarian control of Hungarian destinies." However, he carefully emphasized that such preference did not imply America's willingness to depart from its proclaimed neutrality. As in the case of Greece earlier, Webster's conception of an American intervention did not involve more than using "the vast moral force" of public opinion. President Filmore added to this his own pledge that America would "pray" for Kossuth and the Hungarians whatever might become of them.[13] But beyond the rhetoric most of those involved, in and out of office, agreed with Henry Clay's assertion that "far better it is for ourselves, for Hungary and for the cause of liberty; that adhering to our wise pacific system and avoiding the distant wars of Europe, we should keep our lamp burning brightly on this western shore, as a light to all nations, than to hazard its utter extinction, amid the ruins of fallen and falling republics in Europe." [14]

Isolationism, however, or "American continentalism" as the historian Charles Beard called it, was not a self-denying policy: from the beginning, America's effort to avoid an active role in the world scene was repeatedly challenged not only from within but from without as well.[15] Throughout the nineteenth century, European nations attempted to gain America's participation in the search for international order. But Americans remained adamantly opposed to multilateral intervention, whether by policy, such as the Holy Alliance for which Russia's Czar Alexander offered America full membership, or by mediation, such as when America was asked to help devise a settlement on the future status of the Congo in the Berlin Conference of 1884. At the same time, though, successive administrations in Washington practiced a policy of unilateralism that paid limited attention to the interests of other nations: the naval expeditions against the Barbary Pirates in North Africa (1801–1805), the involvement (mostly diplomatic) in Liberia in the 1820's, the incidents surrounding Commodore Perry's opening of commercial relations with Japan in 1854, the intervention in China where British soldiers were rescued by an American force in 1859, and the shooting in Korea in 1871. In all such cases the United States displayed the flag where and when words were no longer sufficient. Thus, President McKinley's remark, in the aftermath of the war with Spain, that "in a few short months [America] has become a world power" was an erroneous assessment of America's abstention as well as a confused representation of America's rise as a world power.[16] For such a position had been reached much earlier: in the ten years that preceded the "little glorious war of 1898," as Secretary John Hay called it, the United States had decisively coped with Germany over the Samoa scramble in 1889, with Italy over the New Orleans lynching bee in 1891, and with Great Britain over the Venezuela boundary question in 1896. But too serious trouble was avoided and none of these crises erupted into war.

The confusion between isolationism and interventionism reached its peak with World War I. America entered the European war when the aggressive continental land power of Germany was about to achieve hegemony in Europe by defeating the British sea power and to acquire simultaneously the mastery of the Atlantic Ocean. The very month that war was declared by America, Britain lost 880,000 gross tons of shipping, several times more than what it could possibly replace. In that same month, mutinies in the French army made France's future in the war questionable. Russia, the third member of Europe's Triple Entente, was but a few months away from its internal collapse. Much of this, however, was not known to President Wilson at the time and, in justifying America's intervention, Wilson further confused national ideals with principles of national interest. At first, the American president explained his decision to the American people on legalistic grounds by defending ancient concepts of neutral rights upon the seas. Later, in need of popular enthusiasm, Wilson raised his approach to a still higher moralistic level and transformed the war into a philanthropic crusade — "to serve and save the world at whatever cost for America" — a crusade that would end all wars and make the world safe for democracy.[17] "It would be," as Mr. Wilson put it in his Message to Congress on January 18, 1918, "the culminating and final war for human liberty." [18] Speaking in favor of the president's War Message of April 1917, Representative Ferris' words represented a typical public-minded endorsement of the presidential belief: "Ours," he stated, "is a war against crime, against murder, against autocracy, against militarism, against the overthrow of our freedom and liberty, against imperialism; ours is a war for democracy, for justice, for freedom, for liberty, and that the republics of the world may endure and live." [19]

Having oversold the war, the Wilson administration proceeded to oversell the peace. The American people were promised a concert for peace among democratic nations, a "league of honor, a partnership of opinion," which would eliminate the warlike plottings of inner circles.[20] President Wilson further predicted the international abandonment of selfish national purposes for the common and peaceful purposes of enlightened mankind. "The interests of all nations," he declared on September 27, 1918, "are our own also. . . . There is nothing that the United States wants for itself that any other nation has." [21] America was the first nation to substitute goals of self-abnegation for the more traditional ones of self-preservation, Wilson argued throughout 1919. The country had entered the war neither for its redemption, as it had not been directly attacked, nor for its salvation, as it had not been immediately in danger, but only for the salvation of mankind. President Wilson predicted that other nations would follow suit once the way had been shown.

In the aftermath of the war, a comparison was unavoidably made between the causes of intervention (as presented to the American public) and its results. Clearly, great expectations for peacetime had come out of the lofty expectations raised in wartime. These could not be, and were not, satisfied. The compromises secured from President Wilson at the peace conference of Versailles by European statesmen more concerned with security than with moral principle could not easily be understood and accepted by the American people who rejected Wilson, Versailles, and Europe altogether.

It is not surprising that this first total challenge to nonparticipation in world affairs was followed by a counterreaction of withdrawal. Never since the early years of the nineteenth century had the American people been exposed to the realities of either interventionism or isolationism. Their security unaffected by the necessities of national expediency, with no great power neighbor nearby, and developing in a century of relative international order, 1815 to 1914, Americans grew accustomed to equating their ideal expectations with international realities. At a time when standing armies in Europe reached several hundred thousand men, the United States Army was almost always below thirty thousand men between 1817 and 1900. The lesser relevance of world affairs was also illustrated by the ever-diminishing status of America's secretaries of state. In early American history, being secretary of state was a major step on the way to the presidency: before 1861, six secretaries of state became presidents. After the Civil War, however, no secretary of state ever became president.[22] Moreover, the ambiguity of the Western cause during World War I played a substantial part in building a counterreaction to that intervention as historians soon began reappraising the outbreak of the war as well as the causes of American participation in it.

World War II could be more easily understood both idealistically as a just war, particularly as Hitler's rhetoric was being acted upon, and realistically as a necessary war, particularly as Hitler's blitzkrieg was gaining momentum. To accept it as a just war made it a necessary war anyway, regardless of how well the security argument was conveyed.* After the passage of the Lend-Lease bill in 1941, America behaved as if it understood its security interests in Europe. Indeed, to many, Lend-Lease seemed to signify the death of isolationism. "We have tossed Washington's Farewell Address into the discard," Senator Vandenberg, then an ardent isolationist, complained in his diary. "We have thrown ourselves squarely into the power politics and the power wars of Europe, Asia, and Africa. We have taken the first step upon a course from which we can never hereafter retreat." [23]

Not just a change of heart but changes of circumstances seemingly made isolationism, in the words of General Marshall, "just wrong generally." [24] No longer could Great Britain or any other state be counted upon to prevent an expansionist nation from gaining hegemony in Europe. No longer could geography protect America's security as technological developments made obsolete the protection provided by the Atlantic. Conceived as a necessary policy, isolationism became a policy of choice when

---

* That the security argument was well considered is illustrated by a letter that William C. Bullitt, then the United States ambassador in Paris, sent to President Roosevelt on May 16, 1940. Reporting on the need for America's quick support of France and Britain, Bullitt explained: "The moral for us is that unless some nation in Europe stands up to Germany publicly, France and England may face defeat and such defeat would mean the French and British fleets in the hands of the Germans and the Italians. We should then have the Japs in the Pacific and an overwhelming fleet against us in the Pacific." (The *New York Times,* April 26, 1970). The vision of Germany's victory was repugnant to Roosevelt too. On June 10, 1940, he described the United States existing as an island of peace in a world of brutal force as "a delusion." "Such an island," the American president declared, "represents to me and to the overwhelming majority of Americans today a helpless nightmare of a people without freedom — the nightmare of a people . . . fed through the bars from day to day by the contemptuous, unpitying masters of other continents." (Cited in Robert A. Divine, *Roosevelt and World War II* [Baltimore, 1969], p. 31.) Yet, during his campaign Roosevelt pledged, on October 30, 1941: "To you mothers and fathers, I give you one more assurance. I have said this before, but I shall say it again and again and again: Your boys are not going to be sent into any foreign war . . ." (*Ibid,* p. 37).

the weaknesses of the infant Republic appeared overcome and the conditions that made such isolationism possible appeared forgotten. Originally regarded as an "extraordinary" option, intervention became a necessary policy as the American continent drifted closer and closer to Europe and to Asia and as the conditions that had made long periods of isolation possible were irreversibly transformed. In 1945 and thereafter, America was too much of a power to be left out of power politics.

From Isolationism to Globalism

For those in the forties who expressed doubts over America's capability to sustain its interventionist spirit, the controversies of the sixties may have seemed to justify earlier warnings. To President Truman, for example, the isolationist bloc appeared to grow bolder as victory in Europe approached. "The country was being flooded with isolationist propaganda under various guises, and many of us were apprehensive lest the isolationist spirit again become an important political factor." [25] In 1971, President Nixon echoed Truman when he stated in a major foreign policy address, "After a long and unpopular war, there is temptation to turn inward — to withdraw from the world, to back away from our commitments." [26] But granted such inward contemplation, the isolationist spirit of 1971 still presented a character markedly different from that of the late forties. By 1971, neo-isolationism implied a rejection of Asia as the cornerstone of United States national interest, a complaint that allies were not backing up American interventions, and the desire for a negotiated settlement of disputes with the Soviet Union and China. In 1950, neo-isolationism had implied exactly the reverse: a rejection of Europe as the cornerstone of United States national interest, a "the hell with the allies" outlook, and the refusal to negotiate with the communist world. The apprehension of the Truman years — that America might not remain willing to intervene — was transformed, in the late sixties, into the apprehension that it had become excessively eager to intervene. Doubts of America's aptitude in dealing with other nations (because of its alleged inexperience in such matters) were replaced by fears that somehow America had gone from historical immaturity to historical senility as, according to some critics, it persisted in offering outdated solutions for new problems. For, to these same critics, America's timidity in relying upon power had given way to an alleged arrogance of power while old myths, instead of being finally corrected, had simply grown older and hopes of a peaceful and just world had perished in revolutionary warfare.[27]

In the aftermath of World War II, the escalation of interventionism started with the inflated rhetoric of the Truman Doctrine (1947). This doctrine set the conceptual framework that fostered the Atlantic Alliance (1949), through which the United States committed itself to the defense of much of Western and Southern Europe, ANZUS (1951), which committed Washington to the defense of Australia and New Zealand, the Southeast Asia Treaty (SEATO, 1954), and, by association, the Central Treaty (CENTO, 1954), which filled the alliance gap in Asia from Iran to the Philippines. The Middle East Resolution (1957) also pledged America to the defense of the Arab states against internal subversion, and bilateral defense arrangements were concluded with Japan (1951), South Korea (1953), and the Republic of China (1954). Since the Rio Pact (1947), the United States had reaffirmed its commitment to the defense of the entire Western Hemisphere. Finally, the United States continued to endorse all United Nations actions, not only in Korea, but also in the Congo, Rhodesia, the Middle East, and other troubled areas. By 1971, the United States had over 500,000 soldiers stationed in approximately 30 countries, not including the 185,000 troops fighting in Vietnam at the end of the year and the Atlantic and Pacific fleets that amounted to about 650,000 men. At that time, the United States operated 429 major bases overseas and 2,297 lesser bases that cost approximately $4.8 billion a year. A member of four regional defense alliances and an active participant in a fifth alliance, America had signed mutual defense treaties with 42 different nations, was a member of no less than 53 international organizations, and, in 1967, maintained diplomatic missions in 117 countries.[28] Lost among all these, there had been an ambiguous commitment to the noncommunist part of Indochina where the desirability of such a wide distribution of American resources received its first, true public challenge.

It was not so much, then, that the United States had suddenly become morally and politically "overcommitted," to use the expression that was particularly fashionable among foreign policy critics in the second half of the sixties. Overcommitment, if overcommitment there was, had been with America for many years before it became a national issue. But its sudden discovery was related to a "new" perception of American interests and American needs, both abroad and at home, a perception that de-emphasized the urgency and scope of the external threat to American security while it overemphasized the urgency and scope of the domestic threat to America's own order. That foreign policy requirements were less important and more expendable than domestic reforms appeared to be particularly plausible because the test case for foreign policy needs occurred in the worst place (Asia had not been a part of the United States postwar foreign policy consensus) and at the worst time (a growing dismemberment of the domestic consensus followed President John F. Kennedy's assassination).

The Vietnam War:
Limits of Dissent Reexamined

During the second half of the sixties, the uniqueness of domestic dissent on foreign policy questions was not because of the mere existence of dissent, nor even because of the impressive passion and bitterness that frustrations over the war in Vietnam progressively aroused. Such passion and bitterness had occurred on numerous occasions in the past. In April 1847, the Massachusetts legislature had overwhelmingly adopted a set of resolutions against the Mexican War that would have intimidated many of the most ardent dissenters of 1970. The resolution read in part: "That such a war of conquest, so hateful in its objects, so wanton, unjust and unconstitutional in its origin and character, must be regarded as a war against freedom, against humanity, against justice, against the Union . . . and against the free States." [29] What was new in the sixties was the inability of successive administrations to manage the dissent they faced at home, an inability particularly striking in wartime.

President Johnson's failure to manage the dissent was related to the unique opposition he encountered. Going beyond party lines and ideological affiliations, the new dissenters came from the very groups that had provided the main support for American foreign policy since the end of World War II.* These were not professional dissenters. They had faithfully supported the growth of American commitments since World War II and had rejected the arguments used by early foreign policy critics. As the United States system of alliances was spreading, Reinhold Niebuhr, for example, had repeatedly warned against a "budding American imperialism" engineered by "eminent proconsuls . . . partly drawn from the army and partly from business." [30] American power in the service of American imperialism, Niebuhr continued, would create wrong situations, which Americans would be unable to correct because of their very idealism. And Walter Lippmann, speaking out even before the Korean War led to the actual globalization of America's policy of containment of communism, had attacked a policy that required the "recruiting, subsidizing and supporting of a heterogeneous array of satellites, clients, dependents, and puppets." Once completed, Lippmann argued in 1947, such a "coalition of disorganized, disunited, feeble, or disorderly nations, tribes and factions," was bound to present America with "accomplished facts that we did not intend . . . crises for which we are unready . . . [and] an unending series of insoluble dilemmas." [31]

But throughout the sixties, as such prophecies appeared to be proved right, identical arguments were adopted and enlarged upon by an increasing number of national figures who had previously ignored them. Consequently, foreign policy questions were promptly brought to popular attention in various ways, including Senator Fulbright's televised Senate Hearings of 1966 and the 1968 presidential elections, when peace in Vietnam grew

---

* On March 9, 1971, President Nixon described as the "real problem" the defection of America's foreign policy "establishment," namely, "the people who, after World War II, supported the Greek-Turkish aid program, the Marshall Plan, NATO." It is ironic, commented the president, "that the great internationalists of the post–World War II period have become the neo-isolationists of the Vietnam war period and especially of the period accompanying the ending of that war." (The *New York Times*, March 10, 1971.)

into one of the major campaign issues. The growth of dissent continued despite repeated attempts to explain and to justify American policy in Southeast Asia. In turn, these justifications often raised new limits to presidential action. In May 1970, President Nixon's dispatch of troops in Cambodia created enough unrest throughout the country to have the president set specific limits in time and space to the military action he had just ordered.

Significantly, it was not only the war in Vietnam that was brought to public debate. To many of the dissenters, the war could not be accepted as either an accident caused by bad luck or as an aberration stemming from the ineptitude of some high level officials. Instead they described it, and criticized it, as the logical outcome of a policy that had always made such outcomes possible.* Thus, within the framework of the 1960's they were still raising the same unanswered questions that had been asked in the 1820's. How much intervention did America need for its security? How much intervention could it afford? Where, when, and how should it be undertaken? There was one major difference between these questions and those of a century before, however, namely that this time the debate was no longer one between interventionists and isolationists. Instead, this debate pitted interventionists among themselves. As one of these critics put it, "In American policy today, the great controversy arises not so much from the fact that we are intervening abroad as from the scale and character of our interventions . . . the objection is to excess — to a failure of political judgment and discrimination." [32] In sum, dissenters were seeking a limitationist foreign policy that,

---

* According to other critics, America's foreign policy was itself the logical outcome of a system that made such an outcome unavoidable. Some defined this system essentially as bureaucratic (see Richard Barnet, *Intervention and Revolution* [Cleveland, 1968]). Others defined it according to economic needs (see Gabriel Kolko, *The Roots of American Foreign Policy* [Boston, 1969] and Harry Magdoff, *The Age of Imperialism* [New York, 1969]). Implicit in these critiques was an institutional imperative that forced the United States to act the way it did. This is not the place to review and discuss such arguments. Suffice to say that the institutional imperative leaves this author generally unsatisfied. It does not explain, nor even describe, the policy proper — a policy that, after all, is decided upon by individuals operating within a bureaucratic or economic apparatus that is or is not determining, depending upon the specifics of a situation that requires a great deal more concrete, empirical analysis.

however ambiguously, would achieve a reduction of international commitments they considered grossly excessive.

The limitationist argument was further enhanced by the antiwar feelings that the Vietnam War helped substantiate. The astute observer Richard Rovere could write that popular antiwar feelings were "not simply against the war in Vietnam but against war itself, not against bombing Vietnam but against the slaughter of bombing anywhere at any time for any reason, not simply against the slaughter of innocents in an unjust conflict but against the slaughter of those who may be far from innocent in a just conflict." [33] In a way the dissenters' outrage at the war reflected the tremendous impact of television, which ended the anonymity of war deaths and at the same time increased the revulsion of a public already puzzled by the causes and objectives of the war itself. It is this aspect of the war that was instrumental in steering the opposition away from the material costs and toward moral issues. For in Vietnam the material costs alone were *relatively* not more cruel than in other wars America had waged. During the Korean War, in less than a year every major city in both Koreas was leveled. By contrast, in Vietnam, the only city that suffered from a comparable treatment was Hue, during the communist Tet offensive of January 1968. In Korea, civilian casualties were estimated unofficially at a minimum of two million — an average of 700,000 casualties a year, many times superior to the yearly rate of civilian casualties in Vietnam.

Confusion over the war was also translated into general doubt and reappraisal of America's goals and methods, not merely in Vietnam and in the present, but anywhere and throughout its history. No longer did only the war in Vietnam have obscure beginnings and causes. So did the cold war and even the Korean War, as self-styled revisionists derided the findings of an outdated "court history" and offered new explanations, usually harsher on America's role and softer on the communist role. New historical schools found conspiracies everywhere: President Truman's use of the short-lived American atomic monopoly to blackmail the Soviet Union and to force it to withdraw from Eastern Europe; the capitalist manipulation of the Marshall Plan, used to put down the genuine revolt of the European masses; the "crucifixion of Korea" undertaken so that the military commitment of America to the remaining anticommunist regimes in the Far East might be firmly established; the nuclear folly of John Foster Dulles' massive retaliation and the conventional folly of McNamara's flexible response — all these reflected a new state of mind that doubted America's purpose and policies.

In Congress, too, questions were increasingly raised about the respective roles of the executive and legislative in making commitments and waging wars. Neither of America's last two wars — in Korea and in Vietnam — had been formally declared by Congress, and a growing number of congressmen loudly resented this "oversight." They attempted to reverse a trend that had seemingly seen the president gain control of the power to commit the country to war.

Two actions taken by the Senate in 1970 brought to at least a temporary climax the feeling that Congress should assert itself. Adopted on June 30, 1970, by a vote of 58 to 37 after 34 days of debate, the Cooper-Church amendment represented the first time legislative restrictions on the president's capacity as commander in chief were voted by one Chamber during a shooting war. Its significance, however, was essentially symbolic as its main provision required that all American troops be out of Cambodia by July 1, 1970, a situation actually achieved by the time the amendment was voted upon. Any future military activity in Cambodia, specified the amendment, would need the prior approval of the Senate.

Still more ambitious was a second proposed Senate amendment, the Hatfield-McGovern amendment, which attempted to require the withdrawal of all American forces from Vietnam by June 30, 1971. Even though it was rejected by the Senate by a vote of 55 to 39, the proposed Hatfield-McGovern amendment, like the Cooper-Church amendment, implicitly signaled the end of an age of acquiescence during which foreign affairs had been allowed to become nearly the exclusive responsibility of the president.*

---

* The first major victory of critics of the Vietnam War in attempting to find some legislative formula to end the war was achieved in June 1971. Then, over the opposition of the Nixon administration, the Senate adopted by a 55 to 42 vote an amendment calling for the withdrawal of all American forces from Indochina within nine months if American prisoners of war

With the Senate Foreign Relations Committee behaving increasingly as a "counter-Department of State," it appeared that America was now pursuing at least two foreign policies. One was defined by the White House and still operated within a generally interventionist framework, with some minor changes reflected in the so-called "Nixon doctrine" and the looser attitude that the Nixon administration adopted toward Europe. The other policy, defined by an occasional majority in the Senate, displayed a strong desire to break down the interventionist outlook, limit America's involvement in world affairs to areas of major national interest, reduce defense expenditures to a minimum and reestablish the primacy of domestic politics over international matters. But with the limitationist critics seriously failing to define the specific limits they advocated, differences between these two foreign policies remained relatively slight because their common vision of America's predominant power related to a world where changes could occur only in certain ways and where some other changes remained altogether forbidden.

The Truman Doctrine

In a global vein, the war in Vietnam started a chain reaction that called for the overall reappraisal of America's postwar foreign policy. Known as "globalism," this policy was described as worldwide interventionism stemming from a belief in a universal crisis caused by an international communist conspiracy. The globalist believed that such a crisis could successfully be resolved if America backed its commitment to international order with force, not only for its own national interest but also in the general interest of mankind.

The guidelines of this approach to the United States role in world affairs had been stated in President Truman's Message to

---

were released. The Senate action went, in principle at least, against two basic principles of the administration's Vietnam policy. First, it disassociated the pace of withdrawal from the ability of the Saigon government to survive. Second, it set a definite dateline for withdrawal, a step that the administration was unwilling to take at the time. Shortly thereafter the Senate amendment was defeated by the House of Representatives.

the Congress in March 1947. Understood as a policy action, the president's Message was realistic in its motivation, restricted in its application, and moderate in its requirements. Since the early years of the nineteenth century, Great Britain had carefully prevented Russia from gaining control of the Straits of Dardanelles on the assumption that Russian domination there would threaten the European balance of power by providing Moscow with a major outlet in the Mediterranean. But early in 1947, unable to continue to fulfill this function, the London government asked Washington to assume the containing role.[34]

That Russian expansion in the area needed to be contained was sufficiently clear. Greece particularly was on the verge of collapse, economically, militarily, and politically. Yet, Greece was the strategic key to the Middle East and an important psychological key to the future of a Western Europe also on the point of panic. It seemed vital to American security that Greece and Turkey be strengthened, and circumstances were such that only the United States could provide such aid. This support was not an endorsement of the Greek regime: "The extension of aid by this country," emphasized Mr. Truman in his statement, "does not mean that the United States condones everything that the Greek government has done or will do." It was not even to be considered as an endorsement of Great Britain's own excesses and mistakes in dealing, through the established Greek government, with the Greek rebels. It was a decision clearly taken for reasons of national security, a decision that could easily be implemented as the problem in either country was largely within American economic, technical, and financial capabilities. The president asked for $400 million for both countries – a little more than .1 per cent of the money spent during World War II – and no substantial military involvement was foreseen beyond assisting in the reconstruction.

Understood as a policy action, then, Truman's message attempted to satisfy specific objectives for a specific area at a specific time. But understood as a "doctrine" that transpired through Truman's own description of the implications of his policy, the message involved America in the unlimited containment of an ill-defined ideology. Through these implications Greece became, as Truman put it, the symbol of a worldwide ideological clash between alternative ways of life, the totalitarian way and the democratic way. "It must be the policy of the United States," thus concluded the president in his Message, ". . . to help free people maintain their institutions and their national integrity against aggressive movements that seek to impose upon them totalitarian regimes." Such a policy would be "no more than a frank recognition that totalitarian regimes imposed on free peoples by direct or indirect aggression, undermine the foundations of international peace and hence the security of the United States."

Admittedly, the rhetoric of the Truman administration satisfied the need to revive faltering public support for American participation in world affairs. The ideological globalism in Truman's declaration of intentions was also forcefully requested by Republican Senator Vandenberg as the price of bipartisan support in Congress. Such an approach, however, remained particularly unfortunate given the administration's incertitude over Moscow's intentions and how they could best be met. So, the doctrine was followed by a disclaimer over its practical consequences. Dean Acheson, in his testimony to the Senate Foreign Relations Committee, denied that a chain reaction of aggression "wherever it occurs in the world" needed to be met systematically with a chain reaction of intervention. The Truman doctrine, continued the acting secretary of state, "did not state . . . that wherever [subversion] occurs, one must react to it exactly the same way." Quite the contrary: "Any requests of foreign countries for aid will have to be considered according to the circumstances in each individual case." [35] The administration was also eager to deny that America had entered an era of total confrontation with its former war ally. Indeed, within a few weeks, the Marshall Plan was presented in a way that did not exclude communist participation. American aid policy, said General Marshall in a speech made at Harvard University in June 1947, was not directed against any country or ideology. Instead, it was offered to any government willing to assist in international recovery.

But after the North Korean attack, a corollary was appended to the Truman Doctrine: "The attack upon Korea," declared President Truman on June 27, 1950, "makes it plain beyond doubts that Communism has passed beyond the use of subversion to conquer independent nations and will now use armed invasion and war." Earlier hesitations about Soviet ambitions, and the means they would use in fulfilling those ambitions, were thereby dismissed and Truman's doctrine now had a specific target against which it could eventually be applied.

Nevertheless, even after the corollary had been stated the rhetoric of the doctrine remained more impressive than its actual implementation. In their respective ways, the Truman and Eisenhower administrations preserved a relatively limited vision of American interests and did not attempt to translate verbal excesses into practice. The Truman Doctrine was not applied to the coup in Czechoslovakia, when the last democratic state in Eastern Europe was finally subverted by communist forces, or in China in the late forties, or in 1953 during the so-called Posnan riots in East Germany, or in 1954 to help the French forces to avoid defeat in Indochina, or in 1956 to get the Russians out of Hungary.

Risks were taken, over Berlin, over Quemoy and Matsu, and over Cuba, when the consequences of inaction were deemed unfavorable to the national position within the global balance of power. In other words, America continued to speak of international interest but acted on behalf of its own national interests, interests that were, as John F. Kennedy once put it, "more important than ideology." [36]

And this is precisely where Vietnam did not seem to fit quite well: no administration was able to establish a satisfactory relationship between international values, national goals, and the global balance of power. Applauding American involvement in Vietnam because it drew from deep and flowing springs of moral duty was not convincing at a time when the old vision of America's moral duty was being discarded not only in large areas of the world but within large sections of America as well. That American actions should continue to be explained by the indivisibility of international peace was also not convincing at a time when America witnessed the divisibility of its own domestic peace. In the sixties, then, the Vietnam War became the source and symbol of a foreign policy debate. Through that war the abstract and ideological commitments of yesteryear became the concrete and practical realities of the present, although no valid case could be made that these realities still related to the inflated moral rhetoric of the past.[37]

The Intellectual Preconceptions

More than a debate over Vietnam, or over America's foreign policy, the debate of the sixties was also a debate over the American philosophy of international relations — a philosophy unsuited to the circumstances of the time and unrelated to the policies needed to meet such changes. Speaking shortly before he became the special adviser to President Nixon on foreign affairs, Henry Kissinger stated: "Vietnam is more than a failure of policy, it is really a very critical failure of the American philosophy of international relations. . . . We have to assess the whole procedure and concepts that got us involved there . . . if we are not going to have another disaster that may have a quite different look but will have the same essential flaws." [38] The direct outcome of a given experiential context — the isolationist impulse "turned inside out," as Edmund Stillman put it [39] — globalism, and the type of situation that it permitted, reflected some of the most persistent patterns of America's international life.

Foremost among these patterns was America's traditional belief in a utopian community of nations where the struggle for power is forever ended and where the state of war ceases to be the most characteristic feature of international relations. Such utopia had grown out of America's own national experience, an experience so luckily disassociated from that of other countries that the United States lived for two hundred years in a state of "perpetually renewed historical virginity." [40] As a result, Americans merely learned about history from a distance and reluctantly, and liked so little of it that a point was soon reached when the only history America accepted and worshipped was that of its own institutions and culture transposed on the world scene.

One of the characteristics that Americans cited most proudly was the minimal role that power had played in the development of their country. Having had little contact with the distortions that a constant struggle over national self-preservation may have on the fiber of international morality, the United States could easily dispute the role of power in the international arena. With the exception of the Civil War (quite an exception at that!) Americans recalled that the thirteen colonies had peacefully cooperated and integrated into the wealthiest and strongest country ever. Why, then, could not other countries learn from this experience? Why could they not learn to depend less on force and more on good intentions? Similarly, why not compare the unification of the American colonies to that of Europe? Or the American revolution to the national revolutions of the post–World War II period?

Yet, the uniqueness of America's past usually made its projection in the rest of the world inappropriate. When President Madison needed to settle American differences with Great Britain on the Canadian border he sent an expeditionary corp of 6,000 men at about the same time when Napoleon was sending an army of 600,000 men to settle France's quarrel with Russia. Yet, the latter failed while the former succeeded. For better or worse all nations could not measure their adversaries according to the Mexicans and Indians who had impeded the American march forward to the Pacific. Similarly, the states involved in America's unification were colonies with no specific tradition, already united in the same experience of rejection, by and large enclosed within a single linguistical unit. By contrast, in Europe there were a multitude of nations, jealous of their traditions and their prerogatives, speaking different languages, using different currencies, and facing different problems in different ways. America's national revolution had been essentially a domestic struggle, whereas the revolutions of new African and Asian countries were waged, often violently, against an alien colonial power determined to preserve its domination.

The implications of this narcissistic outlook cannot be overlooked. Plunged into a contemplation of its own national virtues and history, America relied on a distorted and simplistic vision of present reality. Instant historical analogies (Hitler and Stalin, Munich and Korea, Korea and Vietnam) distorted this reality even further so that they made both policies and goals irrelevant to specific cases. Beyond all this, America also believed all too easily in its own altruism as the proof of the correctness of its actions. In Stanley Hoffmann's critical words, this was "the *hubris* of believing that others will interpret [our] deeds as we interpret them and that our intentions cancel out our acts." [41]

Nevertheless, in the name of this general utopia the United States continued to wage its wars, and in the sixties the United States still regarded the use of force in Vietnam as an accidental phenomenon that could be eliminated from the system of nations as it had been from the American system of states. "It is a very old dream," noticed President Johnson in April 1965, "but we have the power and now the opportunity to make that dream come true." [42] In the meanwhile, however, the world needed to be policed. It was incumbent upon the forces of intervention to reject any compromise with the disrupters of international order. Only unconditional surrender could assure the peace-loving nations that evil had been crushed and the criminal disturbances altogether settled, ensuring a world that, in President Johnson's words, would be "free of marching invaders and aggressors, free of terror in the night, free of hunger and ignorance and crippling diseases." [43] In sum, when America took up arms, it was not only the flag of America that was waved but that of humanity. "I hope we shall never forget," Wilson had once said, "that we created this Nation not to serve ourselves, but to serve mankind." [44] The assertion of a national interest that entailed conquest and diplomatic pressures at the expense of other nations was deemed somehow unacceptable to the American people. If one fought a war it was in the name of a universal interest, as embodied in the Four Freedoms and the Atlantic Charter during World War II. That same rhetoric was applied to the war in Vietnam where victory would be, according to the then Secretary of State Dean Rusk, "a victory for all mankind . . . a world-wide victory for freedom." [45] Vietnam was the last hurdle before ultimate victory, a victory that would be the prelude to the emergence of what former President Johnson wanted to build: the great society of independent nations, each with their own institutions and each settling their disputes by peaceful means.[46] This feature was still so typically American that it was found even among the most outspoken American critics. Michael Harrington, one of the many self-proclaimed intellectual leaders of the American left, criticized the American establishment for having burdened its people with an excessively good conscience. Yet, his program made the more traditional American utopia modest in comparison. For his program was no less than "to finish the creation of the world." [47]

The utopia had not yet been fulfilled but it was the role of the American people to assure the millennium, and the laissez faire principle inherent in the free enterprise system was, when translated in foreign affairs, a "laissez-nous faire" principle.[48] America was "the watchman on the walls of world freedom" or the self-appointed "guardians at the gate." [49] Former White House adviser Theodore Sorensen said of President Kennedy that he was at his best when his responsibilities did not have to be shared.[50] This was true of American statesmanship as a whole, and Americans never ceased to be amazed when this leadership was being disputed. To dispute American leadership was to dispute its intentions as well. But these intentions were too pure to even tolerate any argument. At all times, even America's real and potential enemies could not but be aware of America's altruism, self-control, and self-mastery. "They [the Russians] know, and the world knows," had claimed Dean Acheson at the time of America's nuclear monopoly, "how foreign is the concept of aggressive war to our philosophy and our political system." [51]

Assuredly, America could be trusted because it was the Chosen Nation, "the justest, the most progressive, the most honorable, the most enlightened nation in the world," and as such it had not only the right but also the duty to use whatever means were necessary, including force, to do justice and to assert the right of mankind.[52] Earlier in the twentieth century, Wilsonian diplomacy, which wanted "to teach the South American republics to elect good men," had found "something sacred and holy in . . . warfare" and thus "refused to cry 'peace' as long as there is sin and wrong in the world." [53] In the late sixties, the time to cry peace had not yet arrived. "When we are gone," asked President Johnson in March 1968, "what other nation in the world is going to stand up and protect the little man's freedom everywhere in the world?" [54] Fifteen months later the same troubled concern was voiced by his successor who was worried over the prospect of an America that might become a "dropout" in assuming the responsibility for defending peace and freedom in the world.[55]

But neither America's utopia nor its faith in the exceptional nature of its mission would have been possible without a strong infusion of romanticism. For America still thought of itself as the last — if not the first and only — romantic nation in the world. It helped its sister nations with no other objective than winning their gratitude. It sought no gain. Wilson had said: "There is nothing so self-destructive as selfishness . . . whereas the nation which denies itself material advantage and seeks those things which are of the spirit works . . . for all generations, and works in the permanent and durable stuffs of humanity." [56] Fifty years later, President Johnson was still measuring America's greatness by its willingness to fulfill its moral obligation to mankind.[57]

Even in war, America was guided by the spiritual hand of God. Consider, for example, President McKinley's much quoted explanation of why he had decided to annex the Philippine Islands: "I walked the floor of the White House night after night until midnight," he said, "and I am not ashamed to tell you . . . that I went down on my knees and prayed to Almighty God for light and guidance. . . . And one night late it came to me . . . (1) that we could not give them [the Philippines] back to Spain — that would be cowardly and dishonorable; (2) that we could not turn them over to France or Germany — that would be bad business and discreditable; (3) that we could not leave them to themselves — they were unfit for self-government . . . and (4) that there was nothing left for us to do but to take them all, and to educate the Filipinos, and uplift and civilize and Christianize them, and by God's grace do the very best we could by them, as our fellowmen for whom Christ also died. And then I went to bed, and to sleep, and slept soundly." [58]

The cynic would have soon pointed out that President McKinley's statement had been made to a group of visiting clergymen and that side by side with God's hands were, as usual, more realistic arguments that could be understood as the real motivation of McKinley's action. Yet, such rhetoric, when repeated as often as it had been through the years, had become credible to a trusting public. Indeed, the American public had grown so sensitive to such rhetoric that the rhetoric seemed indispensable if public support was to be gained. Indoctrinated as an instrument of foreign policy, the public had thus emerged as its directive force. A policy that merely intended to be packaged into a hard-hitting doctrine might soon be absorbed by the doctrine itself, thereby assuring the translation of the doctrine into policy.*

A Nation or an Empire?

In the late sixties, America fought abroad and argued with itself to reaffirm its faith in its illusions and its omnipotence, for some, or to face the consequences of the end of both, for others. With most factions at last recognizing the realities and responsibilities of power, the debate centered on the scope, the nature, and the frequency of its use. Indeed, it is likely that during that debate the American people learned more about international relations than they did during the whole prior history of the American Republic.

Twenty years before, Dean Acheson had warned against unlimited interventionism:

> People will do more damage and create more misrepresentation . . . by saying our interest is merely to stop the spread of Communism than in any other way. Our real interest is in those people as people. . . . It is important to take this attitude not as mere negative reaction to Communism but as the most positive affirmation of the most affirmative truth that we hold, which is in the dignity and right of every nation, of every people, and of every individual to develop in their own way, making their own mistakes, reaching their own triumphs but acting under their own responsibility. . . . On their own, they will make their own decisions. They will attempt to better their own lot and on occasion they will make their own mistakes. But it will be their mis-

* It should be observed that an identical analysis of the critics' style would point to a similar series of intellectual flaws. Among the dissenters could be found a staggering illusion of the enemy's omnipotence — an illusion that suggested that every American action anywhere would be swiftly countered by an overwhelming reaction of the other side everywhere as the enemy's resources appeared to be as unlimited as American resources were limited. Similarly, the critic's utopia often related to an international community that would be peaceful if only America could control its interventionist impulse. As to the intellectual mistake described above as exceptionalism, it was sometimes reversed by the critic in order to fit the "other side," so that the apologist's "laissez-nous faire" principle became the critic's "laissez-les faire" principle.

takes, and they are not going to have their mistakes dictated to them by anybody else. . . . American assistance can be effective when it is the missing component in a situation which might otherwise be solved. The United States cannot furnish all these components to solve this question. It cannot furnish the will, and it cannot furnish the loyalty of a people to its government.[59]

This warning had been increasingly ignored and, in the words of a critic, America now stood with "one foot in genesis and the other in apocalypse, and annihilation . . . always an option." [60]

Undoubtedly, the war in Vietnam tragically has shown that the broad margin of error traditionally permitted to American diplomacy could no longer be counted upon. But the war also put an end to what C. B. Marshall has called "the illusion of perfect efficacy." [61] This illusion seemed all the more to be ended as, throughout the sixties, it became increasingly apparent that the efficacy of a foreign policy, any foreign policy, could no longer be measured, because a policy was all the more successful when nothing happened. Finally, the war in Vietnam also raised questions about America's omnipotence: there were limits to what America could do, and it was over the determination of those limits that the debate unfolded.

Unlike previous eras what was disputed in the sixties was not so much the intervention as its modalities — its causes and its effects, its goals and its means. First in Europe and in Latin America, then everywhere following the war in Korea, interventionism had become an established principle of American foreign policy. It was generally well accepted by the American public, and generally well tolerated by the noncommunist international community. In the sixties, however, repeated military interventions in such places as Vietnam and the Dominican Republic, diplomatic interventions in such places as France and Germany, political and economic interventions almost everywhere, caused people to question whether the United States had not gone beyond the threshold of acceptable ends and available means. What was objectionable in those interventions was the relation tentatively established between America's interest and the methods employed to attain that interest. Granted the existence of the interest, what was also debated was whether the methods chosen had any probability of fulfilling that interest.[62]

Furthermore, a new balance was looked for; a balance between security and purpose, commitments and means, a balance that was much affected by the world's own diversity and by the multiplicity of the possible responses to the many questions which it raises. For beyond the policy dilemmas which the diversity of the world created, another essential question America finally needed to face and answer was whether it could be both a nation and an empire, whether it could build at home a Great Society, or a Just Society, or an Equal Society, as various political slogans of the time had it, *and* police a just and peaceful world abroad. Or should the United States instead do more of one and less of the other, with much of the self-denial that such a choice entailed?

2

The
Politics
of Confrontation

The Strained Alliance

The time of peace is a time of regret. The peacemaker relives yesterday's events so that he will not repeat the mistakes that made the present what it is. The time of peace is a time of hope too, and the peacemaker concerns himself with yesterday's world so that tomorrow's world is the better one to which he aspires.

Peacemaking, like warmaking, is a perennial activity of man. He wages war in the name of peace; he often makes peace as if he wanted more war. That the peace which everyone wanted as World War II was nearing an end was hardly ever given a chance is a particular source of regret when one considers the unanimity with which it was hoped for. In 1945, the victorious allies were all-powerful, at least insofar as their outside adversaries were concerned. The only substantial enemy they faced was an internal one — confrontation among themselves. "If we were to win the peace after winning the war, we had to have Russian help," Truman remembered thinking in the spring of 1945.[1] "The only hope for the world," Churchill wrote as late as January 1945, "is the agreement of the three great powers." [2] And Stalin was to concur as he warned against the "greatest danger" to world peace: "conflict among ourselves. We must . . . think how to secure unity in the future, and how to guarantee that the three Great Powers (and possibly China and France) will maintain a united front." [3]

It is hardly possible to be sure that these statements were made in good faith. Because of the events that had occurred previously, it was everyone's hope that they were. Because of the events that have occurred since, it is everyone's regret that they were not fulfilled. But calling for future collaboration was surely not enough, particularly in view of the various past tensions that had plagued the alliance in wartime. Only if these tensions, often serious, were to be resolved, only if the mutual, and occasionally justified, suspicion that each side of the alliance had displayed for the other could end — only then could the Grand Alliance survive the disappearance of its common enemy and assure the peace that eluded the victorious powers in 1919. That these tensions were not ended provides a first clue to the confrontation between America and the Soviet Union.

From the summer of 1941 on, and even before America's entry into the war, Stalin's complaint that the Germans were not being prevented from moving forces to the Eastern front with impunity placed an immediate and constant strain in the coalition. From Moscow's viewpoint, such a complaint appeared generally warranted as, throughout most of the conflict, the Soviet Union clearly bore the brunt of Germany's war effort in a way that was at first acknowledged by Moscow's allies. For example, reviewing the military operations scheduled for 1943, Winston Churchill himself criticized the "poor contribution" of the Western allies whom he described as "playing about" with half a dozen German army divisions while the Russians were facing 185 divisions. "Everywhere," Churchill wrote to General Ismay in March 1943, "the British and Americans are overloading their operational plans with so many factors of safety that they are ceasing to be capable of making any form of aggressive war." [4] Not surprisingly, what Churchill called "poor" Stalin called "insignificant" and the latter statesman's resentment strengthened his personal prejudices. The Soviet generalissimo told one of Yugoslavia's communist leaders in June 1944, after the long-awaited opening of a second front in Europe,

> Don't think that just because we are allies of the English . . . we have forgotten who they are and who Churchill is. They find nothing sweeter than to trick their allies. During the first World War they constantly tricked the Russians and the French. . . . Churchill is the kind who, if you don't watch him, will slip a kopeck out of your pocket. . . . Roosevelt is not like that. He dips in his hand only for bigger coins.[5]

In order to relieve the German pressure in the East Moscow repeatedly asked for the opening of a second military front. This had been prematurely promised by President Roosevelt after Molotov's first visit to Washington in May 1942, when an ambiguous understanding was reached between the United States and the Soviet Union "with regard to the urgent tasks of creating a second front in Europe in 1942." But due to material and strategic reasons, the implementation of the understanding was postponed for two full years during which each Soviet recrimination was systematically followed by a Western profession of good faith. Even the North African landing, in 1943, did not significantly help the Soviet Union as a momentarily reassured Germany was reported to have shifted twenty-seven of its army divisions to the Eastern front, away from an Atlantic coast that was no longer threatened.[6]

The inability and/or unwillingness of the Western allies to play a more immediate role in the defeat of the German forces apparently confirmed Stalin's suspicion that, under Churchill's direct influence, the strategy of the Western nations consisted in letting the Soviets and the Germans fight with one another until the physical exhaustion of both states. At that point, the Soviet leader reasoned, it would be relatively easy for the West to dictate its conditions of peace to both the Nazis and the communists. Such a suspicion had been considerably aroused by the

1938 Munich Conference. Prior to, and during, that ill-fated meeting between France, Great Britain, and Germany over the fate of Czechoslovakia, the Soviet government attempted to cement a united front against Hitler. How genuine such Soviet efforts were remains a mystery that will probably never be solved. Obviously it was to Moscow's interest to harden Czechoslovakia's resistance as this unfortunate state represented one further step in Germany's eastward advances. But neither Czechoslovakia, nor France or Great Britain were anxious to make Soviet intervention possible.* Did they plan, then, to settle Europe not only without the Soviet Union but against it? The question is worth raising only inasmuch as it illustrates Soviet suspicion, both at the time and later, during and after World War II. Clearly, as Stalin saw it, the Western powers preferred to see Germany fight eastward rather than westward, if it fought at all.[7] Moreover, Moscow's vision of a capitalist "conspiracy" was enlarged, again in Stalin's estimation, by the events in the Far East where Japan was engaged in a full scale conflict with China — one further step in Japan's westward advances. Thus Moscow could implicate Washington in the "conspiracy" whenever the American and the Japanese governments undertook conciliatory negotiations. Ultimately fear of isolation would drive Moscow into the Nazi camp, in August 1939, as the Western powers could not decide upon the value of a military agreement with Moscow. At Yalta, Stalin, in an expansive mood, confided to Churchill: "If the British and French had sent a mission to Moscow in 1939 containing men who really wanted an agreement with Russia the Soviet government would not have signed the pact with Ribbentrop." [8]

Soviet fears of Western treachery were paralleled by fears of the Western allies that Moscow might seek a separate peace, which, eventually, would place it in a position to dictate its own terms at the end of the conflict. From the Peace of Tilsit during the Napoleonic wars (when Czar Alexander signed a separate peace with Napoleon) to the Peace of Brest Litovsk in 1917

---

* Assuming that it was possible at all. Weakened and demoralized by purges which had reached some 30,000 officers, the Soviet army was further hampered by major problems of logistics. For example, it was estimated that it would take the Russians three months to move one single army division into Czechoslovakia through Rumania.

(when Lenin signed a separate peace with Germany), and including the Pact of Non-Aggression of 1939, Russia's modern history emphatically suggested that no Russian government, czarist or communist, would preclude the idea of a separate peace with any one foreign government if Russia's national interest justified a search for an immediate end to the hostilities. Aware of the allies' doubts over each others' staying power, Hitler sought ways whereby charges and countercharges within the opposite coalition would proliferate. Late in the war, therefore, the German High Command shifted the main pressure from one front to another, hoping thereby to give more credibility to the possibility of an impending double cross. "If," Hitler argued in December 1944, "we can deliver a few more heavy blows, then at any moment this artificially-bolstered common front may collapse with a gigantic clap of thunder." [9]

The German chancellor met with little success in raising Western suspicions when he threw his last major offensive in the Ardennes while the Soviet troops were rolling on in the East, now favored by a depleted German front. But when contacts between Germany and the Western nations were attempted in Berne, Switzerland, without the presence of Soviet representatives, Stalin's suspicion reached a new high. Informed of these by his own sources, the Soviet generalissimo attributed Western discretion on such matters to the "strange and unaccountable" absence of German resistance on the Western front. "At this moment," Stalin continued bitterly, "the Germans have stopped fighting against English and Americans while they continue the war against Russia — an ally of England and America." [10]

That the war on the Western front had not stopped, as Stalin claimed, did not contain his indignation. As to the substance of the disagreement the whole incident was blown out of proportion and proved awkward to President Roosevelt personally and to the Allies in general. For Roosevelt it dealt a considerable blow to his conviction that Stalin had the same high confidence in his truthfulness and reliability as he had in Stalin's. In part at least, this incident accounted for Roosevelt's growing change of attitude shortly before his death. The American president was all the more distressed because the Western allies had actually notified the Russians that their interest in pursuing the

German overtures did not go beyond a willingness to present German emissaries (who never came to Berne) with a draft copy of Germany's capitulation. Seen from Washington, Soviet recriminations implicitly reflected both Soviet ideological opposition, which was irreversible despite the previous Western concessions, and Stalin's desire or reflex to inflate any minor incident into a major confrontation. Seen from Moscow, this attempt at separate negotiations clearly illustrated Western bad faith. Seen from Berlin, the incident appeared to confirm Hitler's earlier assumption. Thus, in a last desperate measure following the sudden death of Roosevelt and reminiscent of Prussia's mode of terminating the Seven Years' War, Himmler, the German Gestapo Chief, formally offered to surrender his forces on the Western front, while resistance would be continued on the Eastern front, "at least for a time." [11] Once again both Washington and London rejected any part of this offer even though from Paris, Charles de Gaulle found in the offer and in the analysis that came with it "an element of truth." [12] When the war finally ended, Moscow had become so conditioned to the possibility of a separate peace that its own announcement of Germany's final and unconditional surrender was delayed as Stalin assumed that the fighting against the Russian troops might go on indefinitely.

From Roosevelt to Truman

Obviously, the alliance between the Soviet Union and the Western democracies was a convenient arrangement, concluded in urgent circumstances to face an immediate threat and despite the many differences and profound mistrust that existed between the new partners. But a few years of common fighting, combined with a wartime rhetoric that extolled the virtues of the Russian people — "one hell of a people," claimed the March 1943 issue of *Life*, "who look like Americans, dress like Americans, and think like Americans" [13] — had aroused expectation in the United States that the alliance would survive the disappearance of the common enemy. Foremost among the optimists was President Roosevelt, who believed that a sincere correction of earlier errors made by Western democracies in their dealing with the

Soviet Union would help overcome Stalin's hesitations. "The only way to have a friend is to be one," he stated wishfully in his final inaugural address of January 20, 1945, in an obvious reference to the Soviet Union. Friendship between the two nations, Roosevelt believed, would be cemented by America's patience until Moscow's confidence in the West was sufficiently built up.

President Roosevelt, however, died on April 12, 1945. Less than two weeks later, Senator Vandenberg, already one of the most influential men in shaping American foreign policy, approvingly wrote in his diary, in the aftermath of a meeting between Truman and Molotov: "FDR's appeasement of Russia is over." [14] Earlier on the day of that meeting, April 24, President Truman had told his advisers that the "one-way street" that the United States had been traveling when dealing with the Soviet Union would now have to be reversed. He agreed with Secretary James Forrestal's view that "if the Russians were to be rigid in their attitude we had better have a showdown with them now rather than later." [15] Was there indeed a sharp change in American policy toward the Soviet Union following Roosevelt's death? If so, what were the conditions and objectives of that change?

In retrospect, policy changes might well have occurred even if President Truman, as the more traditional cold war analysts argue, had carefully carried out all the agreements that Roosevelt had entered.[16] Yet, there was little in the new president's background that indicated a personal desire on his part to follow the conciliatory policies of his predecessor. His lack of expertise in international affairs placed him under the constant influence of a State Department already frustrated over Roosevelt's personal handling of America's foreign relations. From the very moment of Moscow's entry into the war, the State Department had looked upon President Roosevelt's willingness to come to Russia's assistance with marked resentment, and it advised against extending aid to Stalin, whose brusque style and perceived greed for territory caused alarm. Subsequently, bureaucratic snarls that slowed down American aid annoyed Roosevelt who felt that the Russians were getting "the run around in the United States." He appointed a special assistant to direct the supply effort, and sent another one to Moscow to look into the pessimistic appraisals that were made by State Department and military experts about Moscow's staying power.[17] As the years passed by, Roosevelt increasingly abstained from consulting the State Department in his major diplomatic actions. But with Roosevelt gone, renewed pressure was exerted to have the positions of the State Department known and implemented, all the more so because these views coincided with the more belligerent attitude displayed by the new president. As a much quoted example, Truman, while a senator, had suggested, following the German invasion of the Soviet Union: "If we see that Germany is winning the war we ought to help Russia, and if Russia is winning we ought to help Germany, and in that way let them kill as many as possible."[18] Although not too much significance ought to be placed on a statement probably dictated, in part at least, by domestic considerations, it still reflected Truman's profound mistrust toward the Soviet regime. At any rate it did not do much to further Stalin's trust in the new American president.

In Truman's personality there was an impatience that would be of noticeable importance in the forthcoming negotiations with the Russians, whose bargaining style, if nothing else, required much patience indeed. At Potsdam, for instance, Truman often interrupted the conference over which he presided with the warning that "if they did not get to the main issues [he] was going to pack up and go home."[19] He finally did resort to such behavior when, following the failure of the London Conference of September 1945, the frustrated president announced that no more such conferences would take place.

Truman's character may have become all the more impatient as the successful testing of the first atomic weapons provided him with a new sense of national strength. It was Churchill's evaluation that the fortified Truman now became "a changed man" and, in a most emphatic manner, "told the Russians just when they got on and off and generally bossed the whole meeting."[20] Yet the intransigence that Truman was to display toward the Russians had manifested itself long before the New Mexico test of July. The new president had decided as early as April 17, five days after he had assumed the presidency, to "lay it on the line with Molotov."[21] And three days later, to Averell Harriman, who had just reminded the president that in any international negotiation reciprocal concessions by both sides are necessary, Truman's reply was that "he [Truman] understood that and [he] would not expect 100 percent of what he proposed. But [he] felt that [America] should be able to get 85 percent." [22]

Truman's attitude was itself related to the Munich syndrome of the time, a syndrome that described any search for accommodation as appeasement, and any appeasement as the prelude to a new world war. The Munich syndrome, the source of numerous future policies (including, as will be seen, the "domino theory") was persuasive in view of Truman's constant reliance on history. A self-styled interpreter of history, Truman strongly believed that most of the problems a president faced had their roots in the past. "I had trained myself," Truman confided, "to look back into history for precedents, because instinctively I sought perspective in the span of history for the decisions I had to make. That is why I read and re-read history." [23] The Munich syndrome became particularly harmful when the Kremlin too began to act and react *as if* it believed in its educative function. Said Zhdanov, one of the most influential men in Moscow in the forties: "Just as in the past the Munich policy untied the hands of the Nazi aggressors, so today concessions to the new course of the United States and the imperialist camp may encourage its inspirers to be even more insolent and aggressive." [24]

Both sides had learned their lesson seemingly too well. Understandably the guidelines that security policies attempt to follow are anchored in the past. But unfortunately the past is not always fully comprehensible either to the policymaker or to the observer. Thus, one of the major ideas that contributed to the formation of the Munich syndrome was that, in 1938, a show of force would have deterred Hitler from using any force in the future. But a show of force did take place that year, in May, when military measures were adopted by Czechoslovakia to compel a diplomatic retreat by Hitler. Yet, the very success of Czechoslovakia's policy made the adversary more determined, as Hitler, now angered by his "humiliation," cancelled a previous directive that had repudiated military action against Czechoslovakia. At the same time, Prague's show of force *weakened* British-French support for Czechoslovakia whose perceived aggressiveness was not to the taste of its Western allies. Coercive diplomacy and appeasement come hand in hand: Hitler's appeasement in the spring had become coercion in the fall, while Czechoslovakia's coercion led to the West's frightened appeasement. The case against the Anglo-French policy of appeasement was completed by the subsequent discovery that Germany was not prepared for war in September 1938 and that Hitler's ambitions were unlimited. If met with Western coercion, Hitler's attempted take-over of Czechoslovakia might have turned into another with-drawal, at least until he was better prepared. But such favorable components of the situation were not known at the time.

Another significant aspect of the Munich syndrome was Washington's refusal to associate itself with the search for a settlement. In his appeal to Hitler on September 27, 1938, Roose-velt had proposed a major international conference, which, how-ever, the United States would not attend. "With no political involvements in Europe," Roosevelt informed Hitler, the United States would assume "no obligations in the conduct of the present negotiations." [25] In that indirect way, it was reasoned, Roosevelt bore part of the responsibility for the Munich debacle. In sum, through the Munich syndrome, America relived in the late forties the Munich Conference by doing not only what it thought it should have done itself in the late thirties (enter into a formal commitment with Europe) but also what it thought European democracies should have done themselves (use force to deter aggression in its early stage).

Truman alone, though, could not bring about a reversal of American policy from one of conciliation to one of showdown. Thus, economic pressure to soften Stalin's position had been ad-vocated in Washington for some time prior to Roosevelt's death.[26] Throughout the war, many in the State Department, in Congress, and within the Cabinet, steadfastly rejected any accommodation and insisted that peace would have to be secured *against* Russian wishes. They regarded the wartime collaboration as a reprieve from an inevitable opposition between two irreconcilable ide-ologies. For that matter, these "hard-liners" could not overcome the surprise they had experienced when the Soviet Union had revealed itself capable of resisting the awesome German war machine. So, on the day after Germany's invasion of the Soviet Union, Secretary of War Henry Stimson had predicted Russia's defeat within three months at the most while Secretary of the Navy Frank Knox indicated that "the best opinion" available gave Hitler "from six weeks to two months . . . to clean up on Russia." [27] The "surprising" Soviet military stamina further increased their long-term fears.

As early as November 1941, Congress had shown some displeasure over Roosevelt's request that the Lend-Lease Program be extended to the Soviet Union, thus placing Soviet territory within the defensive perimeter of the United States. Under the bill, the president was authorized as he saw fit to lend, lease, sell, and barter arms, ammunition, food, and any defense information to the participating nations. By the end of the war American deliveries to the government of the Soviet Union added up to more than eleven billion dollars worth of the widest variety of requirements — including such items as tire plants, chemical factories, petroleum refineries, food, machinery, metal, diverse vehicles, and even $1,647,000 worth of buttons. The aid given to Russia amounted to approximately one-fourth of total Lend-Lease aid from America to the Allies.[28] But during the last year of the war congressional opposition to the renewed extension of Lend-Lease to the Soviet Union had become even more determined. As a result, the Fourth Russian Supply Protocol was delayed from July 1944 until April 1945. In fact, the deciding vote was cast by then Vice-President Truman who, as president of the senate, broke the tie on a Republican-sponsored amendment that called for the prohibition of Lend-Lease deliveries for postwar relief and reconstruction — a direct allusion to the increased Soviet requests for industrial equipment and machinery.

Truman's precipitous decision to end Lend-Lease shipments to Russia, whether it was accidental, as Truman claimed, or whether it was a conscious decision as his critics have argued, could not be understood as a unilateral decision suddenly reached within a deliberative vacuum. Foreign policy hardly lends itself to the dramatic reversals that, throughout the sixties, a new breed of (revisionist) cold war historians grew fond of describing. Some historians, for example, after having recognized Truman's "unwillingness" to change Roosevelt's policy *one* week after the latter's death,[29] dated the president's decision in favor of an immediate showdown at April 23, but then described his change of mind and his reversed decision two days later in favor of a delayed showdown, following a conversation that Truman held with Secretary of War Stimson who supposedly "explained" the effect that atomic weapons would have on Russo-American relations. This reversal is all the more out of character with Truman's subsequent streaks of stubbornness: "By nature not given to make snap judgments or easy decisions I required all available facts and information before coming to a decision. But once a decision was made, I did not worry about it afterward." [30]

By 1945 international relations were less involved with men than with circumstances. At Yalta and at Potsdam, three men signed agreements that reflected strategic conditions as they were understood to exist then. Occasionally, several varying interpretations of these agreements were possible, and, in such cases, the interpretation most closely connected to the strategic landscape of the moment prevailed. Later on, of course, as these temporary circumstances faded away, criticism, now related to a different "reality," became somewhat fashionable. For example, General Patrick Hurley, former United States ambassador to Peking, said in June 1951: "America was in a position at Yalta to speak the only language the Communists understand, the language of power." [31] But could it really? Substantially delayed by the last great German counteroffensive in the Ardennes, Western forces did not reach the Rhine until March 2, 1945 (after the Yalta Conference), though the Soviets had reached the Oder River, near Frankfurt, by February 7 (during Yalta). With a Soviet army in possession of almost all prewar Poland, approximately forty miles away from Berlin and within eighty miles of Vienna, the question faced by the Western allies was less one of determining what they would allow the Russians to do than one of determining what the West could persuade them to do. As Dean Acheson put it: "The Russians had in their power not only to take what was conceded to them, but much more besides." Yalta, therefore, merely gave them the basis for a legal claim to something considerably less than they might have taken without a legal claim.[32] And to this relative and limited extent, in the words of the then Secretary of State Stettinius, the Soviet Union made more concessions to the United States and Great Britain than were made to the Soviet Union.[33]

Furthermore, whatever concessions were made at Yalta to the Russians, they were ultimately based on Washington's explicit need to secure Soviet assistance in the war against Japan.* While the Yalta Conference was being held, the Combined (United States and British) Chiefs of Staff still foresaw that the end of the war against Japan would take eighteen months beyond the end of the war against Germany.[34] Japan, it was estimated at the time, had stationed approximately 700,000 troops in Manchuria and 1,235,000 troops in China, all of whom MacArthur would later describe as "as fine ground troops as I have ever known." [35] Later it would be learned that these Japanese armies in Manchuria and Korea had been greatly depleted, both in quality and in quantity as Tokyo wanted to counter American assaults elsewhere. But this information was unavailable to the policymakers in early 1945. And because the impending campaign was based on the assumption that American ground forces should not engage the Japanese army on the Asian continent, Soviet help was judged to be indispensable.

The decision to spare American ground forces from further confrontation with Japanese ground forces was itself understandable within the perspective of the slaughters that had just occurred on the two islands of Iwo Jima and Okinawa. When Iwo Jima was finally secured, in March 1945, the American marines had lost 4,891 men, and the wounded amounted to 15,594. Out of a Japanese garrison of 22,000 men, 212, all wounded, were taken as prisoners. All others had died in battle, in line with the Japanese military code of honor. The following month at Okinawa, 11,939 marines died, and 35,905 were wounded, while, on the other side 7,400 Japanese soldiers were taken prisoner and 131,000 of them died.[36] Partly on the basis of these events, the anticipated losses for an invasion of the Japanese islands were placed at a minimum of 500,000 killed for the American forces, with many more for the Japanese, and still on the premise that the invasion, scheduled to start on November 1, 1945, would be

* The most significant and questionable concession made to the Soviets at Yalta was probably the restoration to Russia of a share in the Chinese Eastern and Southern Manchurian Railroads. This, together with the lease of Port Arthur as a naval base could have well lead to a Soviet domination of the Yellow Sea and of Manchuria, unless China emerged, after the war, as a strong and unified state — a prospect already unlikely at the time.

able to bypass the Asian mainland thanks to the Russian intervention.

In February 1945, shortly after the Yalta Conference, General MacArthur still argued that the invasion of Japan proper should not be undertaken unless the Russian army was previously committed to action in Manchuria.[37] His estimate was confirmed by all the Joint Chiefs of Staff. MacArthur himself felt that at least sixty Russian army divisions were needed for the invasion to be successful. The Joint Chiefs of Staff additionally planned to clear a Pacific supply route through the Soviet Union and such plans were not canceled until April 24, the very day of Truman's stormy meeting with Molotov.[38] What could be disputed is whether such concessions as President Roosevelt made at Yalta were needed to secure Russia's agreement to enter the war against Japan. For, granted that Russian help was needed, such aid had already been pledged by Stalin, even before the Yalta Conference was held. In other words, as George Kennan has suggested, the political payment was made to Stalin for something he had every intention of doing "anyway, perhaps even without any reimbursement, we cannot know." [39] But even then, the American president's action at Yalta could still reflect a desire to let no loophole or frustration prevent implementing what was regarded as indispensable to American capabilities and objectives.

Several months after Yalta and on the eve of his journey to Potsdam, Roosevelt's successor continued to regard Russia's entry into the war against Japan as the "compelling reason" for holding a conference.[40] Even after the successful atomic test of July 16, 1945, no one was able to measure with any certitude the immediate and practical capability of these new weapons, so that most of the existing military plans for Japan's invasion were actually maintained just in case these new weapons proved ineffective.[41]

Yet, during the last months of the war in the Pacific, a tripolar confrontation slowly evolved with Japan playing less and less active a role, caught between the United States and the Soviet Union. Such a confrontation was particularly significant with regard to the use of atomic bombs at Hiroshima and Nagasaki. Two seemingly contradictory factors were predominant in shaping Washington's policy — on the one hand, the automaticity with which the decision to use these weapons was reached. Truman said afterwards that he never had any doubt that they should be used, and, with very few exceptions including then General Eisenhower, everyone within the political, military, and scientific communities concurred with the president. The Committee on the Atomic Bomb recommended that the bomb be used against the enemy as soon as it could be done. They recommended further that it should be dropped without specific warning and against a target that would clearly show its devastating strength. Their debates always centered on *how* to use the bomb, never on *whether* to use it. Yet, on the other hand, everyone agreed that the Japanese had already been militarily defeated, with or without atomic weapons. More than half of Japan's main cities had been burnt to the ground — Tokyo, Osaka, Nagoya, Kobe, Yokohama — and with them, the major industrial areas that had supported Japan's war effort. Short of planes, skilled pilots, gasoline, and parts the Japanese air force was almost inactive and American bombers could now come and go as they pleased and without escort. Less than one-fourth of the Japanese navy was still floating. And Japan was seeking mediation from Stalin, an effort duly communicated to Truman at Potsdam. Indeed, it was the opinion of each of the Joint Chiefs of Staff that, if they were patient enough, the "unconditional" surrender of Japan was most likely to occur without the bomb and without the invasion. Should they be wrong in their assumption, the invasion itself was not scheduled to start before November 1, and the rate of casualties would probably remain very low during the summer that preceded the invasion, as the Japanese leaders wanted to preserve their scarce remaining forces for the expected invasion of the homeland.[42]

That these atomic bombs would nevertheless have been dropped, somewhat precipitatedly and automatically, reflects America's concern not only with the military requirements that the war against Japan raised in August 1945 (for all practical purposes it was virtually and admittedly over), but also with the political requirements imposed by the imminence of a Soviet intervention in the Far East. Such intervention had been contractually sought at Yalta when it seemed imperative to secure it. Now, atomic weapons, if they were to work properly, looked like the most effective way of concluding the war in the Pacific with the shortest delays, thus not allowing Soviet claims for active participation in the future occupation of Japan. By making its own impression the bomb would also contain the Soviet armies who might otherwise go further into Manchuria even after Japan had been defeated. Such concern with this additional function of the bomb was voiced afterward. "I would not allow the Russians any part in the control of Japan," confided Truman in his *Memoirs*, "I decided to take no chances in a joint setup with the Russians. . . . We were not going to be disturbed by Russian tactics in the Pacific." [43] And Secretary Stimson confirmed it: "The thing to do was to get this surrender through as quickly as we can before Russia could get down in reach of the Japanese homeland . . . [and] before the Russians could put in any substantial claim to occupy it and help rule it." [44] Stalin had pledged to enter the war within three months following the end of the conflict in Europe: the dateline was August 8. The Soviet army was then to begin to fulfill whatever political and military objectives Moscow might have had in the Far East. Occurring as they did on August 6 and 9, the bombings of Hiroshima and Nagasaki, which led to Japan's surrender on August 14 — six days after the beginning of the Soviet offensive in Manchuria — represented both the last military acts of World War II and the first acts of the cold war.

The Cold War in Historical Perspective

By the late sixties, historians had as usual gone the full swing of the pendulum. The earlier revisionists of the right had attacked American policies for supposedly turning over the fruits of World War II victory to the Russians; the later revisionists of the left described American postwar policies as the unnecessary containment of a destroyed and impotent Soviet Union whose only postwar claims were legitimate: compensation for the enormous destruction caused by Germany and security from a potential revival of German militarism. These later revisionists overlooked several major points. First, they ignored the ideological outlook of the Soviet regime and the political psychology of its rulers. While not "the" cause of the cold war, these factors could not be put aside as if they did not exist. Second, and related to this ideology, the revisionists of the left overlooked Western perception of Soviet intentions: they overlooked Western fears. To dismiss them as unjustified because of the alleged Soviet weakness or as not genuine but part of a jingoistic mentality aimed at frustrating a rising movement for social justice is not sufficiently convincing. To the extent that these fears were indeed perceived at the time, America's policy could still be regarded as a policy of response after all. Third, the revisionists of the left gave too little credit to America's restraint (at least until the Korean War). To be sure, as will be seen, the United States did not attempt to share its nuclear monopoly and it did make many mistakes of great importance that justified in part Soviet fears of Western intentions. But the United States did not attempt to exploit directly its nuclear monopoly. Nor did it attempt, until after June 1950, to build up its nuclear and/or conventional forces in a way that would have made an American military attack on the Soviet Union possible. Finally, and tying these together, the revisionists of the left plainly ignored the security interests that American policy sought to achieve. The assumption can be made now that these interests were not threatened then in view of Moscow's reduced capabilities and limited ambitions. Whether or not this assumption is true, it is not surprising that a convincing case could not be made at the time. In retrospect, the tragedy is that the only policy either side could have legitimately regarded as one that did not present any serious threat was a policy that placed that state's security at the mercy of the other. In sum, the revisionists of the left paid too much attention to American ideology, Soviet fears, Soviet restraint, and Soviet security and not enough to the Soviet ideology, American fears, American restraint, and American security.

Nobody wanted the cold war. The United States and the Soviet Union had been foreseen for a long time as the two main actors on the international scene. In the 1830's, Tocqueville described the two nations as "marked out by the will of heaven to sway the destinies of half the globe." [45] By that time they were already two of the greatest land empires in the world, and over the following decades both became inhabited with a larger population than the Great Powers of the late nineteenth century — Great Britain, France, and Germany. At however different a pace, America and Russia were both on their way toward unparalleled industrialization. Only a somewhat mythical belief in isolationist principles in the United States and a domestic upheaval in Russia postponed their status as superpowers in 1919. By 1945, the collapse of the traditional sources of power in Europe combined with continued or renewed growth in the United States and Russia made them superpowers by position if not by choice. Their confrontation too was one of position, if not of choice, as the island power of the West instinctively sought to prevent the land power of the East from filling the various power vacuums then existing within the international system. Such divisive factors as the Soviet Union's communist ideology and America's short-lived monopoly of atomic weapons enlarged the conflict further, shaping some of its unique features, even though, admittedly, these factors did not actually cause it.

As such then, the cold war was the fourth great hegemonial struggle fought during the past 150 years to maintain or to restore the balance of power in Europe. And as in the previous struggles, the American people were involved, whether they wanted to be or not.* In several respects, however, the cold war was quite different from previous general European wars. First, there was a new distribution of power that deprived of any significant meaning the former power multipolarity. The new superpower bipolarity preempted any national claim of independence by the old nation states, especially those of Europe whose decline

---

* A listing of the long sequence of European wars presents a vivid picture of the seeming inevitability of American involvement: 1688–1697, War of League of Augsburg (known in America as King William's War, 1689–1697); 1701–1713, War of Spanish Succession (Queen Anne's War, 1702–1713); 1740–1748, War of Austrian Succession (King George's War, 1744–1748); 1756–1763, Seven Years' War (French and Indian War, 1754–1763); 1778–1783, War of the American Revolution (American Revolution, 1775–1783); 1793–1802, Wars of the French Revolution (Undeclared French War, 1798–1800); 1803–1815, Napoleonic wars (War of 1812, 1812–1814); 1914–1918, World War I (World War I, 1917–1918); 1939–1945, World War II (World War II, 1941–1945). (Thomas A. Bailey, *A Diplomatic History of the American People* [Sixth ed.; New York: Appleton-Century-Crofts, Inc., 1955], pp. 23–24.)

was accentuated by the rising expectations of their colonial possessions.[46] Within this bipolar framework ideological antagonism intensified superpower rivalry. Other European wars too had implied a measure of ideological opposition, but never before had the lines been so clearly drawn according to ideological criteria. In repeated instances, communist ideology could be adapted to the requirements of anticolonial revolutions so that the advent of postwar nationalism in the third world also became part of the cold war. Yet, the challenge of such a revolutionary ideology was greatly and unfortunately overemphasized. Often communism merely displayed great opportunism in taking advantage of domestic weaknesses and eventually worsening these weaknesses, rather than causing them. Yet, to the extent that each side allowed itself to believe in the ideological rhetoric of the other, each side could conceivably be understood as seeking to establish its rule all over the world, even though military means were physically and psychologically unavailable to both sides. The homeland of communism, evidently tired by a war it had been most instrumental in winning, could not seriously think of militarily exporting its avowed gospel. Nor were the Western democracies capable of a serious effort at rolling communism back across an already devastated European battleground. Hence, a second peculiarity of the cold war — both Moscow and Washington implicitly resolved that they would avoid employing force against each other. At first the decision was largely motivated by fear of the other whose resources were inflated far beyond what they were.* Later, such a mutual fear became

---

* Paradoxically enough, in the midst of this nascent confrontation both nations proceeded with an accelerated demobilization of their respective armed forces. The Truman Administration lost no time in "bringing the boys back home." By June 30, 1949, the military personnel had been reduced from approximately 12 million four years before to 1,450,000. Most of these remaining troops, as it was to be shown during the first few months of the fighting in Korea, were insufficiently trained and generally not ready for combat action. By that time, the Soviet military resources had also been considerably reduced, from the wartime high of 11.4 million to a possible low of 2.9 million. The Soviet demobilization easily matched America's, given the huge land borders that these forces had to protect plus the domestic needs which the Army may be called upon to fulfill in the Soviet Union. Besides, American forces were one part only of the Western forces that still included among others, the 750,000 men made available by Great

more realistic with perfected nuclear devices of ever greater destructive capability: the more the superpowers thought about the unthinkable, the less tempting the unthinkable became.

Nevertheless, at first both nations took relatively great risks. They spread their confrontation in an unparalleled manner, extensively throughout the world and intensively throughout national and international activity, threatening one another with all the paraphernalia of indirect aggression and subversion that they could devise. In this game of action and reaction, probing and containment, each party helped the pendulum move from one side to the other. Ultimately, the two sides had to face the consequences of their diplomatic bluffs being called. During the Hungarian crisis of October 1956, the Eisenhower administration tacitly conceded that it had neither the resources nor the desire to move into the Soviet sphere of interest in Eastern Europe. During the Cuban missile crisis of October 1962, it was shown that Soviet infiltration in Latin America, the American sphere, had precise limitations that were not to be overstepped. Once the two superpowers understood the limits of the action they might take against one another, the areas of accommodation began to proliferate, at least until the war in Vietnam intensified.

Side by side with such an evolution grew the seeds of a better understanding of each nation's respective goals. Everywhere and about everything, ideological as well as political, yet by and large demilitarized, the cold war had developed within a framework of total opposition and inability to communicate. Given the almost complete opposition that characterized the past experiences and character of the two protagonists, there was a basic incomprehension of the other side's historical past. So, Russia, always aware of its national weakness and territorial insecurity in the face of the ever possible invasion from the West, faced a self-assured America, certain of its national strength and geographic security. Similarly, an often humiliated Russia, whose military successes had usually been the culmination of a series of defeats and which had traditionally looked at the world out-

---

Britain. (See Adam Ulam, *Expansion and Containment* [New York, 1968], pp. 403–4; and Thomas Wolfe, *Soviet Power and Europe, 1945–1970* [Baltimore, 1971], pp. 10–11.)

side for much-needed help in completing its modernization, coped with a self-righteous America, supposedly never defeated in war, proud of its greatness, and eager to propagate it abroad.

But each nation also misunderstood the other's future, as neither side could understand why the other side was not living up to its expectations. The Soviet Union assumed that, following the conclusion of the war, a bitter and frustrated America would soon lapse into isolation, in order to face the enormous problems of reconversion, recession, and unemployment. At Yalta, Roosevelt himself had stated that the withdrawal of American forces from the Continent would be completed less than two years after the end of the war. Why then, asked the Russians, was Truman now speaking as if he foresaw an unlimited involvement of his country in the affairs of Europe? Why this departure from what the Soviets understood to be the traditional policy of the United States? Why these friendly overtures toward the Western zone of Germany and why such concern with the remilitarization of the Western European states *as if* they were indeed to undertake the "liberation" of the Eastern European states from Soviet control? Why such American amity and generosity toward Japan, a traditional threat to Russia? As Adam Ulam states in his highly perceptive analysis of Soviet foreign policy, "Was the construction put upon American policy in the summer of 1947 much more extravagant than the belief held in the West between 1945 and 1949 that the USSR was about to unloose her armed hordes across Europe to the English Channel?" [47] Seemingly, both Washington and Moscow lacked the empathy that was needed if they were to understand one another. Within each country hardly any substantial expertise existed on the other — only, at best, varying degrees of ignorance. Disillusion with misrepresented expectations thus maximized each country's suspicions.

America too faced its own illusions. A weakened Russia was expected to give in to the requests of an America made irresistible by atomic weapons. In the spring of 1945, Truman was being repeatedly advised that "the bomb might well put us in a position to dictate our own terms at the end of the war." [48] Secretary of State James Byrnes hoped with others that America's atomic monopoly, which he thought would last between seven and ten years, might force Russia to agree to an American plan for a lasting world peace. Such weapons might be, in Truman's words, "the greatest thing in history." [49] Furthermore, Russian losses in the previous war went far beyond what America could conceptualize as "acceptable." Between fifteen and twenty million Soviet citizens had been killed and another twenty-five million had been deprived of shelter, through the destruction, complete or partial, of fifteen large cities and innumerable towns and villages. In the words of a sympathetic Western observer, Russia's economic situation was "little short of disastrous." [50] In the aftermath of such suffering and destruction how, Americans asked, could the Russian people long accept the yoke of communist dictatorship? Already the Kremlin was reported as having lost the allegiance of several million representatives of minority groups. How much longer, then, would it be possible to keep the demobilized Russian soldiers harassed and deprived of their fundamental liberties? Had not the time come for the long-awaited collapse of the Soviet regime? And what about the "orgy of good feeling" that seemed to have spread over Russia, whose "almost delirious friendship" toward the American people was significantly recorded by George Kennan from his post at the Moscow embassy? [51] But instead of fulfilling Washington's expectations, Moscow appeared to implement, ever forcefully, its plan of Sovietizing what it regarded as the legitimate fruits of the war. Suspicion bred still more suspicion.

To examine the outbreak of the cold war is to travel through the sinuous paths of conditional history. What would have happened if the allies had been in a position to satisfy faster the Soviet request for a second front? What would have happened if the Soviets had been led by a man other than Stalin, a man who according to Khrushchev's later analysis, "everywhere and in everything . . . saw 'enemies,' 'two-facers' and 'spies.'" [52] As hardly anyone could ever determine what Stalin was up to, it became everyone's prudent behavior to assume that he was up to the worst. What would have happened if Roosevelt had not died, or if Wallace had not been replaced in 1944 as Roosevelt's running mate, or if Churchill had been reelected? But, above all, what would have happened if the United States had been more amenable to a Soviet sphere of influence in Europe?

Such a principle had been recognized in an agreement concluded between Churchill and Stalin in October 1944.[53] According to this agreement, Stalin was to be left free to organize his own favored elements in Rumania and Bulgaria, while Hungary and Yugoslavia were equally split and Greece left to the control of Great Britain. By and large, Stalin lived up to the agreement, which he regarded as a natural extension of traditional European history. In Bulgaria, a part of "his" sphere, the "coalition" government was practically ended as early as August 1945, when the parties of the opposition — the Agrarian and Social Democratic parties — were captured by communist nominees following the forced resignation of their leaders.[54] In Rumania, the second half of the Soviet sphere, Moscow's takeover was implemented through the early and forced "resignation" of King Michael in favor of a so-called National Democratic Front government. In Hungary, on the other hand, relatively free elections were held in the fall of 1945 and the communist take-over did not occur until 1947, with the imprisonment of the Hungarian leaders, Bela Kovacs and Imre Nagy. The communization of Yugoslavia was essentially domestic, initiated with the destruction, through Germany's invasion, of the old political structure. Tito gained power from within. When he tried to export his own revolutionary fervor (in Greece for instance), he encountered the opposition of Stalin, anxious in 1945 to respect Britain's free hand and in 1947 not to engage American forces, now openly committed to the defense of Greece.[*]

Yet, spheres of influence were intrinsically unacceptable to American political philosophy. World War II would not be a war to end all wars, but at least it would bring forth an alternative to power politics and the related evils of secret or open alliances, balances of power, and spheres of influence where the weaker state had its fate decided upon by the stronger state. All these

[*] Much more critical were the questions raised with regard to Poland. Two of these questions were what would be the boundaries of postwar Poland and who would rule it. At Yalta, it had been decided that a "democratic" Poland would receive compensation in the West for the substantial territories acquired by Russia in the East. At Potsdam, Poland's eastern frontier was tentatively agreed upon but neither the question of Poland's western frontier nor that of its democratization were settled. By that time already, and in a way that mixed symbolic, political, and strategic considerations, Poland had become too complex an issue to permit concessions by either side.

were to be replaced, in Roosevelt's words, by a "universal organization in which all peace-loving nations will finally have a chance to join." [55] This goal had been the essential objective of Cordell Hull's wartime tenure as secretary of state, the high tide of which had been reached, in his own estimation, with the Moscow declaration on general security of November 1, 1943. At that time, the United States, the Soviet Union, Great Britain, and China had pledged to establish at the earliest practical date a general international organization, based on the sovereign equality of all peace-loving states, and open to membership by all such states, for the maintenance of international peace and security.

But America's refusal to recognize de facto Soviet gains in Eastern Europe dealt a decisive blow to any remaining hope of continued collaboration. Soviet suspicions of American high-spirited ideals were all the more aroused as they saw the United States practice with a good conscience the very principle against which they preached. The place was, of course, Latin America, "our little region over here which never has bothered anybody," as Secretary Stimson once put it. [56] For the United States, just like Russia, was behaving according to tradition. Collective security for the one already endowed with continental security, regional security for the other, who is little concerned with global security when the potential aggressor is at its door — this was the old pattern of the idealist employing realist means while facing the realist, who was using idealist cover. Those ultimately responsible for the outbreak of the cold war were those long departed — the Founding Fathers of each country who had been naturally unable to prepare their respective societies for the strange world in which they were called upon to assume super status.

Indeed a strange world evolved out of the military victories of a strange alliance. In August 1945, the dawn of the cold war also meant the dawn of the nuclear era. It would take many years to grasp the full meaning of this technological revolution. Meanwhile, in the background, the turmoil of another revolution — the political revolution of rising expectations — added to the cacophony of an international community where the United States itself was going through a diplomatic revolution. It was a strange world, indeed, and for whatever reasons it took form, it remained with us all for a very long time.

3

Expansion and Containment

The Collapse of Europe

"What is Europe now?" asked Winston Churchill in mid-1947. "It is a rubble heap, a charnel house, a breeding ground of pestilence and hate." [1] Indeed it was. Five years of war had left the entire European continent in shambles, a collection of hopeless nations in the most complete state of hunger, poverty, desperation, and chaos. In the relative affluence of the early seventies, it is hard for us to recall Europe's agony and the general atmosphere of past atrocities, actual collapse, and future disturbances. We cannot visualize the millions of people unemployed in England, where almost half the factories were closed in the spring of 1947. A nation that had resisted the onslaught of the German armies could not face an endless and devastating winter. As Louis Halle put it, the country was like "a soldier wounded in war who, now the fighting was over, was bleeding to death." [2] Cigarettes were used as wages in Germany, a nation that only a few years earlier was building a new empire expected to last a thousand years. Germany now lay prostrate, divided into four occupied and ravaged areas. The diet of bread and potatoes for the European urban dweller without access to farm products, the lack of clothing and the scarcity of shoes, the desperate search for coal, the innumerable black markets, and the rampant prostituting — all these appear remote one generation later.

Continental Europe alone, exclusive of England, needed twelve million tons of food in 1946 in order to avoid large-scale starvation. Food production had fallen by 25 per cent from its prewar levels, with seventeen million more people than before the war. In the thirties, too, most European countries had been unable to feed their people out of their own resources. In England, only one-third of the total food consumed had been home grown; it had amounted to less than one-half in Belgium and four-fifths in France. But after 1945, the capability of each nation to produce foodstuff was further reduced, not only by war damages but also by a dramatic succession of "acts of God." In the summer of 1945, drought struck in France. In 1947, an exceptionally harsh winter ruined the wheat crops in England, France, and Germany. The winter was followed by severe floods in the spring, and more damages and disruption were caused in the summer by excessively dry weather.

Industrial output had also collapsed. It reached only one-third of the prewar (1938) volume in Belgium, slightly over 50 per cent in Italy, less than 80 per cent in France. By 1947, Europe's industrial production was 15 per cent less than prewar levels. Inadequately fed and sheltered, without much incentive to work as the increase in prices and taxes steadily reduced their purchasing power (in France, for instance, wholesale prices rose 80 per cent in 1946), Europeans showed little enthusiasm in the reconstruction effort. In Marshall's words, beyond the human losses, beyond the physical destruction of cities, factories, mines, railroads, the war had actually created a "dislocation of the entire fabric of European economy." [3]

Not only was Europe unable to regain on its own the limited standard of living it enjoyed before the war, it was not even in a position to prevent further deterioration. Everything had to be imported — food, raw material, industrial equipment, agricultural machinery — but these imports needed to be paid for, and Europe had no substantial foreign exchange reserves left. In 1947 alone, Western Europe's dollar deficit totaled over $8 billion. During the period between the end of the war and the beginning of the Marshall Plan, America supplied Western and Southern Europe with roughly $11.3 billion to help these countries face interim problems.[4]

The collapse of Europe, however, was not simply economic or financial. It was also military, political, and social. The military establishments of all continental nations had been not only weakened but discredited as well. Defeated was the French army, supposedly the strongest and most dependable continental force in the thirties, but so outfought, outmaneuvered, and outequipped that, in June 1940, it surrendered to Germany after a mere few weeks of serious fighting. Gone too was the German army and its short-lived aura of invincibility, as well as the Italian army whose moment of national glory did not long survive the Ethiopian campaigns of 1936. With manpower made plentiful by chronic unemployment, military forces might possibly be reconstituted. But there was no collective desire to fight, hence genuine neutralist pressures were exerted by populations thoroughly exhausted by war and reluctant to enter new conflicts for which, as usual, Europe would provide the battleground.

Political establishments too had been discredited, before and during the war, and a widespread crisis of political confidence afflicted each nation. The old accounts of the thirties were being settled under cover of an assumed postwar justice. Collaborators were found everywhere, and everywhere they were eliminated, personally or professionally. In France alone, 2,000 death sentences were passed, together with 40,000 detentions and 48,000 condemnations for national indignity.[5] Many of these affected individuals at one level or another had occupied official positions that now needed to be filled by new men, not always available and not always competent. Thus, in most European countries a leadership vacuum existed, and there could not be found a lasting majority able to revive the will of the nation and to reorganize its productive resources.

Such a political crisis was especially convenient for local communist parties. Forced to go underground in the aftermath of the Russo-German Pact of 1939, European communists had joined national movements of resistance when the Soviet Union entered the war against Germany. Their organization helped them to become rapidly the main force of these movements, a status symbolically enhanced because German forces everywhere persecuted them. These parties were now rewarded by the electorate — 19 per cent of the total vote in Italy (June 1946) and 28 per cent in France (November 1946). In France, in Italy, in Belgium, the communists were active members of governments of national unity. But such national unity was conceivable only as long as the facade of East-West unity was maintained. In these countries, therefore, small cold wars grew together with the cold war proper, and none of these governments long survived America's Truman Doctrine. With the presidential Message to Congress actually delivered on March 11, the communists ceased to be part of the government on March 12 in Belgium, on May 4 in France, and on May 31 in Italy: the threat to Europe's security was now seen as coming from within as well as from without.

When the German armies swept across Europe in 1940 all European states were transformed, willingly or unwillingly, into dependencies of the Nazi Empire. In every one of these states, thousands of people had turned against their own countrymen and fought alongside the enemy. The very notion of the nation state had been dismembered (completely dismembered when Germany too was defeated), thereby compounding the ineffectiveness with which postwar problems of reconstruction were tackled. Consequently, in 1945, throughout Europe — with the possible exceptions of England and such neutral countries as Switzerland and Sweden — nationalism appeared suspect. Source of all evil, the nation state was transcended, at least for a while, by movements in favor of European unification. It was not surprising that in the three major countries on the continent some of the leading political figures came from borderlands. Robert Schuman in France, and Alcide de Gasperi in Italy, had formerly held dual nationality; Konrad Adenauer in Germany had promoted separatist movements in the aftermath of World War I. Everywhere, public and private figures called for the creation of a United States of Europe. But born out of destruction and misery, these calls failed to survive subsequent reconstruction and recovery.

The postwar years enlarged the vacuum that the war had created in Europe. Economically deprived, politically unstable, and militarily impotent, the old European states faced the world outside with uncertainty and weariness. In traditionally predominant nations, such as France and Great Britain, policymakers wondered what direction they should give to their policies. What was the status of their countries now? Were they still great powers in their own right? Could they find salvation in neutrality, or should they seek their security through an alliance with one of the superpowers? In France, under de Gaulle's leadership, old diplomatic patterns reappeared even before the conclusion of the war. Signed on December 10, 1944, the Franco-Russian alliance pledged automatic cooperation in preventing a resurgence of Germany's power and any action that might render possible a new attempt at German aggression. Diplomatically, Moscow greeted the new treaty as a sign of France's reentry among the great powers: "On the continent Germany will remain placed between Russia and France," declared the Soviet ambassador to France. "That is why the Franco-Soviet pact allows us to think that Frenchmen and Russians with all their allies, will be able to assure to Europe a stable and durable peace." [6] To increase America's weight in dealing with de Gaulle, American policy planners also recommended satisfying French wishes and treating this embattled nation in all respects according to its potential power and influence rather than its present strength. [7]

The British government was also resuming traditional attitudes in areas of perennial British interest such as the Middle East and Southern Europe. But these governmental attempts to reassert national prestige and independence often offended public wishes for new, a-national solutions. Such efforts also conflicted with the compelling necessity of relying upon outside aid for economic recovery and military defense. For Europe, the choice was one of means, and policies were, as always, being dictated by circumstances. That most states decided to go along with the United States is hardly surprising, not only because of previously established links between these nations and America, but also because America alone was able and willing to provide the much-needed assistance. Nevertheless, such decisions were not always approved of by a highly suspicious general public. As a result a gap developed between official thinking, characterized by an expressed decision not to remain isolated, and public thinking, which often regarded the growing schism between Moscow and Washington as a choice between two evils. To Washington, European doubts, whenever perceived, appeared horrendous. They were often dismissed as an obvious communist ploy.

Western Europe's internal debate, however, was a real one. What could Western Europeans do? Where could they go? If the military threat raised by Moscow was realistically assessed by Washington, Western European states were too weak to join in any protective alliances. If the perception of that threat was not realistic, then Western European states were too divided at home to join in any political or ideological challenge to the communist doctrine. Western Europe was deterred from endorsing American policy by the fear of offending Stalin, whose counteraction they could ill afford to face. But it was also deterred from rejecting that policy by the fear of offending Truman, whose assistance they could ill afford to lose.

The delicacy of Europe's attempted balance between Washington and Moscow was particularly apparent in the Atlantic Alliance that was entered into by states (Great Britain and France) that had signed prior treaties with the Soviet Union.[8] These treaties had pledged the contracting parties not to conclude any alliance or take part in any coalition directed against either party. To satisfy the requirements of an alliance with America without risking an automatic invalidation of the alliance with Russia, Western Europeans wanted to diminish the anti-Soviet direction of the Atlantic Alliance by discarding the high phraseology that was characteristic of the Truman Doctrine. Yet, Western Europeans also attempted to impale the American administration and the senate on the specifics of their commitment to Europe even though the European denial of an immediate Soviet threat largely diminished, in theory at least, America's primary interest in the alliance.

An unstable France was a good example of the differences that existed between America and its European partners at the start of their association. Like most of its neighbors, France had a postwar electorate almost evenly divided between the political right and the political left. Every new action taken by Washington found at least one part of the electorate generally eager to criticize it. The Truman Doctrine was regarded as an interference in domestic affairs inasmuch as it described any communist party in the world as a threat to American security. The Marshall Plan was found to be divisive since it might freeze the East-West split in Europe by keeping Eastern Europe out of a general European economic recovery. Later, it would be argued that the war in Korea had been instigated by Washington to create a more compelling sense of urgency and thus accelerate European rearmament.[9]

Whether or not these charges were justified is less important, for our immediate purposes, than the state of mind they reflected. For such a state of mind was by no means expressed in France alone, and by communists only. It was also shared by many Western Europeans who were as hostile to Moscow's ideology as they were to Washington's. It was a state of mind born out of a European nationalism of frustration, bitterness, and humiliation. It was a state of mind that looked upon the United States as a strong country, but one whose strength might become dangerous because of America's innocence and inexperience: consider, for example, the visit taken in late 1950 by British Prime Minister Clement Attlee to "lecture" President Truman on nuclear power and the direction of Soviet diplomacy.[10] Europeans looked upon this country as a rich and generous country, but one whose wealth and generosity could become embarrassing and, at times, shocking: consider, for example, their angered reaction to the specific directions outlined in the aid agreements that were part of the Marshall Plan.[11] Europeans agreed that this was a well-intentioned country, but one whose good intentions were too often misled by a misunderstanding or misrepresentation of what the Europeans regarded as the realities of the world.

But the necessities of the situation made financial aid and military protection indispensable. Despite their divisions, their fears, and their criticisms, Europeans eagerly seized the opportunity of the Marshall Plan and actually promoted the Atlantic Alliance as an alliance of nations that might provide national problems with international solutions. But when the indispensability of aid and protection became more questionable, such divisions, fears, and criticism reappeared to disrupt the relations between America and Western Europe and to impose national solutions on international problems.

The Strategy of Containment

Following the end of World War II, America thought of Western Europe as "an organism with a soft shell," as Dean Acheson put it.[12] Most of those countries feared subversion, and America's primary concern was to reorganize the states that faced the Soviet lines. "Europe," said President Truman, "is still the key to world peace." [13]

United States policy also aimed at displacing Soviet influence in Eastern Europe, expecting that the Soviets would inevitably withdraw. But such a withdrawal would occur only if the Western nations held firm in the face of Soviet pressure. Washington applied the lessons it had learned from two previous world conflicts: cooperation between the two sides of the Atlantic needed to be formally recorded, and a multilateral (as opposed to bilateral) alliance was the best way to assure such cooperation. Said Dean Acheson in March 1949: "If the free nations do not stand together, they will fall one by one. . . . We and the free nations of Europe are determined that history shall not repeat itself in that melancholy particular." [14]

The task and the interest of the United States was in helping "contain" communist expansion in Europe. The strategic dependence of American security on that of Europe was not substantially and persuasively disputed at the time. In retrospect, it might be argued that this dependence was exaggerated. But then, as now, there could be hardly any doubt that the "fall" of Western Europe would make America if not insecure at least much less secure. At the most, a Soviet domination of Western Europe would shift the global distribution of power against the United

States and ultimately create a direct threat to America's physical security. At the least, a Soviet domination of Western Europe would create an indirect threat to America's security by forcing the creation of an American fortress that would strain the nation's resources, which were already depleted by the loss of European resources, and slowly erode its democratic institutions.

America's nascent policy of containment was attributed to George Kennan, whose controversial "X article" (a lengthy cable that he sent from the American embassy in Moscow, in January 1947, on the request of then Secretary of the Navy James Forrestal) provided the Truman administration with the theoretical framework eagerly sought at the time.[15] Kennan's analysis indicated that the main thread of Soviet communism was unlimited domestic authority. Having seized power while they were still a small minority, the communists had wanted to secure their rule against both internal and external enemies. "Until such time as that security might be achieved, they placed far down on their scale of operational priorities the comforts and happiness of the peoples entrusted to their care."

With time, Kennan continued, this Soviet absolutist conduct could not be successfuly completed. On the contrary, it produced a violent counterreaction as the ruthlessness of the party steadily increased potential opposition to a level even higher than in 1917. In the aftermath of World War II, therefore, the Soviets found themselves taken in by their own ideological logic. Because capitalism no longer existed inside Russia, opposition to their rule was attributed to foreign agitators, and the retention of their dictatorial power justified by the menace of capitalism abroad.

Because of its quest for security, the main objective of the Soviet regime in foreign affairs was to fill every vacuum by exerting a "cautious, persistent pressure toward the disruption and weakening of all rival influence and rival power." This pressure, Kennan argued, could be contained by America through the "long term, patient but firm and vigilant" application of "counter-forces, at a series of constantly shifting geographic and political points, corresponding to the shifts and maneuvers of Soviet policy." (Later, Kennan more specifically limited the task of containment as that of preventing the "fall" of the three areas of the world other than the United States and the Soviet

Union where "the sinews of modern military strength could be produced in quantity" — the Rhine valley with its adjacent industrial areas, England, and Japan.) [16]

If successfully managed, containment would also imply rollback, as American actions were expected to influence the internal developments of a state that had "within it the seeds of its own decay." Faced with America's external pressure, burdened with unsolvable domestic problems, and subjected to the additional strains of their political dominion in Eastern Europe, Soviet Russia, predicted Kennan, "might be changed overnight from one of the strongest to one of the weakest and most pitiable of national societies. Thus, the future of Soviet power may not be by any means as secure as Russian capacity for self-delusion would make it appear to the men in the Kremlin."

Kennan's exposé too easily granted the worldwide character of Soviet expansionist aims without indicating how Soviet expansion would take place and how it should be contained. That Kennan himself later criticized his own analysis as ambiguous, careless and indiscriminate is a meager solace.[17] That he disapproved of the Truman Doctrine, which was after all in line with his exposé, merely points to the problem of communication between those who plan or devise policies and those who implement them. That the Russians may have never seriously contemplated a military invasion of Western Europe is now academic, although probably true.* For now armed with the rhetoric of the Truman Doctrine (to which, Kennan feared, Moscow might respond with no less than a declaration of war) [18] and the tools of unlimited containment, America resolved to revive, stabilize, and strengthen Western Europe to restrain Stalin from his perceived expansionist impulse.

---

* In April 1948, Kennan attempted to explain his view of containment in a letter, which he never sent, written to Walter Lippmann, whose columns spearheaded the controversy over containment in the late summer and fall of 1947. "The Russians don't want," he insisted, "to invade anyone. It is not in their tradition. . . . They . . . prefer to do the job politically . . . that does not mean without violence. But it means that the violence is nominally *domestic*, not *international*, violence. . . . The policy of containment related to the effort to encourage other peoples to resist this type of violence and to defend the internal integrity of their countries." (*Memoirs* [Boston, 1967], p. 361.)

The Marshall Plan

Very few policies in modern times have succeeded as well as the Marshall Plan. When it officially ended in 1951, the economic systems of sixteen European countries had been rehabilitated at a cost of $13.5 billion for the United States, approximately $4 billion less than the anticipated cost.[19] By 1951, industrial production in the Marshall Plan area was 35 per cent higher than in 1938, and agricultural output had climbed to more than 10 per cent above prewar output, thus largely balancing the increase in population.[20] The revival of European trade had, by that time, begun to close the dollar gap. Inflationary pressures had been alleviated and national currencies stabilized. It is precisely because such policies never abound that they should not be forgotten. Said Mr. Hugh Gaitskell, then a leader of the British Labor party and Chancellor of the Exchequer:

> We are not an emotional people, and we are not always very articulate. But these characteristics should not be allowed to hide the very real and profound sense of gratitude which we feel toward the American people, not only for the material help they have given us but also for the spirit of understanding and friendship in which it has been given.[21]

The character and success of the Marshall Plan were fundamentally shaped by two basic decisions. The first one related to Washington's insistence that the initiative come from Europe and that requests for aid take a multinational form. Two programs were being simultaneously undertaken. One called explicitly for American support of the economic revitalization of Europe, and the other stressed implicitly American support of Europe's political unification. That the United States should try to secure European initiative in both domains was indicative of Washington's effective sensitivity to Europe's concern with national sovereignty. In all probability, had the United States not insisted on such a multilateral, all-European approach to these problems it would have been faced with competing national demands, somewhat padded for competitive purposes. The United States would have had to make choices between these demands, choices bound to be politically unpopular in "neglected" areas. Finally, America's choices would have left European governments in a position to blame Washington for any features of the programs that were disagreeable to their electorates and for any part of the program that was plainly unsuccessful.[22]

The second major decision of the Marshall Plan was to invite the Soviet Union and its allies to participate in the common recovery program. A sensible effort was made by American policymakers to define the plan not according to communism proper but according to the economic maladjustment that made European society vulnerable to exploitation by extremist movements. Moscow's rejection of the Western invitation was delayed a few days, and Soviet Foreign Minister Molotov attended the all-European conference that was hastily convened in Paris to organize the details and the implementation of the American plan. But, from the Soviet viewpoint, the drawbacks of a communist participation were numerous: the possible opening of Eastern Europe to Western economic control, the requested extension of detailed information pertaining to the Soviet economy, the connection that the Marshall Plan appeared to have, despite all disclaimers, with the Truman Doctrine, the Soviet unwillingness to cooperate with Germany, to which the offer had also been extended. Also, Stalin might have been aware of the American planners' intention to welcome the Soviets on a basis of full participation in bearing the burdens of the plan.[23] Yet, Soviet participation would have certainly reduced and conceivably voided the effectiveness of the Marshall Plan. It might even have caused its cancellation altogether as Congress was in no mood to extend American economic assistance to the Soviet Union. American legislators, on the other hand, were eager to support anything that Stalin opposed. "Top target" on the Kremlin's list, the Marshall Plan became "top priority" on Washington's list,[24] and, in retrospect, Stalin's decision to combat the Marshall Plan from without was doubtless one of his major, postwar diplomatic mistakes.

However successsful, the Marshall Plan failed to fulfill several of its objectives. From a national viewpoint, the plan helped bring about economic recovery but it did not succeed in ending the communist electoral appeal in France and Italy. Inadequate information was in part responsible for this failure: a survey of French opinion conducted early in the program revealed that 70 per cent of those Frenchmen who had heard of the Marshall Plan felt that it was bad for them.[25] Clearly, political struggles fought in the economic domain need to be translated into political victories at the polls, but these victories did not take place in national elections. In 1953, 22.7 per cent of the electorate still voted for the communist party in Italy, as opposed to 19 per cent in 1946. In the summer of the same year, 26 per cent of the French electorate voted communist, as opposed to 28 per cent five years earlier.

From a regional viewpoint, the plan did not succeed in moving Western Europe toward unity. The Organization for European Economic Cooperation (OEEC), which was set up to determine the long-term economic needs of the area and to supervise the most effective satisfaction of these needs, was never accepted by most of its eighteen members as a major vehicle for European unification. Its secretariat remained ineffective and without real power despite initial efforts by the French government to have the Marshall Plan handled by a supranational organization. Furthermore, the OEEC could not easily be conceived as both an inducement for prompt economic recovery and a vehicle for economic unification. It was doubtful that the economic recovery of Western European states could help achieve their political unification. On the whole, a united Europe remained, in Europe, an intellectual idea with little mass support. It gathered political momentum essentially in time of crisis. Thus, the more successful the Marshall Plan, the less likely it was to generate European unity — the impetus for which, however, was provided in the early fifties by another crisis caused this time by Germany's rearmament.

The Birth of the Western Coalition

The immediate aim of the Marshall Plan was to help the participating countries regain a self-reliance that would render them economically independent by 1952. But although Western

Europe had its economic health and vigor restored, it needed to be protected from direct aggression as well. Whether or not such aggression was ever seriously contemplated by Stalin is questionable. Most Kremlinologists in the late sixties found behind the Soviet dictator's irrational quirks considerable calculation and caution in foreign affairs.[26] Nevertheless, by February 1948, following the communist coup in Czechoslovakia, all Eastern European states had become Soviet satellites, and Iran, Greece, and Turkey continued to be under strong communist pressure. One could well argue that the Soviets were attempting to fulfill traditional national interests and that, by staying carefully away from the American sphere, they were in no way challenging American power. It would then follow that a settlement between the two superstates was still obtainable with a mutual recognition of each other's interests. Former Vice-President Henry Wallace was advocating this position when he ran for the presidency on a third-party ticket in 1948. But, however convincing now, is it surprising that such an interpretation was not seriously considered by policymakers then? How was it possible to distinguish between direct and indirect aggression when the leaders of the French and Italian communist parties were announcing that they would welcome indeed Soviet troops in Paris and in Rome — troops already stationed in occupied Germany and elsewhere in Eastern Europe? [27] In the 1940's, then, the United States guarantee against direct and indirect aggression would finally take the form Europe had sought since 1919: a formal alliance linking America's security to that of Europe. The initiative, however, rested not with the Truman administration, but with Europe to request the alliance and with the United States senate to approve it.

Europe's initiative was taken through the Brussels Pact, which was signed by France, England, Belgium, Luxembourg, and the Netherlands in March 1948. Unlike the Anglo-French treaty of Dunkerque, concluded the previous year, the Brussels Pact had no anti-German focus. It provided automatic assistance in the event of an unspecified aggression in Europe against any one of the participants. The pact also envisaged the creation of a permanent consultative council. Clearly, these features were welcome in Washington as they repeated the pattern set by the

Marshall Plan. That the pact was concluded so rapidly was in part a reaction to the February coup in Czechoslovakia. In the United States, approval of the pact came at once. On the day of its signing, following requests by the French and British Foreign Ministers, President Truman officially pledged that American willingness to help Europe would match Europe's willingness to help itself, with collective (regional) action.[28]

To make this promise constitutionally possible, Truman sought prior support from the senate, which provided this support in the 1948 Vandenberg Resolution. The resolution stated the senate's approval of American participation in "such regional and other collective arrangements as are based on continuous and effective self help and mutual aid, and as affect [United States] national security." By relying on Article 51 of the United Nations Charter, which permitted regional defense, the resolution enabled the United States to operate within the United Nations, but outside the veto constraints of the Security Council. Most importantly, the Vandenberg Resolution indicated that, for the first time in its history, America was now willing to conclude peacetime alliances outside the Western Hemisphere.

The resolution was aproved by the Senate with only four dissenting votes. Less than four weeks later negotiations officially began between the United States, Canada, and the members of the Brussels Pact. During the next few months, five new participants (Italy, Iceland, Norway, Denmark, and Portugal) joined the talks. When signed, on April 4, 1949, the NATO treaty contemplated optimum defense exertions from the twelve participating countries and maximum aid and supplies from the United States. After the Korean War, further institutional arrangements for military, diplomatic, and financial cooperation progressively transformed the Atlantic Alliance into a regional organization as well as a guarantee pact.[29] Ultimately, this organization involved a Permanent Council, to coordinate the activities of the alliance; a Military Committee, responsible to the Council and consisting of the Chiefs of Staff of the member states (with the exception of Iceland which had no army); several regional planning groups, foremost among them the European Command, under the Supreme Allied Commander, Europe (SACEUR); a Secretary General, appointed by the Council for an undefined period; and an international staff of several hundred. Three more states were subsequently admitted in the alliance — Greece and Turkey in 1951, and West Germany in 1955. For ideological reasons, and despite its strategic importance, Spain was excluded from the alliance, as well as Yugoslavia, whose participation was briefly considered by the Western states.

The NATO treaty, like most treaties, was a general declaration of intentions. The pledge of mutual support was open to substantial escape clauses, and little in its text justified Senator Robert A. Taft's fear that it had placed America "at the mercy of the foreign policies of eleven nations." [30] The treaty was strictly defensive. It was applicable only in case of armed attack. Should an armed attack occur, each nation was to take, individually or collectively, "such action as it deemed necessary." This commitment did not mean, as Dean Acheson told the Senate Foreign Relations Committee, that "the United States would be automatically at war if one of the nations covered by the pact is subjected to armed attack." [31] The gravity of the armed attack, and its effect upon America's vital interests, would be considered and acted upon ad hoc. Thus, the report of the Senate Committee stated: "What we may do to carry out that commitment . . . will depend upon our own independent decision in each particular instance." Contrary to what was subsequently argued, in no part of the treaty was the United States obligated to react to an attack on Paris or Copenhagen in the same way it would react to an attack on New York City.[32] Finally, each government was expected to operate within strict constitutional restrictions, a requirement carefully inserted in Article 11 of the treaty.

Should an indirect aggression threaten the territorial integrity, political independence, and security of any member, only consultation was pledged. But, should a revolution be aided and abetted from without, such foreign assistance might be considered an armed attack. NATO intervention in a civil war within a Western European state was therefore conceivable. In later years, the status of Algeria (specifically mentioned by name in the treaty) became a potential source of dispute among the Atlantic allies. But the French government refused to consider the hostilities in Algeria as an external war. Instead, it argued that the Algerian situation was a purely domestic matter, and as the

French refused to appeal for aid or consultation the alliance remained officially unconcerned with it.

The treaty of April 1949 was also limited in space and in time. It extended to a finite geographical area including the member states alone, excluding major colonial areas of the participating European nations, in South and Southeast Asia, in Africa, and in the Middle East. Nothing in the language of the treaty compelled the NATO partners to render aid to the French in Indochina, to the British in Malaya, and to the United States in Korea. If there were doubt as to whether or not an armed attack had indeed occurred within the "North Atlantic area" (an attack upon a ship or an aircraft, for example), each member state was left conveniently free to determine on its own the nature and the significance of the attack. The treaty could be modified after ten years, and each nation reserved the right to withdraw after twenty years, on a one-year notice. Europe's efforts to obtain a fifty-year commitment were opposed by America's open objection to forecasting international developments in such a distant future.[33]

In 1949, it was essentially believed in Washington that a statement of American intentions was sufficient to deter aggression in Europe. Despite the occasional tenseness of the situation, there was no sustained fear of a military attack on Western Europe. With the information he had gathered from the United States government and from the heads of European governments, John Foster Dulles, who was a senator from New York at the time when NATO was being debated, had concluded: "The Soviet Union does not now contemplate large-scale military aggression in Europe."[34] Vis-à-vis the Russians, the treaty would set up a new Monroe Doctrine that warned them to stay out of Western Europe.[35] The Europeans hoped that the treaty would be the bolt of lightning that transformed apathy and despair into hope and confidence in facing the staggering problems of reconstruction and defense with American assistance.[36] To everyone, the treaty was a vivid reminder of America's "Europe first" policy. If peace and security could be achieved in the North Atlantic area, it could easily be achieved in other areas as well.[37]

Already, however, this partnership was a troubled one, and within the alliance itself each nation looked at its partners with suspicion and uncertainty. America could not easily overcome the surprise caused by France's early military and political collapse in June 1940. It saw in France a weakness that needed to be strengthened if a unified Western coalition was ever to exist. Conversely, the French were suspicious of what they regarded as collusion between Washington and London. The French government was anxious to establish, in the eyes of the American government, its leadership of continental Europe. Yet, it thought that somehow America was "more generous" and "more friendly" toward the British government.[38] The Italians, too, entered the alliance with mixed emotions. Riots broke out throughout the country, and some fist fights occurred at parliament. The issue became a domestic one as the majority coalition identified the Italian communist opposition with the "threat" raised by the Soviet Union. Great Britain was still trying to reconcile its relationship to Europe, its obligations to the Commonwealth, and its "special partnership" with the United States. It ultimately antagonized them all.

The Atlantic Alliance was all things to all people. The French presented it as a follow-up on the Franco-Russian alliance of December 1944; they still looked upon Germany as a major menace to their security. The British regarded the alliance as the restoration of the old power game in Europe where, thanks to their influence in Washington, they would still continue to hold the balance. To the Italian government, the alliance provided the best available means to seek an early revision of its peace treaties with the United States, Great Britain, and France, while securing more support against Yugoslavia for Italy's claims over the port of Trieste.

Paradoxically enough, the war in Korea helped bridge these differences by providing the new allies with a recognizable danger and urgency. In June 1950, Western Europe, which had remained relatively passive while the Soviet territorial expansion in Eastern Europe had become a fait accompli, now grew more responsive to America's call for general and accelerated rearmament. "From now on," emphasized Dean Acheson, "it is action which counts and not further resolutions or further plans or further meetings." [39] The war in Korea provided the alliance with a new unity. It was, as McGeorge Bundy has suggested, a good opportunity "to adopt openly a policy urgently recommended in private for some months previously." [40] But the unity achieved was at most military; political and strategic differences between allies were not resolved. They were merely postponed and, in the sixties, the lessening of the external threat revealed these differences again.[41]

The unanimity reached periodically at every interallied meeting was founded on a general agreement about its basic aims. "Special groups," "liaison teams," and "standing committees," regularly agreed first to build up defense forces sufficiently, second to devise a common defense strategy, and third to preserve the sound and stable economy necessary to support such a defense effort. Such agreement, however, was not always extended to the way these objectives could be satisfied or even, in some instances, reconciled. For instance, how far could the alliance go in building up adequate strength and at the same time preserve a sound and stable economy? With a per capita income of approximately one-third that of America, Europe faced obvious difficulties in diverting its scarce resources toward rearmament. Everywhere, popular reactions demanded lesser taxes, better food, more houses, and more consumer goods even if fewer guns, planes, and tanks were manufactured. But Europe's minimal contribution in turn irritated America, particularly as the costs and burdens of Western defense continued to rise though military targets were not attained. For in America too the claim was made that military expenditures covered too large a share of national wealth, thus endangering economic stability.

Regardless of the cost, the efficacy of conventional rearmament was also disputed by European allies. Could the alliance ever devise conventional forces strong enough to face Russia's? In 1949, the military power of the Soviet Union was assumed (not necessarily rightly) to exceed the combined military power of both Russia and Germany in 1939. Yet, during the war, 200 German divisions, well armed and well led, had been unable to defend the Third Reich. How, then, could 40 or 60 army divisions now defend the whole continent against a Russian invasion? Conventional defense might be effective if, and only if, 100 or 150 American divisions were deployed in Europe even before the beginning of the hostilities.

This at least was Western Europe's response to America's call for strengthening the conventional forces of the alliance. Washington, however, did not look with much favor upon a large American ground presence in Europe. "Are we going to be expected to send substantial numbers of troops over there as a more or less permanent contribution?" Senator Bourke Hickenlooper asked Secretary Acheson during the NATO hearings. "The answer to that question," Acheson replied, "is a clear and absolute 'no.' " [42] An American air force (supplemented with American atomic capability), a British navy, and a European ground force would be sufficient to deter the Soviets. But assuming that this division of military labor was acceptable to most European allies — and it was not — what would be the place of West Germany within this force? The Atlantic Alliance could not dedicate itself to the defense of a Europe that included Germany without having the Germans themselves participate in the common effort. Yet, how could one secure Germany's military participation without some German rearmament? One answer was to have German soldiers but no German army, or even a German army that would be strong enough to defeat the Soviet army and yet weak enough to be defeated by the French or British army. Obviously this was not possible. [43]

To the Europeans, still feeling the ravages of the last war, Germany could not easily be dismissed as a threat of the past. At least part of the protection they sought was related to a potential revival of Germany's military capability. To Washington, however, the threat that needed to be deterred came from the Soviet Union. The more urgently Washington perceived that threat, the less attention it paid to other problems. As part of a regional grouping or as a single entity, Germany had to be rearmed if the defense of Europe was to be organized in any effective way at all. So, despite repeated pledges to the contrary, the Truman administration officially asked, in September 1950, that Germany contribute 10 of the 60 army divisions that were expected from the Western European allies. [44]

As has been often true since 1945, France took the lead in expressing Europe's opposition to the United States request. In October 1950, the French response was to use European unity as the framework within which Germany might altogether disappear as a nation. The idea of European unity had already been used the year before by France. Unable to convince its Western allies that the industrial resources of Germany's Ruhr complex should be internationalized, the French government had successfully sponsored the formation of the Coal and Steel Community, a supranational organization wherein France, Germany, Italy, Belgium, the Netherlands, and Luxembourg pooled together their coal and steel resources. With Washington now requesting Germany's rearmament, the new French offer, the so-called Pleven Plan, was to set up a European Defense Community (EDC) under the executive command of a European Political Community. The purpose of this plan was not so much to create a unified Europe as it was one to contain the revival of Germany's military capability. "Europe" was the means chosen for the absorption of a country that, it had now been demonstrated, could neither be dismembered nor neutralized, neither disarmed nor pastoralized. But even such a framework was acceptable to France only if Great Britain's participation was secured on top of further American guarantees. These guarantees would ensure that the European "experience" was still conducted within an Atlantic framework. France would not take the risk of locking itself up in a "small dark box," where it might ultimately be unable to match German dynamism and where, therefore, no counterpoise to Germany's early domination of the new entity could be perceived.

Ultimately, the collapse of the EDC was guaranteed by Great Britain's reluctance to join it in 1951–1952, even though its death certificate was signed by the French Assembly when it refused to ratify the treaty in August 1954. The whole history of Great Britain explained such a distaste for the integration of the British army into a supranational, European army. It was only during these early years that the combined threat of Russian imperialism and German militarism might have generated a Europe-wide consensus for the EDC and defeated France's own distaste. But by 1953, it was already too late. With the war in Korea ended, with Stalin dead, and with renewed hopes that East-West détente was on its way, the apparent need for European unity had lost its urgency. That Washington continued to insist on it made the EDC episode one of the gravest crises experienced by the Atlantic Alliance in the fifties. American threats to undertake an "agonizing reappraisal" were matched by the reemergence of various European groups asking for cold war neutrality for Europe.

After the demise of the EDC, Great Britain made its commitment to the Continent and pledged to keep a few contingents of British forces there as long as its European allies wanted them. For Great Britain this step alone was revolutionary: never before in modern times had British forces been specifically committed to service on the Continent, except in wartime. This commitment paved the way for the Paris Pact (October 1954), which recognized the full sovereignty of West Germany. The Brussels Treaty Organization of 1948 was enlarged into a Western European Union (WEU), which was joined by West Germany and Italy. Through WEU West Germany was to contribute 12 army divisions to the defense of Europe, more than what President Truman had asked for in the first place. But several safeguards were included: West Germany renounced the right to manufacture atomic, biological, and chemical weapons, as well as guided missiles, large naval vessels, and bombers. At the same time, the American and British pledges to maintain their continental forces were restated, thus paving the way, in May of the following year, 1955, to the admission of West Germany in NATO. In 1971, American forces in Western Europe still amounted to over 300,000 men.

Expansion and Containment

It is common to observe the wide divergence between the world as it is and the world as men perceive it. A further source of distortion is added when one seeks to perceive, and understand, the world as it *was*. Any historical record ought to be read in relation to the conditions prevailing when the events in question occurred. Unfortunately, the record is too often read in retrospective relation to subsequent developments.

America's containment policy in Western Europe succeeded inasmuch as nothing happened: Soviet aggression, assuming that it was ever planned, never occurred. Yet, the success of American policy may also have spelled its undoing. Achieved thanks to America's assistance, the recovery of Western Europe placed the

Soviet Union in a new defense posture. Admittedly, Stalin's main recourse in the military field lay in balancing American atomic and air power with Soviet land power. With no strategic weapons capable of reaching continental United States, the Soviet military posture lent itself to deterrence only if the Soviet capacity to overrun Europe to the Atlantic was made to be credible.[45] Should the Soviets be unable to preserve the credibility of their conventional superiority, they could conceivably be served with an atomic ultimatum from Washington whose policy, as *they* might have perceived it, was to expel Moscow from Eastern Europe. Washington described its policy as the containment of Soviet expansion. But to Moscow this policy reflected America's decision of expanding beyond its traditional sphere of influence. Should such expansion go unchecked, it would ultimately roll back Moscow's own line of containment. In a striking instance of the reversal of cause and effect, America's very success in the containment of the Soviet Union in Western Europe went far toward creating the necessity for containment.

The success of containment also ensured its adoption in other areas — particularly in Asia, as will be seen. The American recipe for global containment of communism thus came to include the three major ingredients that were used in Europe: at the economic level, foreign assistance; at the political level, regional unification; at the military level, formal alliances.

Western Europe's receptiveness to foreign aid was unique. Western European states already possessed an integrated economic infrastructure, lived in a market economy, had an impressive array of managerial and technological skills and a long-established entrepreneurial tradition. Europe did not lack the many intangible factors that, in other areas, made economic growth so laborious. What was needed for Europe's economic recovery could be defined and provided within a limited period of time. In other words, there was in Europe a short-term problem that had but a distant relation to the long-term dilemmas that foreign aid attempted to resolve elsewhere.

America's receptiveness to the idea of a united Europe was understandable considering America's own background. Yet it seemed that throughout the fifties, American policy lost the sensitivity to European aspirations that it displayed in earlier years. America based its thought too much on the cold war, and not enough on those problems that Europe had encountered traditionally. America's entry into an "entangling alliance" was indeed a major revolution in its foreign policy — a revolution that accounted for some of the initial errors. But to think of a European army where France and Germany, Belgium and Italy shared the same uniform only five years after the agonies of World War II was also a major revolution in Europe's foreign policies — a revolution that accounted for the soul searching and the quest for ever more guarantees. Neither side displayed much empathy for the other's hesitation. At any rate, integration in other areas of the world — in Asia, Africa, and Latin America — went counter to a pattern that aimed at creating new political units rather than at integrating old ones.

Finally, the alliance that constituted the backbone of American containment policy in Europe became overmilitarized as too much was made of the assumption that a major Soviet military attack was imminent. As Washington believed that the rearmament of the NATO countries had prevented such an attack from taking place, it was tempted to establish NATO-like alliances everywhere else, without first examining the differences that another place, another enemy, and another time might introduce in America's interests and commitments. These differences were still being debated in the early seventies.

4

The Globalization of Containment

The Communization of China

In contrast with Europe, the nature and scope of America's interests in Asia remained under review throughout the postwar period. Thus, on November 1, 1945, Secretary of War Robert Patterson requested from Secretary of State James Byrnes political guidance on what involvement the United States would accept and what consequences it would tolerate in order to preserve "minimum interests" in the Far East, particularly in Manchuria, Inner Mongolia, North China, and Korea. An answer to this question, the secretary of war insisted, was urgently needed if military plans were to be made coherently against unacceptable aggression in that region.[1] The department's ambiguous answer at the time reflected their doubts as to what such interests were — assuming that some existed. Only in a negative sense could an agreement be reached between all concerned: American ground forces should not be used for combat on the mainland of Asia.

Dean Acheson, then secretary of state, attempted to elucidate this issue of minimal interests in January 1950, in a speech that was to become famous after the outbreak of the Korean War. "It must be clear that no person can guarantee these areas against military attacks," Acheson said of a defensive perimeter that did not include Korea, Taiwan, and Southeast Asia. Military aggression, the origin of which Acheson was unable to foresee ("one hesitates to say where such an attack could come from"), would have to be met not by the United States alone, but by the "peoples attacked . . . and . . . the commitments of the entire civilized world under the charter of the United Nations." Thus, the Asian peoples were expected to be "on their own." "We can help," continued Acheson, "only where we are wanted and only where the conditions of help are really sensible and possible." But after the war in Korea, America drastically revised and enlarged its vision of what was "sensible and possible." [2] Ironically, America obtained what it had previously agreed to rule out: two ground wars, one in Korea and the other in Southeast Asia.

The extension of America's policy of containment to Asia paradoxically grew from America's refusal to intervene in the Chinese civil war. After the formal surrender of Japan in August 1945, China was, in the words of President Truman, a "geographic expression" led by a fragile government that had been fighting for its survival since 1927.[3] From within, the nationalist government of Chiang Kai-shek faced a communist opposition that controlled one-sixth of the country proper (exclusive of Manchuria) and one-fourth of the overall population (116 million people). On the field the communists had over 1 million troops, generally well trained, well led, and moderately well equipped with captured Japanese weapons. Unlike the situation in Greece, the communists formed an entity of their own. They had a government of their own, an army of their own, in fact, a separate country of their own.[4]

Government forces, on the other hand, comprised approximately three million men. They held an undisputed 5-to-1 superiority in basic weapons such as rifles, a near monopoly of heavy equipment and transport, and total mastery of the air.[5]

Throughout 1946, these forces were successful in achieving major advances, occupying areas formerly controlled by the communists and clearing lines of communication. But, they overextended themselves as they had neither the military resources nor the political skills to garrison and administer these holdings.

Mao's troops seized the initiative in 1947. They exerted superior pressure at points of greatest government overextension, destroyed isolated bodies of troops, and cut communications. They also seized much-needed weapons. For example, one offensive that the communists mounted in May 1947, netted over 20,000 captured rifles in its opening operation.[6] By 1949, it was estimated that 75 per cent of all the material the United States had furnished to the nationalist government, both during and after the war against Japan, had been captured by the communist forces.[7] As communist victories multiplied, nationalist opposition disintegrated. The latter had entered 1948 with an estimated 3-to-1 numerical superiority, an advantage that remained generally constant through mid-September. Yet, by February 1, 1949, the communist forces outnumbered the total nationalist strength and had even achieved a 3-to-2 superiority in combat effectiveness.[8]

President Truman's decision against intervention in the Chinese civil war clearly reflected limitations on existing military capabilities. By June 30, 1946, when the fighting in Manchuria began to spread systematically throughout the country, the forces America had available in the entire Pacific area amounted to 830,000 men. Within one month following the defeat of Japan, American troops were discharged at the rate of 15,200 a day. This rate had reached 25,000 a day by January 1946, and by the end of 1946 all American forces amounted to approximately 1.3 million, with 12,000 soldiers and marines designated for service in China proper. By February 1948, a date now generally regarded as having been the last feasible opportunity for an effective large-scale American intervention, 890,000 men were in the United States army and air force, with total force level in the Far East amounting to 140,000 men.[9]

American action in China also faced a problem of political efficacy. Admittedly, military forces alone could not eliminate Chinese communism. The issue of victory in the civil war had

been a political puzzle long before it became a military question.[10] Yet, the United States had no control over the political
means needed to solve these political problems. Referring to his
own unsuccessful efforts, General Marshall bitterly emphasized
that American "advice [was] always listened to very politely but
not infrequently ignored when deemed unpalatable."[11] In time,
the Chiang government grew incapable of adapting its policies
to the requirements of the situation. The head of the American
military mission, Major General David Barr, called it "the world's
worst leadership."[12] The American ambassador, Leighton Stuart,
found it, by August 1948, "no longer capable of changing and
reforming or discarding inefficient associates in favor of competent ones. . . . It [the nationalist government] ignores competent military advice and fails to take advantage of military
opportunities offered, due . . . to the fact that . . . the Generalissimo selects men on the basis of personal reliability rather than
military competence."[13]

America had neither the capability nor the will to fight
against Mao. It neither could nor wanted to fight for Chiang. Two
options were still technically available: either to work out a
reconciliation between the two embattled factions, or to create a
political third force by gathering various moderate elements that
might be found throughout China.

The first possibility was explored throughout 1946 during the
so-called Marshall Mission. As spelled out by the president,
General Marshall's mission was "to persuade the Chinese government to call a national conference of representatives of the major
political elements to bring about the unification of China, and,
concurrently, to affect a cessation of hostilities."[14] The Marshall
Mission notwithstanding, Truman's overriding objective was to
support Chiang and help him reestablish his authority as far as
possible within what were judged to be the capabilities of the
United States.[15] During the first half of the year, General
Marshall's efforts of mediation met with relative success. Procedures for political and military unification were discussed at
length, and compromises were suggested. An unconditional and
immediate cease-fire was secured in early January 1946, and a
Political Consultative Conference was organized, pending the
convocation of a national assembly, scheduled for the following

May. Late in February, an agreement was reached that provided for a unified Chinese army of sixty divisions, with 50 nationalist divisions and 10 communist divisions. But both sides then chose not to implement the parts of these agreements most unfavorable to them, and complete failure of Marshall's effort became unavoidable. American inability to intervene militarily limited the pressure that Marshall could exert on the communist forces. But American inability to generate an alternative to Chiang Kai-shek also limited the pressure that Marshall could exert on the nationalist forces. Assuming that they had ever existed, the possibilities of mediation formally disappeared on November 15, 1946, when the Chinese National Assembly was convened without communist approval or participation.

A third force had neither the personalities nor the resources to survive alone. Outside of the communists, no alternative to Chiang could be found. "He is the one who holds this vast country together," reluctantly admitted Ambassador Leighton Stuart in his previously quoted report.[16] Such a third force would have required America's willingness to support it politically, economically, and militarily until it had gathered sufficient domestic support to stand on its own against the communists. But America had neither the resources nor the will to provide such assistance in a struggle that many in Truman's official entourage already perceived as lost.

The decision against armed intervention was clearly the fundamental element of American policy in China. Chiang could not win the civil war unless he undertook economic, political, and social reforms opposed by those very forces that had kept Chiang in power through the years. Without direct intervention, America could not promote a third force that could undertake such reforms since, devoid of much initial support within China, such a third force would have been largely an American creation requiring American protection. Finally, without direct armed intervention, America could not prevent the Chinese communists from defeating Chiang militarily, as his troops had neither the morale, the leadership, nor the stamina to resist their opponents. In short, to quote Dean Acheson: "Nothing that this country did or could have done within the reasonable limits of its capabilities could have changed that result; nothing that was left undone by this country had contributed to it. It was the product of internal Chinese forces, which this country tried to influence but could not." [17]

After Mao's triumph, the Truman administration still attempted to pursue a policy of neutrality.* American policymakers still reasoned that China might be used as a counterpoise to Russia in the Far East, as it was felt, correctly it later turned out, that border disputes and other historical antagonism would ultimately eradicate ideological links. Any other policy, warned Dean Acheson, "would deflect from the Russians to ourselves the . . . anger, and the wrath and the hatred of the Chinese people." [18] Thus, Washington's objective continued to be one of nonintervention in the pending Chinese civil conflict over Taiwan, last stronghold of Chiang's defeated armies. On December 23, 1949, the State Department sent a "secret" memorandum to all its diplomats abroad to prepare for the expected fall of Taiwan. Following unavoidable leaks to the press and pressure from his domestic opposition, President Truman issued on January 5, 1950, a formal, written statement that first, the United States would not give military aid or advice to Chiang, second, it would refrain from any action that might lead to involvement in the Chinese civil conflict, and third, it confirmed China's territorial sovereignty over Taiwan, as stated in wartime conferences.

But this hands-off policy was drastically altered following North Korea's invasion of South Korea. "I have ordered the Seventh Fleet to prevent any attack on Formosa," announced President Truman on June 25, 1950. "The determination of the future status of Formosa must await the restoration of security in the Pacific, a peace settlement with Japan or consideration by the United Nations." For the first time, then, American forces were directly involved in the Chinese civil war, because the communist victory in China would remain incomplete as long as Chiang held Formosa. By 1971, as President Nixon was preparing his dramatic visit to Peking, the status of Formosa was still a main obstacle to a rapprochement between the United States and China. Yet, the presidential trip indicated that America was now moving back to

* Nanking, the nationalist capital, fell to the communists on April 24, 1949. On October 15, the new capital at Canton also fell. By December 8, 1949, the Nationalist capital was on the island of Formosa.

the policy that the Truman administration had begun to outline prior to the outbreak of the Korean War.

The Partition of Korea

Decided at the 1943 Cairo Conference, the postwar partition of Korea was expected to be a five-year arrangement based on military convenience and even courtesy from the Russians. The demarcation line was convenient because it determined which nation, America or Russia, would accept Japan's surrender in a given locality.[19] The dividing agreement was also an act of Russian courtesy because the 38th parallel was chosen despite America's military inability to reach it, so that the United States might preserve the symbolic satisfaction of accepting the Japanese surrender in Korea's ancient capital city of Seoul. "If we had been guided solely by how far north we could get our troops [in Korea] if there was opposition," President Truman has testified, "the line would have had to be drawn considerably further south on the peninsula." [20]

Soon, however, it became apparent that the two superpowers, if left alone, could not implement their trusteeship policy, and assure the reunification of Korea into a free and independent nation. In September 1947, therefore, the Truman administration brought the matter to the General Assembly of the United Nations with the hope that that international body might break the deadlock and achieve the reunification of the Korean peninsula. Actually coming when the United Nations was being frequently bypassed by American actions elsewhere, such reliance on the international organization conceivably reflected Washington's desire to reduce its commitment in the area. Such an interpretation was confirmed in October 1947 when the Joint Chiefs of Staff, of whom General Eisenhower was the unofficial chairman, asked that the 45,000 American troops stationed in Korea be evacuated. The Joint Chiefs reasoned that in the context of a general war, Korea was indefensible and of "little strategic value" to the United States.[21] With America about to withdraw from Korea, the General Assembly recommended that free elections be held throughout the country under its supervision. The North Korean authorities, however, refused to grant the United Nations' Control Commission access to North Korea, and the election was limited to South Korea. The General Assembly voted to recognize the newly elected government of Syngman Rhee as the "only lawful government" in Korea. Within a few months the Soviets countered by setting up, north of the 38th parallel, the Democratic People's Republic of Korea. By the end of 1948, with or without the approval of the United Nations, there were two Republics of Korea, with different social outlooks, economic structures, and political organizations.

During the first half of 1949 both the Soviet Union and the United States hurriedly completed the military evacuation of their respective zones of occupation — the Soviet Union in January, and the United States in June. But within one year after the American military withdrawal, on June 25, 1950, an invading force of approximately 90,000 North Korean troops crossed the 38th parallel. Within twenty-four hours, the Rhee government's request for military assistance had been satisfied by Truman's authorization to use American air and naval forces to support South Korean troops. Within two days, the Security Council of the United Nations had declared North Korea the aggressor and pledged its commitment to the restoration of peace in the whole peninsula. Within five days, the use of American ground units had also been approved by the Truman administration. Thus began a "police action" that was to last three years and cost America 142,000 casualties, including approximately 34,000 dead.

The Korean War

"It seemed close to certain," has stated Dean Acheson, "that the [North Korean] attack had been mounted, supplied and instigated by the Soviet Union." [22] The United States military action in Korea was conceived from the start as a prolongation in Asia of the containment effort undertaken in Europe. It was not South Korea proper that needed to be defended, a South Korea that even in the midst of the war, was still not regarded as "vital" to American security. [23] The Truman administration assumed that the North Korean action against South Korea and the impending

Chinese action against Taiwan were both part of a worldwide communist military offensive that was being directed from Moscow. Accordingly, American strategy was reappraised at three different levels: in Europe, the rearmament of the North Atlantic area was accelerated; in Korea, American troops hastily returned; in the Taiwan Straits, the Seventh Fleet was sent in with the avowed purpose of neutralizing the area.

However convincing it may have been at the time, American policy did not reflect adequately the position of China, whose involvement in planning North Korea's aggression was limited.[24] First, Mao's influence in North Korea was minimal. Most North Korean leaders had been trained in Moscow where they continued to pledge their allegiance. The new Chinese government did not have any diplomatic representation in North Korea until August 1950. Already, it had publicly endorsed a blueprint for the future, a blueprint that called for localized "wars of liberation" as opposed to the overt force employed by the North Korean government. Furthermore, China's interest demanded that it complete its unity through the recovery of the Tibet territories and, more particularly, through the absorption of Formosa whose invasion was knowingly scheduled for the summer of 1950. Implicitly, the forthcoming "loss" of Formosa had been accepted by President Truman in his previously quoted January statements. Why, then, would the Peking government risk losing Washington's repeated pledge of neutrality in the Chinese civil war? If China's objective was to replace Stalin's revolutionary influence in Asia, then the backing of the North Korean action was ill chosen in space, given North Korea's ideological preference for Moscow. But if China's objective was the more traditional one of creating a buffer zone between itself and Japan, who was on the verge of signing a peace treaty with the United States, then too the means were ill chosen since they allowed for the possibility (regardless of what Dean Acheson might have previously said) of American troops returning to a neighboring area that they had just evacuated, and at a time when China was about to recover an essential part of its national territory.

Similarly, the assumption that China's involvement in the Korean War was part of a combined action arranged with the Soviet Union is doubtful. It implies both a close harmony of views between the two communist giants and their rulers and China's acceptance of having to face American forces for its Soviet ally should the United States choose to intervene. But this does not appear to have happened. The Moscow-Peking "axis" was unstable even before it was formed, and Mao's victory on China's mainland did little to reduce the disagreements that alienated him from Stalin.[25] In 1927, Stalin had tacitly endorsed Chiang's repressive action against the Chinese communist party, and, throughout the thirties, he continued to support the anti-Maoist faction within the party. During the war against Japan, most of the assistance provided by the Soviet government went directly to the Chiang government, which Moscow recognized until 1949. After his victory, Mao still had to fight Stalin's protracted attempt to carve a Soviet sphere of influence in both Manchuria and the Sinkiang area, and, during the negotiations of the Sino-Soviet Pact of February 1950, the Chinese leader sharply criticized Moscow's refusal to honor its 1924 pledge that Outer Mongolia be returned to China.

When China decided to enter the Korean War it also did so reluctantly. Despite occasional boasting of its military assistance to North Korea, Peking carefully warned Washington of the specific conditions that would make its own military intervention unavoidable. On September 30, 1950, Chou En-lai publicly declared that the Chinese people would not "tolerate . . . seeing their neighbors [North Korea] being . . . invaded." [26] Similar pronouncements were issued through New Delhi. All such signals clearly identified the crossing of the 38th parallel by American–United Nations forces as *casus belli*. The evidence subsequently disclosed also indicated how carefully the Chinese weighed their intervention, particularly during the first week of October 1950, as the 38th parallel was about to be crossed by United Nations forces. The Chinese intervention itself was undertaken with many of the old weapons that had been salvaged from the war against Chiang Kai-shek, and massive shipments of Soviet-made weapons did not begin to arrive until later.[27] In short, the Chinese entered the war because of the direct threat to their security, which, as they perceived it, would be created by further unopposed American victories in North Korea.[28] "Everybody," suggested Senator McMahon to General MacArthur during the

latter's 1951 Hearings, "that had to do with it [China's intervention in Korea] turned out to be wrong." To which the general
replied: "Practically, although . . . everybody realized that that
risk was involved." [29] Actually, America's misreading of Chinese
policy intentions existed throughout the Korean episode, for no
convincing evidence of Chinese participation in the planning
and preparation of the Korean War exists.[30]

By contrast, Soviet interests in sponsoring the Korean War
were considerable and varied. First of all, South Korea might
have constituted, in Stalin's eyes, a rare opportunity to establish
his presence in Asia, influence the impending peace treaty with
Japan, and alter favorably the distribution of ideological power
between himself and Mao. With Korea seemingly placed outside
the American defensive perimeter, the risks of American intervention there could be regarded as minimal, especially in view
of the lacking domestic concern for the area. Unlike Poland, or
any other Eastern European country, no influential Korean ethnic
group lived in the United States. Furthermore, Americans had
strong misgivings about the Syngman Rhee government. Early
in 1950, the United States State Department publicly protested
Rhee's disregard of basic constitutional rights, and Truman described the South Korean president as a man who had "little
patience with those who differ with him. . . . I did not care,"
the American president indicated, "for the methods used by
Rhee's police to break up political meetings and control political
enemies." [31] Indeed, America's distrust of Rhee was reminiscent
of its distrust of Chiang. In the elections of May 30, 1950, anti-
Rhee factions within South Korea won more than half of the
National Assembly, and the South Korean president had been
forced to form a coalition government that promised to be
precarious, bitterly contested, and possibly short-lived. If Washington had been unwilling to intervene in Korea to defend
Chiang Kai-shek, why would it intervene in Korea to defend
Syngman Rhee? In Stalin's view, the small risk of Washington's
intervention was worth taking against the gains that would certainly result from a North Korean victory (which the military
unpreparedness of South Korea made all the more probable)
should the United States choose not to intervene. First, the
victory might preempt the impending alliance between Japan

and the United States by serving notice to Japan, and to the other countries of the area as well, that no arrangement in Asia or elsewhere could be worked out without the prior agreement, if not participation, of the Soviet Union. Moreover, a Moscow-sponsored invasion of South Korea would restore Moscow's prestige as the true revolutionary center in Asia, as it was in Europe, at a time when this position was being challenged in both areas. A North Korean victory would thus be as much a communist victory over the capitalistic camp as it would be a Russian victory within its own camp.

Substantial gains were possible for the Soviet Union even if Washington, despite its previous announcements, opted for military intervention. Such intervention would weaken America's hand in Europe as it would divert American resources away from the European continent to Asia. Consequently, Soviet situations of strength could rapidly be created not only in Western Europe but also in Eastern Europe, particularly in Yugoslavia and Bulgaria, countries much opposed to Stalin's rule. Assuming the worst, a military defeat of North Korea would still be of some profit to Stalin: on top of establishing Moscow's revolutionary élan, it would place the Soviets in the position of peacemakers defending the weak hybrid state against the powerful industrial superstate. This peacemaking function was actually assumed by the Soviets from the start of the hostilities, more or less eagerly depending on the fluctuations registered on the battlefield.

Although Soviet participation in planning the war is beyond doubt, some questions may be asked about their participation in its actual execution. If the Soviet's immediate objective was to gain control of South Korea, other means short of using force were still available. From without, North Korea had far from exhausted the potentialities for fulfilling their objectives through guerrilla and psychological warfare, political pressure and intimidation. From within, the very weakness of the Rhee government made it probable that an enlarged Rhee coalition would become more amenable to "negotiating" with North Korea over the reunification.

Up to the Korean War, in the words of George Kennan, the Soviet policy in Asia had been generally "a fluid resilient policy of maximum power with minimum responsibility." [32] Undoubtedly, open warfare in Korea might lead to maximum Soviet responsibility for, regardless of past American pronouncements on the matter, a Soviet-sponsored attack in Korea did present considerable risks to those who had initiated it. Obviously enough, to stop the confrontation of the two armies would be more difficult than to end frontier maneuvers, as in the Turkish affair, or to lift a blockade, as in Berlin. If past experience could be relied on, the only thing predictable about American behavior was its unpredictability. An America that had refused to intervene for Poland and Czechoslovakia had sent an ultimatum to Moscow for the Republic of Azerbaidjan. Similarly, an America that had refused to fight for China might now decide to fight for South Korea. Since January, the Soviet Union had been boycotting the Security Council of the United Nations. With Moscow deprived of its veto power, the United Nations retaliatory capability was left entirely in American hands. The advantage for Moscow in returning to the Security Council's meetings would be considerably enhanced as of August 1, when the Soviet representative was scheduled to assume the presidency of the Council.

With time working on its side because of South Korea's domestic situation, and with other means of action available to it meanwhile, Moscow did not need to hurry North Korea's military attack. This fact leads to two possible interpretations, neither of which can be adequately tested because the necessary documents are not accessible. Either the North Koreans, hurried by repeated border incidents from which Rhee was not always innocent, jumped the gun and initiated their action on a carte blanche that had been previously given to them by the Soviet government, or, as Stalin saw it, the Korean conflict was an effective means of diverting the Chinese away from their planned invasion of Taiwan. The latter was a development Stalin might have opposed either on the basis of its foreseeable ideological repercussions in Asia or on the basis of his genuine fear that such occurrence would be unacceptable to the Truman administration and lead to an armed conflict between the United States and the Soviet Union.

The Truman administration, however, did not pause to ponder the extent of Sino-Soviet involvement. Instead it maximalized this involvement in a swift and instinctive reaction, which reflected the prevailing anti-Munich mood of the postwar era. As previously described, the Munich syndrome led to the assumption that aggression met by appeasement inevitably bred more aggression until ultimately it generalized into a world war. President Truman reflected the dominant mood of the country when, in the plane taking him back to Washington on June 25, he recalled other occasions when his generation had seen the "strong" attack the "weak."

> I recalled some earlier instances: Manchuria, Ethiopia, Austria. I remembered how each time that the democracies failed to act it had encouraged the aggressors to keep going ahead. Communism was acting in Korea just as Hitler, Mussolini and the Japanese had acted ten, fifteen and twenty years earlier. I felt certain that if South Korea was allowed to fall Communist leaders would be emboldened to override nations closer to our own shores. . . . If this was allowed to go unchallenged it would mean a third world war, just as similar incidents had brought on the second world war . . .[33]

The application of the Munich syndrome was greatly facilitated by the apparent certitude with which the aggressor could be identified. Moscow's immediate claim that the invasion had been launched from and by South Korea was invalidated by the massive presence of North Korean forces ten to fifteen miles deep in southern territory within a few hours after the hostilities broke out.

The North Korean attack was widely interpreted as a test by the Soviet Union of America's capability and determination to meet force with force. In the easy language of historical analogies, Stalin was now investigating how much of Chamberlain there was in Truman. Of course, one might have argued that a test over Korea did not necessarily involve more than Korea itself or, at most, Northeast Asia. Other "tests" had been held in other places and they had been met — how many such tests would it take, and where, to establish the credibility of America's will to resist? But an American administration increasingly anticipating an all-out confrontation thought in global terms. Korea proper might not be essential to American security — a proposition readily granted by officials in Washington before, during, and after the war — but its fall was nevertheless unacceptable inasmuch as it weakened those organizations and alliances to which American security was clearly related.

The collapse of the League of Nations was attributed (somewhat erroneously) to the unwillingness of the member states to face military aggression in Manchuria and Ethiopia in the thirties. It was felt that the North Korean aggression now tested the very foundations and principles of the new international organization. On June 26, 1945, President Truman had appraised the past and prophesied the future when he stated: "If we had this Charter a few years ago and above all the will to use it — millions now dead would be alive. If we should falter in the future in our will to use it, millions now living will surely die." [34] In Korea, then, collective security was being challenged and there could be no United Nations (and no international peace and order) without collective security. Thanks to the United Nations, American intervention was also, conveniently, provided with the additional respectability of a multinational endorsement that the absence of the Soviet delegate from the Security Council made possible. Ultimately, forty-one member states, besides the United States, offered some material assistance, and fifteen of these contributed armed forces, even though the American share of United Nations forces in Korea still amounted to 50 per cent of the land forces, 86 per cent of the Navy and 93 per cent of the air forces.[35] The war itself was fought under the flag of the United Nations, even though on the field the United States preserved full command. Said General MacArthur: "The controls over me were exactly the same as though the forces under me were all American." [36]

The strengthening of America's alliances too was of paramount importance, especially as it was anticipated that Korean-type aggression might occur elsewhere in the world at any moment, particularly in Europe where the threat of "disguised aggression through a satellite" was openly alluded to by Dean Acheson. "In the absence of defense forces in being," he warned in February 1951, "satellites might be used for such disguised aggression in the hope that they could get away with it." [37] Throughout the fighting in Korea maintaining adequate forces in Europe remained one of the major concerns of a Truman administration that was worried by the possibility that Moscow might be attempting to take advantage of Washington's involvement away from the main theater of confrontation.[38]

Another potential American ally was Japan. A few weeks before the outbreak of hostilities in Korea, President Truman had announced that a peace treaty with Japan had the highest priority and that it would be signed on the basis of Japanese independence and the long-term presence of American military bases throughout Japan. The announcement had been greeted in the communist world with a series of actions that showed an intense determination to oppose it as best they could.[39] An American unwillingness to meet the communist challenge in an Asian country would reduce America's credibility in Asia still more surely than it would in Europe. To John Foster Dulles, then an "adviser" to the State Department, a North Korean victory would place Japan "between the upper and lower jaws of the Russian bear." [40]

Korea was thus regarded as the first military encounter of a global war that was still avoidable provided that such communist aggressions were defeated. "Our best hope of peace," said Dean Acheson, "lies in our ability to make absolutely plain to aggressors that aggression cannot succeed." [41] To place the conflict in a global perspective helped to limit it even though such a global interpretation was based on a fallacious understanding of the situation — a wrong understanding from which the right decisions were made but the wrong conclusions drawn.

Limiting or Expanding the War

The United States intervened in Korea because the Truman administration believed, rightly or wrongly, that in Korea the Soviets were "probing" for weaknesses in America's commitments; that they were "testing" America's will to fight; and that they were taking advantage of "opportunities" where America itself had uncovered them. Such intervention remained limited because the Truman administration also assumed that one of Moscow's main objectives was to divert American resources away from other more strategic points, so that when the real attack took place American capabilities would be too depleted to withstand it. President Truman remained determined to keep America's commitment, and consequently its objectives, as limited as possible: "We would not become so deeply committed in Korea that we could not take care of such other situations as might develop." [42] Only for a short period were American objectives escalated beyond a restoration of the status quo ante bellum. This occurred when, following MacArthur's crossing of the 38th parallel, the United Nations Resolution of October 7 advised United Nations forces to seek the reunification of the whole Korean peninsula. It would be "sheer madness," said Dean Acheson, for China to intervene. [43] As events came to prove, it was instead "sheer madness" to expect that they would *not* intervene when they had made it clear that they would. By March 1951, as a result of China's intervention, the status quo ante bellum had become once again the stated American objective in Korea.

In short, the war in Korea remained limited less out of choice than out of necessity. In limiting the conflict Washington had two objectives: to keep the Russians out of the war while saving scarce military resources for possible military confrontations elsewhere. The deterrent effect exercised by Moscow was candidly recognized by General Marshall, then secretary of defense, during the MacArthur Hearings: "If . . . there was no danger whatsoever of a Soviet intervention, I would say that certainly the bombing you mention [in China] would start almost immediately." [44] The motivation was quite obvious. A Soviet intervention implied an escalation that was most likely to transform the Korean "police action" into World War III. As the police action had been undertaken in the first place to prevent a world conflict, Korea had to remain limited as much as possible — a proposition readily endorsed by the other side.

The major limitation that both sides agreed to respect was undoubtedly their refusal to employ the most potent weapons at their disposal. America's decision not to use atomic weapons was first dictated by tactical considerations. No target in Korea seemed to justify their use. [45] Furthermore, the scarcity of these weapons and means of delivery made it imperative at the time that they be used with the utmost efficiency. As late as July 10, 1951, Strategic Air Command had only eighty-seven B36 bombers ready for action, and the production rate was only two or three a month.[46] A very limited atomic stockpile needed to be guarded and preserved for more decisive encounters.* The United States probably could have delivered a major assault on China's or Russia's urban-industrial centers, but such a blow could not have been decisive. The Soviet Union was already capable of a small retaliatory blow against the United States or, more probably, against the hostage cities of Europe. As an ultimate although unlikely gesture, Moscow might have "loaned" some of its very few atomic bombs to China for retaliatory raids in South Korea, Japan, and Okinawa. As for the Chinese, they were eager to dispel the notion that such weapons might deter them from undertaking actions they deemed vital to their national security. "Atomic bombs," admitted General Nieh Jung-chen, a Chinese Deputy Chief of Staff, "may kill a few million people." But, he went on, "China lives on the farms. What can atom bombs do there?"[47]

The United States also had the capability, which it did not use, of launching conventional air attacks on China. Such attacks could have closed the Manchurian air bases, disrupted the supply lines, and seriously damaged the Chinese economy by destroying the industrial centers or blockading the coast. This possibility was so carefully avoided that even the bombing of bridges over the Yalu river was ordered to be confined to their Korean half only. In North Korea, too, major targets such as some hydroelectric plants were not touched for two full years after the outbreak of the war. Deep concern with Soviet reaction further prevented

* The question of nuclear weapons is one shrouded in utmost secrecy. In 1950, nowhere, in any document in the president's office, in the Atomic Energy Commission, in any governmental agency, could anyone find the exact number of bombs available or scheduled for production. Nevertheless, the evolution of America's arsenal from a position of inadequacy to one of "sufficiency" during the Truman presidency can be followed, without any specific quantitative measures, through Truman's own remarks. Such evolution appears to be as follows: in 1946, the number of bombs was "disappointing" and those available had not been assembled yet (*Memoirs*, Vol. II, p. 296). In 1947, it was still "inadequate" both quantitatively and qualitatively, and the progress was "dangerously slow" (p. 299). By early 1949, America was beginning to have a stockpile, but it was still regarded as "inadequate in number and not keeping up with technological progress" (p. 304). But in July 1949, the president strongly urged that "production of atomic weapons should be stepped up," and by January 1953, two months after the first successful explosion of an H-bomb, Truman could boast that he had left his successor with "a stockpile of atomic bombs, together with the means for delivering these bombs to the target" (p. 314).

the bombing of targets close to Soviet territory. On the ground no American unit was allowed within approximately fifteen miles of the border of northeast Korea along Siberia.[48] But, in return, communist forces did not attempt, in however limited a way, to attack excellent and crucial targets in South Korea (such as Inchon or Pusan) or American airfields in Japan and in Okinawa. American naval vessels were also spared from air attacks.

Finally, both sides avoided using military personnel that the other might find offensive. No "Russian volunteer" was ever reported in the war even though Moscow had numerous forces not too far away in the vicinity of Vladivostok, Dairen-Port Arthur, and Harbin. Chiang Kai-shek's forces were not used either. On June 29, 1950, his offer of 330,000 troops was turned down as America's Joint Chiefs of Staff felt that the troops would be as "helpless as Syngman Rhee's army against the North Korean attacks." [49] Besides, they were needed for the defense of Taiwan. Later on, larger offers of help by Chiang were still ignored explicitly to avoid any escalation of the conflict.

These self-imposed retraints led to a momentous debate when General MacArthur, following his repeated public demands that most of these limitations be lifted after the Chinese intervention, was fired by the president for insubordination.[50] In the narrow sense, MacArthur's insubordination stemmed from a conflict over strategy. Administration spokesmen viewed warfare as a means to an end and found a substitute to victory in the diplomatic search for an accommodation of mutual disagreements, even while the fighting was going on. In Truman's words, "warfare, no matter what weapons it employs, is a means to an end, and if that end can be achieved by negotiated settlements of conditional surrender, there is no need for war." [51] Such a limited view of warfare as a continuation of politics by other means was rejected by MacArthur.* Instead, he viewed it as the end of politics on the assumption that by using force both sides implicitly admitted the impossibility of reaching any peaceful settlement. "Once war is forced upon us," analyzed MacArthur in his dramatic address to a joint meeting of Congress on April 19,

---

* MacArthur was not alone in his opposition. Apart from Generals Ridgway and Taylor, it appears that every single American commander involved in the Korean War disagreed with the "die-for-tie" approach of limiting hostilities.

1951, "there is no other alternative than to apply every available means to bring it to a swift end. War's very object is victory — not prolonged indecision. In war, indeed, there can be no substitute for victory." [52] MacArthur felt that China's intervention had created a new war that required the "release [of] the power that we now possess so that it can be utilized." [53] "China," MacArthur further complained, "is using the maximum of her force against us . . . and we are not using the maximum of ours against her." [54] No more American ground forces would be needed if 500,000 of Chiang Kai-shek's troops were released against China while major Chinese targets were attacked from the air (possibly with atomic weapons) and the Chinese coast was blockaded. MacArthur's forecast of the "decisive and victorious end" that would reward his strategy was skeptically received by his critics. As was often the case, Dean Acheson best summarized the administration's position:

> We are being asked to undertake a large risk of general war with China, risk of war with the Soviet Union, and a demonstrable weakening of our collective security system — all of this in return for what? In return for measures whose effectiveness in bringing the conflict to an early conclusion are judged doubtful by our responsible military authorities.[55]

MacArthur denied that in the face of an overwhelming American offensive Moscow would be willing to enter the war. The Soviet Union, he argued, did not have the capabilities needed to undertake a major military campaign in Asia.[56] Nor was any part of Stalin's strategy, as MacArthur saw it, related to events in Korea: "[nothing] that happens in Korea, or Asia," declared the general, "would affect his basic decision. . . . He will make his decisions on a higher basis." [57] MacArthur did not believe either that his strategy implied an American participation in a ground war in China, which he staunchly opposed as a "master folly," or the thinking of a man "not in his proper sense." [58] Such an outcome would be avoided because China's inherent weakness prevented it from absorbing long, if any, sustained American air attacks, combined with ground engagements in Korea plus Chiang's diversionary attacks either in China proper or on the periphery.

But the Truman administration, still reacting to the shock

of past underestimations of Chinese communist capabilities and intentions, refused to risk a major war with China in Asia while the major enemy was Russia in Europe, and when America's capability of facing either one in either place was open to question.[59] For the United States to go to war with China over Korea would be to fight the wrong war in the wrong place at the wrong time and against the wrong enemy.[60] The administration further argued that such a war would have to be fought essentially alone, a likelihood that was actually welcomed by the MacArthur forces: "If the other nations of the world," said MacArthur, "haven't got enough sense to see where appeasement leads after the appeasement which led to the second war in Europe . . . why then we had better protect ourselves and go it alone." [61]

In a broader perspective, the confrontation between the president and the general was a classic manifestation of the dispute between civilian and military authorities. In his *Memoirs* Truman emphasized: "If there is one basic element in our constitution, it is civilian control of the military. Policies are to be made by the elected political officials, not by generals or admirals." [62] So, when announcing MacArthur's dismissal, Truman made clear that "it is fundamental that military commanders must be governed by the policies and directives issued to them in the manner provided by our laws and constitution." [63] What he sought was the unconditional approval by the men in the field of the policy goals set by Washington, once these goals had been set. MacArthur at first argued that his policy was in line with the directives sent him by the Joint Chiefs of Staff whose views, he said, were "practically identical" to his own.[64] Thus, MacArthur could emphatically recognize, as he did, Truman's basic assumption of civilian control over the global strategy. These directives, however, had been issued in the first week of January 1951, when it was possible for United Nations troops to be forced out of Korea if the Chinese chose to do it — a possibility that "seemed at the time to be verging on a probability." [65] But MacArthur next contended that the administration had no coherent policy at all in Korea, hence no concrete guidelines for him to follow. Indeed, MacArthur argued, he had followed the only policy that the administration had clearly stated, namely that one outlined in the Truman Doctrine. Reporting on an earlier visit with MacArthur, Averell Harriman had confirmed to President Truman that the celebrated general considered his doctrine "great" — only he felt that it should be carried out "more vigorously," a wish that MacArthur was now attempting to fulfill.[66] "Who is overwhelmingly the main enemy?" asked for example, Senator McMahon. And MacArthur replied a la Truman, "Communism. . . . All over the world including the interior of many of the fine democratic countries of the world." [67]

Essentially, the Truman-MacArthur controversy mirrored the policy vacuum that existed when the decision to intervene in Korea was taken. Still in the aftermath of the communist victory in China and faced with increasing charges of having "lost" China and being "soft on communism," the Truman administration had failed to articulate a coherent general policy for the Far East. At best, America's Asian policy was in a state of flux and uncertainty. Decisive policy formulation and implementation was reached only slowly during the war years and it resulted in measures to which we must now turn.

The Extension of Containment to Asia

Immediately following World War II, American foreign policy objectives were relatively moderate: to restore political stability in the areas in which hostilities against Germany had taken place. In most cases, and despite certain diplomatic errors, Washington was acutely aware that no permanent stability could be achieved without Soviet cooperation, and it was prepared to seek that cooperation through accommodation and coercion.

By 1947, however, the growth of Soviet power and the emergence of a Soviet bloc seemingly waging a war of subversive attrition against the democratic nations led to a shift of priorities. The Truman Doctrine was the earliest indication of that shift, as the program of reconstruction and stabilization that it advocated for Greece and Turkey became part of a general denunciation of totalitarian forces, with Moscow as the obvious target. But, simultaneously conceived, the Marshall Plan reflected the hesitancy with which that shift was taking place because Washington still included, however dubiously, the Soviets into this common venture of political and economic restoration.

From then onward other programs of economic reconstruction and political stabilization became increasingly the instruments of a policy of military coalition under American guidance as the only way to contain Soviet expansion. East and West, North and South, there was now but one world, one peace, and one enemy. "We have no intention to sacrifice the East in order to gain time for the West," claimed the Republican platform of 1952. What made such a statement palatable to a large section of the American people was precisely the rhetoric of the Democrats.

Even before Korea, a Democratic secretary of state, Dean Acheson, had defined the policy of meeting strength with strength that a Republican secretary of state, John Foster Dulles, would soon apply so faithfully. "The only way to deal with the Soviet Union," Mr. Acheson said in February 1950,

> is to create situations of strength. . . . Every time one of these situations [of weakness] exists . . . it is . . . an irresistible invitation for the Soviet government to fish in those troubled waters. . . . You can't argue with a river — it is going to flow. You can dam it up, you can put it to useful purposes, you can deflect it, but you can't argue with it.[68]

In 1951, the Truman administration dismissed MacArthur but almost simultaneously adopted parts of his policy, a policy that was further implemented by Truman's successor. "The first line of defense for Europe," MacArthur argued, was "right where we are fighting over there in Korea." [69] Hurriedly, then, the policy vacuum of 1950 was filled so that the first lines of defense could be manned. During the last eighteen months of the Truman administration and the first two years of the Eisenhower administration, the containing wall of security alliances that had been devised for Europe was rapidly extended to Asia: on August 30, 1951, to the Philippines; two days later to Australia and New Zealand; on September 8, 1951, to Japan; on October 1, 1953, to South Korea; on September 8, 1954, to Australia, France, Great Britain, New Zealand, Philippines, Pakistan, and Thailand within the Southeast Asia Treaty Organization; and on December 2,

1954, to Taiwan. In all these places an armed attack on any country was now formally described as dangerous to America's own peace and security, and the United States was contractually committed to "act to meet the common dangers in accordance with its constitutional process." This understanding was somewhat more general than the so-called NATO principle. But these treaties were thought to be only a first step toward the global implementation of a Pacific Pact regarded as the "desirable ultimate objective of United States policy in the Pacific." [70]

The wisdom of this extension of the containment policy to Asia did not go undisputed. That such a policy could be applied to Europe against the Soviet Union had been regarded by some as doubtful. That it could be applied in Asia primarily to prevent Chinese expansion was regarded by many as absurd. It was then argued, and it continued to be so argued during the war in Vietnam, that in Europe military containment was undertaken primarily to provide a shield behind which European nations could recover, whereas in Asia such containment would help nations not yet formed, where disruption mainly took the form of civil conflicts. The threat that had to be met in Asia was an internal threat, based upon conditions that were genuinely revolutionary, with or without external assistance. Asia needed the political containment of a political threat, not the military containment of a military threat. Furthermore, such an expansion of containment to Asia would commit America to protecting highly volatile regimes whose survivability would become dependent upon American assistance, creating imperial relations that might ultimately overextend America's military burdens. In other words, such an involvement in Asia would consist of supporting local governments and not peoples, taking charge of problems that were essentially domestic and that these governments could no longer face themselves, not only because of the external pressure to which they were subjected but also because of their own inability to create a more stable domestic consensus upon which they could satisfactorily rely for support.

These differences were ignored and, twenty years after Korea, America was still fashioning the military instruments capable of cementing the containing wall that its own mistaken interpretation of the Korean War had led it to devise.

5

The
Irony
of Power

The Dulles Leadership

Not surprisingly, from one American administration to another, there is an uneven distribution of influence and prestige
between the president and his staff, the secretary of state, and
the State Department and other agencies. During the Roosevelt
administration individual advisers to the president, such as Harry
Hopkins, and lesser officials, such as Undersecretary Sumner
Welles, were generally more influential in helping the president
reach a decision in foreign affairs than was Secretary of State
Hull. Yet, Cordell Hull remained in office for almost twelve
years. But upon resigning he expressed bitterness and frustration at the way in which the president had neglected to consult
with him on foreign policy. "I am tired of intrigue," he confided
privately, "of being by-passed . . . of being relied upon in pub-

lic and ignored in private." [1] In Harry Hopkins, who moved into the White House to be constantly at the side of the president, could be seen the precursor of latter day's Presidential Assistant for National Security Affairs.[2]

During the Truman administration, Secretary Acheson worked very closely with the State Department and with the president, as did his predecessor, George Marshall, who had left the handling of the department to his subordinates, including Dean Acheson himself, then an undersecretary. Everything, reasoned Secretary Marshall, would come to him through the undersecretary with his recommendation, unless the undersecretary elected to settle the matter himself. In turn, everything from the secretary would go to the Department through the undersecretary.[3] As secretary of state, Dean Acheson worked under a chief executive who believed in delegating much power to the members of his cabinet in their various fields. But in so doing Truman did not intend, as he himself indicated, to turn over the authority of the president nor to forego the president's prerogative to make the final decision.[4] In effect, Truman's first appointed secretary of state, James Byrnes, lost the president's favor when, in Truman's words, he began to think of himself as "an Assistant President in full charge of foreign policy." [5] Acheson hardly fell into a similar predicament and, in words and in deeds, he truly became Truman's chief adviser on foreign affairs. Conferences between the secretary and the president were held several times a day, and messages exchanged regularly when either one was away. So informed, the president almost always followed Acheson's recommendations and their relationship developed into the closest postwar approximation of an ideal administrative model of foreign policymaking.

In the Kennedy administration the president's ultimate rule was to avoid total reliance on any of his many advisers between whom he kept a careful balance of influence. During Kennedy's one thousand days the president's brother, Robert, then the attorney general, often played a more important role in foreign policy formation than did Dean Rusk and the State Department. Surrounded in his own department by figures of greater public stature — including Adlai Stevenson, Averell Harriman, and Chester Bowles — and interfered with by a prestigious and somewhat hostile White House staff — including Arthur Schlesinger, Jr., and McGeorge Bundy — Dean Rusk was ultimately dominated by a president who wanted to be his own secretary of state. Kennedy also relied heavily on individuals out of the government (Dean Acheson, for example, undertook a variety of unofficial tasks for the Kennedy administration) and unlike many presidents before him, he frequently sought the advice of ambassadors, some of whom he had himself selected. These included George Kennan in Yugoslavia, John Kenneth Galbraith in India, and Llewellyn E. Thomson, whom Kennedy ultimately asked to return from his post in Moscow to serve as his special adviser on Soviet affairs.

During the Johnson administration, the predominant source of policy input changed quite often. Still secretary of state, Dean Rusk developed with President Johnson a much closer working relationship than he had with Kennedy. Rusk himself had been assistant secretary for Far Eastern affairs during the Acheson years. His duties then had included serving as chief liaison officer between State and Defense. During his tenure at the Department of State, Rusk shared some of his influence with the secretary of defense, first Robert McNamara, then Clark Clifford. All these individuals greatly influenced a president relatively inexperienced in world affairs, even though both McNamara and Clifford ultimately fell out of grace. At times, though, policy input moved away from either department to such trusted advisers as Walt Rostow, who was also a leftover from the Kennedy administration.

Finally, during the Nixon administration, the role, power, and prestige of the secretary of state further declined, with Secretary Rogers caught between a president obviously interested in foreign policy and a presidential adviser, Henry Kissinger, whose own role, power, and prestige were steadily growing. "No one doubts . . . the importance of Kissinger's role in the Nixon administration," wrote columnist Joseph Kraft in a penetrating essay on Kissinger.

> He sees the President alone almost every morning . . . speaks to him on the phone two or three times during a routine day. . . . On special occasions such as trips abroad, or before

speeches or press conferences, he is almost constantly with the President. . . . He negotiates with heads of state, foreign ministers, and ambassadors galore . . .[6]

Yet, where one would speak of Roosevelt's foreign policy, or Truman's, or Kennedy's, or Johnson's, or Nixon's policies, one spoke of Dulles' foreign policy. For during the Eisenhower administration it appeared early that foreign policy was the sole concern of its secretary of state whose personality colored, dominated, and personified American diplomacy to an extent rarely equaled. Supremely confident of his knowledge, experience, and insight, John Foster Dulles hardly paid attention to his staff, to the State Department, or to America's allies. From January 1953 till May 1959 (when he died from cancer) Dulles had no known confidant at his own level and he pursued publicly a one-man diplomacy that relegated everyone else to glorified research assistants for the preparation of policies that Dulles himself formulated and that were rarely submitted to much add-and-omit discussion within the department. Christian Herter, then undersecretary and soon to become Dulles' successor, once acknowledged the plight of Dulles' subordinates: "It is hard to know what use I am around here. . . . I have been given no authority, and no area of work is specifically my task. Everyone finds it difficult to know what Foster [Dulles] is either doing or thinking. So . . . I just keep trotting around after events, trying to piece together the true shape of them." [7] As he perceived it, Herter was a number two man in a one-man show.

Nor was much attention paid to career diplomats who occasionally had to rely upon airmail editions of New York newspapers to gain some information and insight into Dulles' policies in their own areas.[8] As to the allies, they were at best ignored, at worst treated as adversaries in protracted arguments. In the fall of 1957, an article in *Look* magazine read: "Not since Hitler has any foreigner been so scorned and disliked in Britain as Secretary of State John Foster Dulles." [9] Althought this undoubtedly was a strong way of stating known disagreements between Washington and London, the fact remained that Dulles created across the Atlantic a communication gap of rare magnitude. Indeed the gap reached such proportion that it used to be said, and believed, that the English way of getting their information across to the American secretary of state was to plant it on American intelligence in the hope that this information would be relayed to the secretary by his younger brother, Allen Dulles, who was at that time the head of the Central Intelligence Agency.

None of this should be understood to imply that the president did not preserve and exercise the final say in foreign affairs. Indeed, omnipotent at the State Department, Dulles remained always respectful of the president's ultimate authority. Every new speech, every new action, every new policy was generally cleared with the White House. At first not especially impressed by Dulles, Eisenhower grew increasingly so respectful of his skill that he delegated to the secretary an unusual flexibility as his representative in international conferences.

Disarmament was the only major exception and the only recurrent disagreement between the president and his chief diplomat. Nevertheless, Dulles' known hostility toward Eisenhower's periodical peace initiatives was never too active or outspoken. These initiatives included the president's "Chance for Peace" address in April 1953, when Eisenhower placed emphasis on the mutual benefits that might be gained by the United States and the Soviet Union from substantial disarmament; the "Atoms for Peace" address in December 1953, when Eisenhower proposed that both superpowers donate part of their respective stockpiles of fissionable material for use in peaceful projects under United Nations supervision; and the "Open Skies" proposal in July 1955, when the American president proposed to exchange plans of each nation's military facilities and to allow air inspection of military bases as an insurance against surprise attacks. In all these cases, the proposals were generated and directed by special assistants or staff aides to the president. Such disagreement remained scarce, and in protecting the presidential delegation of power, Dulles practiced close surveillance over officials having or seeking direct access to the president. In effect, most of the president's advisers on foreign affairs — including Nelson Rockefeller and Harold Stassen — left the government after clashing with the secretary of state.[10]

For this job, Dulles had been particularly well prepared. Since 1907 when he had accompanied his grandfather at the international conference held at The Hague, the new head of the State Department had been thinking, speaking, and writing about the various problems faced by America in the world. In fact, Dulles believed that he had a family commitment to seek a position two of his relatives had occupied during the previous fifty years — John W. Foster, his grandfather, who had served briefly in the cabinet of President Benjamin Harrison and Robert Lansing, his uncle, who had served under President Wilson. To Dulles himself, there was a providential and foreordained design in his assuming the leadership of American diplomacy. This faith further strengthened his confidence in the objectives he defined for America and the rest of the world. Dulles was fond of quoting his Bible (one of the three books he always kept near him, the other two being the *Federalist* and Lenin's work on communism): "All things work together for good to them that love God, to them who are called according to His purpose." Indeed, the American secretary of state had no doubt about God's allegiance, and he confided to the president at the outset of their official partnership: "With my understanding of the intricate relationships between the peoples of the world and your sensitiveness to the political considerations involved, we will make the most successful team in history." [11] Ultimately, it was perhaps unfortunate that a man so supremely confident in his intellectual capacity to master "the intricate relationships between the peoples of the world" should have assumed the role he did when America's military superiority was itself at its peak. For his perception of America's might reinforced too conveniently a deeply felt perception of America's righteousness.

Coping with Friends and Enemies

John Foster Dulles was a lawyer for a long time before he became secretary of state, shortly before his sixty-fifth birthday. As secretary, he often reasoned, spoke, and acted like a lawyer. The court he faced was the Court of History where he prosecuted the Soviet Union for crimes against God, liberty, and peace. The legal code he used was that of a God-made moral law, which determined right and wrong and assured the ultimate victory of those who conformed to its canons. For a while, due to the war, moral law had been necessarily put aside in favor of military expediency. But with the war ended, principle and morality should have been reestablished in the world, as a guide to international conflict. America's mission, Dulles thought, was to assure such a belated restoration. "What we need to do," he pleaded, "is to recapture . . . the kind of crusading spirit of the early days when we were darn sure that what we had was a lot better than what anybody else had. . . . The missionaries, the doctors, the educators, and the merchants carried the knowledge of the great American experiment to all four corners of the globe." [12] As secretary of state, John Foster Dulles was to become such a disseminator of the American way as he traveled almost half a million miles outside the United States while visiting forty-seven different nations.[13]

A preacher in the world of politics, the new secretary of state found in the international community a protracted conflict between the forces of good and evil, in the literal sense. More specifically, the forces of evil were those of the international communist conspiracy, a conspiracy against God that needed to be defeated in His name. "When your Secretary and I are discussing matters," once said an Indian diplomat of Dulles, "God always gets between us." "Surely," Dulles had predicted in 1942, "the catastrophies that inevitably overtake those who operate on anti-Christian principles powerfully argue that it is those principles which are true." [14]

Nevertheless, John Foster Dulles was also a politician before he became a preacher, and his legalistic, moralistic, and ideological references were subtly set within a framework that was nonlegalistic, nonmoralistic, and nonideological. During the interwar period, Dulles had criticized the popularity of the "devil" theory of causation as an ultimate escape from responsibility. Dulles had found at the time little differences between states: "All nations," he wrote then, "are inherently selfish and we are no different from any other." [15] Side by side with a Manichean vision of international politics existed a Machiavellian vision that recognized the primacy of power and national interest; and Dulles, who in the fifties came to be known for his pactomania, had discarded international agreements that did not respond to the necessities of power and national interest. Shortly before being named secretary of state he observed: "Treaties of alliance and mutual aid mean little except as they spell out what the people concerned would do anyway." [16] Earlier, in his *War, Peace and Change,* he had commented, even more abruptly:

> In the absence of any central authority to pass judgments one cannot consider treaties, as such, to be sacred, nor can we identify treaty observance in the abstract with law and order. If we do not realize that treaties as such are neither "law" nor "sacred" we will fall into the common error of thinking that treaties provide a mechanism whereby international peace can be assured. [17]

Within this Machiavellian framework, Dulles simply distinguished between "static" and "dynamic" nations — a distinction that was strictly nonethical. Static nations he regarded as the main obstacle to peace, and he made the need for change the dominant theme of his career. "The concepts and words that matter, in all we say," he once confided to Emmet Hughes, an occasional speech writer for the president, "are simply peace and change. We live in an age of deep change. You can't stop it. What you can do is to bend every effort to direct it — to see that it is evolutionary rather than revolutionary." [18] Only change, Dulles felt, would prevent the institutionalization of injustice: "Change is the law of life and new conditions are constantly arising which call for remedy lest there be injustice." [19] By canceling injustice, change would help promote peace.

> A frequent cause of war has been the effort of satisfied peoples to identify peace as a perpetuation of the status quo. Change is the law of life, of international life as well as national and personal. . . . World order cannot be measured merely by the elimination of violence. There must also be processes of peaceful change whereby justice manifests itself. [20]

But change that involved a possible compromise with forces unwilling to recognize the basic principles of moral law he strictly ruled out. "If we rely on freedom," reasoned Dulles, "then it follows that we must abstain from diplomatic moves which would seem to endorse captivity. That would in effect be a conspiracy against freedom." [21] At this juncture, Dulles displaced the source of international conflicts from the international system and the related problems of assuring change toward malignant states with which coexistence was impossible unless they abandoned their nonmoral principles. "This [moral] law," concluded Dulles, "has been trampled by the Soviet rulers and, for that violation, they can and should be made to pay." [22]

The identification of the Soviet Union as "the" malignant state was relatively slow to take shape and it paralleled the reorientation of Dulles' thinking about the sources of Soviet policy. As late as 1947 he still characterized Russian expansion outside its frontiers as a traditional search for security, but by the time he became secretary of state, Dulles had irreversibly concluded that the Soviet rulers were enslaved by the doctrine of international communism and that Soviet policy was nothing but a means to communist ideology. The immediate inference from Dulles' conclusion was that although problems between states could be worked out, they could not be worked out between two opposite ideologies, one of which started from "an atheistic Godless premise." Between Russia and America there was no real dispute at all — the dispute was with an ideology that had captured the minds and bodies of hundreds of millions of people, including the Soviet people. Said Dulles: "If only the government of Russia was interested in looking out for the welfare of Russia, the people of Russia, we would have a state of non-tension right away." [23]

Such a single-minded, totalistic perception of international communism as the enemy, with the Soviet Union as its agent, closed the secretary's mind to the possibility of reconciliation unless the Soviets and their allies were to abandon altogether the communist way and endorse the American way. Within this Manichean framework, any decrease in Soviet hostility appeared as the realistic consequence of the pressure that America had brought to bear on Moscow, and it provided further "proof" that such pressure needed to be maintained, if not increased. For example, in April 1953, shortly after Stalin's death, early Soviet pronouncements in favor of détente between the two superpowers were dismissed by Dulles as "rotten apples": "It's obvious," he said, "that what they are doing is because of outside pressures, and I don't know anything better we can do than to keep up these pressures right now." [24] By July 1953, following the settlement of the Korean War, Dulles wanted to increase these pressures further: "This is the kind of time when we ought to be *doubling* our bets, not reducing them. . . . This is the time to *crowd* the enemy — and maybe *finish* him, once and for all." [25] Paradoxically, any Soviet action toward accommodation would now be interpreted as evidence of the correctness of America's decision to stand firm until final victory. Should the Soviets agree to a summit meeting as they did in 1955, or should they reduce their armed forces, as they did by 1.2 million men in 1956, they would do so for economic reasons or because of problems of leadership, rather than to shift their foreign policy intentions. Such force-level reductions might also be interpreted as a further display of Moscow's treacheries: to a newspaperman who had asked Dulles whether it was not a "fair conclusion" that he would have preferred "to have the Soviet Union keep these men in their armed forces," the secretary of state replied: "Well, it's a fair conclusion that I would rather have them standing around doing guard duty than making atomic bombs." [26] Should Peking respond favorably to a proposed Indian compromise for a settlement in Korea, as it was rumored in early 1953, Dulles would react with "sorrow" to the prospect of a "premature" settlement: "I don't think we can get much out of a Korean settlement until we have shown — before all Asia — our clear superiority by giving the Chinese one hell of a licking." [27] The intrinsic problem of negotiations between the Soviet Union and the United States in the fifties was well expressed in an exchange that the American secretary of state had with one member of his staff during the Berlin Conference in 1954. Dulles asked his aide whether he would be satisfied if the Soviet foreign minister suddenly accepted the allies' request for free elections in Germany. To the official's positive reply Dulles retorted: "Well, that's where you and I part company — because I wouldn't. There'd be a catch in it." [28] As indeed there might have been — but this was hardly the best way to find out.*

---

* The initial suggestion for the summit meeting came from Winston Churchill in May 1953. In the aftermath of Stalin's death, Churchill called for an early meeting of "the smallest number of powers and persons possi-

Convinced of the effectiveness of his policies, Dulles could then describe the failures of Soviet policies and forecast the imminent collapse of the communist ideology. As one announcement among many, he stated before the Senate Foreign Relations Committee in February 1955:

> The fact is that they have failed, and they have got to devise new policies. . . . Those Soviet policies have gradually ceased to produce any results for them. The free nations have banded together, shown their strength, shown their unity to an increasing degree so that that policy was not producing any positive results. The result is, they have got to review their whole creed, from A to Z.

This statement prompted one senator to comment: "I do not recognize the world of which Mr. Dulles is speaking." [29] Three months later, this time before a House hearing, Dulles spoke no longer of the collapse of Soviet policies but of the collapse of the Soviet system altogether: "My analysis of the whole world situation is that the Soviets are over-extended . . . [and that] their system . . . is on the point of collapsing." [30]

Ironically, the Manichean framework of Dulles' policies was dictated by his Machiavellian perception of the international situation and of America's role within such a situation. Viewing the Soviet menace in a true Kennan optique as a natural, long-range, and stimulating challenge to America and Western democracies, Dulles found it necessary to assure America's continued involvement in the struggle by tightening the screws of American inflexibility. But in so doing, the secretary of state became a captive of the resulting national mood that he himself had helped shape by giving credit, in such indictments as the Re-

---

ble." America's participation was made dependent upon prior evidence from Russia that the conference would be worthwhile. This condition was met with the Austrian treaty in May 1955 and, the following month, final arrangements for the July meeting were settled. The Summit Conference itself was not very successful. On the one hand, the Soviets were now eager to disprove the claims that their concessions had been made out of weakness. The Americans, on the other hand, were eager to exploit the weakness that had been perceived in Moscow's first "retreat" (in Austria) since the end of World War II. (See Coral Bell, *Negotiations from Strength* [New York, 1963], pp. 100–136.)

publican platform in 1952, to the foreign policy charges of the McCarthy era.

The outcome of his tactics was made ironical by international circumstances as well. Was Dulles' reference to a conspiratorial movement for the overthrow of capitalist society still plausible after Stalin's death? In 1953, the Soviet government abandoned its territorial demands in Turkey, thus unfreezing the hostility that had prevailed since 1945; it extended a hand of friendship to Iran and reestablished diplomatic relations with Israel, relations that had been broken by Stalin, following the discovery of the so-called doctors' plot in December 1952; it began a rapprochement with Greece, and nonalignment for the first time began to be spoken of with favor; the war in Korea was ended. In 1954–1955, other Soviet moves included its withdrawal from Austria; a public apology to Tito for past Soviet errors and a public recognition that all socialist states should be left free to follow their own socialism; the evacuation of Port Arthur and the return to Finland of the naval base of Porkalla; offers for the reunification of Germany (in an extension of Stalin's offer of May 1952 for a unified, rearmed, and neutral Germany within its Potsdam frontiers); attempts to normalize relations with Japan; and certain concessions on disarmament.* Finally, in February 1956, at the Twentieth Party Congress, Khrushchev harshly denounced Stalin and Stalinism and spelled out the new Soviet foreign policy of strengthening its relations with other communist states, improving relations with the Western states, and sup-

* Among these steps Soviet policies over Austria and Germany were probably the most dramatic expressions of Moscow's new flexibility. Concluded on May 15, 1955, the Austrian State Treaty signified the withdrawal of Soviet occupation forces from the Soviet-occupied portion of Austria in return for permanent Austrian neutrality. By driving a 500-mile neutral wedge between West Germany and Italy, the Soviets were effectively splitting the zone of Atlantic defense. With regard to Germany, Soviet proposals in early 1954 and 1955 consisted essentially in calling for an all-European collective security system that would tentatively exclude the United States. Such a security system would be linked to a settlement of the German question, possibly on the basis of general elections that would *follow* the formation of a coalition government between the Bonn government and the East German communist regime. Offers of this type, because they were not properly tested, or because they were tested too late, may have been lost opportunities for reaching a basic agreement that could have altered the cold war.

porting nonalignment. Clearly, an American policy that had been at best conceived to satisfy a national mood of inflexibility and an international situation of confrontation built a momentum that made it unresponsive to international changes and incapable of modifying the mood that that policy had brought with it. In May 1950, one month prior to the Korean War, Dulles had criticized America's habit of behaving "as though God had appointed us to be the Committee of Admissions to the Free World and as though the qualifications for membership were to be found by our looking into a mirror." [31] In a position of power, however, he quickly found a need to reassert America's chairmanship of that committee and to bar from the committee any nation that did not fulfill the requirements set by America's own image.

Liberation, Brinksmanship, and Massive Retaliation

The precepts of foreign policy that John Foster Dulles devised and defined, and America followed during his six years as secretary of state, were consistent with both Dulles' and America's theological principles and political temperament. These precepts were also shaped by the political atmosphere of the time. The new Republican administration took office after twenty years of exile in the aftermath of a three year campaign that had vilified the secretary of state, the policies he had pursued, and the institutions that had tried to implement those policies. Indeed, the bitterness and hatred this campaign had aroused were such that in 1961, upon learning of Dean Acheson's appointment as an adviser on NATO, some Republicans expressed amazement that he was still in America.[32]

These attacks had begun to gain momentum in February 1950 when the junior senator from Wisconsin, Joseph R. McCarthy, suggested that a group in the State Department promoted at every moment the communist cause.[33] His charges were endorsed by numerous legislators, and hardly anyone in official Washington escaped the folly of the era. Senator William E. Jenner, a Republican from Indiana, attacked General Marshall, then secretary of defense, as a "living lie . . . an errand boy, a front man, a stooge, or a co-conspirator for the [Truman] administration's crazy assortment of collectivist cut-throat, crackpots and communist fellow-traveling appeasers." [34] From 1950 to 1953, in the "night of the long knives," as Dean Acheson has called it, charges and counter-charges, resignations and dismissals, the growing intolerance of opposition and the unstated fear of not being "loyal enough," caused an incalculable damage to the governance of the nation and the formulation of its foreign policy. To prove his virtue, the secretary of state had to spend much of his time explaining that he was not a communist and that there were not "a lot" of communists known to him within the State Department. To prove its collective virtue, the State Department had to sacrifice many qualified and irreplaceable career officers who had been attacked by McCarthy. Thus, between February and August 1953 the personnel strength of the State Department dropped by more than half, from approximately 42,000 to 20,000. About 16,000 of this reduction was by transfer to other agencies, but 5,000 involved terminations, primarily under the president's "security program" — this latter despite the fact that during the entire McCarthy era not a single case of disloyalty was ever proved.[35]

In 1953, John Foster Dulles faced the problem of gaining national confidence for himself as secretary of state and support of his foreign policy as that of America. From the days when he had served under President Wilson at the Versailles Peace Conference, Dulles had learned the indispensability of securing congressional support for his policies. In 1953, he also needed to quiet Senator McCarthy's attacks, or at least to preempt his devastating influence over public opinion. To this effect, on his very first day in office, the new secretary of state asked of all State Department employees a pledge of "positive loyalty" to the policies of the president and the Congress.[36] From then on, it would be difficult for a large number of the nation's foreign affairs personnel to know how safe or practical it was to ignore official sensibilities and express views or report facts that might differ from those of the administration.

But the new administration was also anxious to impress upon the public the newness of its approach to world affairs. In his

Inaugural Address, the president pointedly underlined the general spirit in which American foreign policy would now be conducted — a spirit that "once again" would "know and observe the difference between . . . a thoughtfully calculated goal and spasmodic reaction to the stimulus of emergencies." Shortly thereafter, in his first State of the Union Message, the Republican president proudly announced that in less than a fortnight he had "begun the definition of a new positive foreign policy." [37] In other words, under a new Republican administration, America would have a "new" foreign policy employing "new" means toward the fulfillment of "new" objectives issued from a renewed faith in traditional principles.

The first of these policies was the policy of liberation. Throughout 1952 the Republican platform announced that under a Republican administration America's policy of containment would be discarded as "an example of non-moral diplomacy." Instead, claimed the Republican presidential platform, the 800 million people who had been abandoned to the forces of evil by Acheson's hold-and-wait policy were to be liberated by rolling the communist empire ever further east. In May 1952, a campaigning Dulles asked the United States "to make it publicly known that it wants and expects liberation to occur." [38] That such a commitment would have immediate political gains was evident enough. As one of the major areas of liberation lay in Eastern Europe, the endorsement of the principle alone carried over countless Americans of East European extraction. Beyond that Dulles assumed that the espousal of high moral principles was a tremendously potent force that ought not to appear as the monopoly of the communist world.

The policy was nothing more or less than a principle itself; during his preconfirmation testimony at the Senate Foreign Relations Committee, Dulles firmly rejected the warlike implications of the liberation doctrine: "A policy which only aims at containing Russia where it now is, is in itself, an unsound policy." But, Dulles continued, liberation "can be done and must be done in ways which will not provoke a general war . . . in ways which will be . . . a peaceful process . . . by moral pressures, by the weight of propaganda." [39] The new sound that a believing

America would use to dismantle the Soviet empire would be the sound of freedom, upon which "America had stood as a Christian nation and for which the Church of Christ [stood]." [40] In practice, to use the image of one of Dulles' most favorable biographers, John Beale, liberation would be no more warlike than Joshua's march around the walls of Jericho. [41]

Never had the illusion of American omnipotence received a more perfect tribute than through the assertion that a mere declaration of principles would suffice to bring down the communist colossus. Under American leadership, "political task forces" were to be formed. These forces would then develop "freedom programs" for each one of the "captive" nations. Such programs would rely not on military power, nor even on economic power, but on the intangibles of power, moral judgment, and world opinion. Yet, could these intangibles be sufficient if they were not substantiated by military force if and when needed? And would America be willing to provide such force as might be needed?

An early answer to these questions was provided during an uprising in East Germany in June 1953. Angered by an increase in "work norms" (which was the equivalent of a cut in wages), East Germans staged mass demonstrations, first in East Berlin, then in most other German cities and in part of the countryside. These were dispersed only after Soviet forces — as many as three army divisions — were called in by the government of communist leader Walter Ulbricht. These riots appeared to prove Dulles' belief in the internal erosion of the Soviet empire by the indomitable call for freedom. Yet, they also proved that such calls against Soviet troops could not be answered by psychological warfare experts only. In June 1953, there was no reaction from Washington because there could be none. The requirements of power were such that American intervention in Eastern Europe could not be seriously considered unless America was willing to wage war with the Soviet Union, which it was not. In practice, liberation meant either war or futility. In 1953, as later in 1956, war was wisely discarded and liberation was implemented via a note of protest and a multimillion dollar offer of free food to East Germany.

Following the East German uprising, the evidence is strong that Dulles became fully aware of the limits of his own Eastern European pronouncements.[42] But, a prisoner of his own rhetoric, the American secretary of state could not suddenly and easily discard his earlier commitments; he continued to provide vocal support for a liberated Eastern Europe. A necessarily demilitarized objective within an unavoidable arena of power politics, liberation thus found its logical end when it was tested again in Hungary in late October 1956.

It will probably never be clear how much American policy led Hungarians into believing that they would receive American military assistance if they rose against Soviet domination.[43] Most probably, the Hungarian revolution was the product of domestic forces and its tragic outcome resulted partly from the miscalculations of a Hungarian leadership that misjudged the pace and the scope of the destalinization. Nevertheless, American pledges of support and exhortations to fight were not conducive to more prudence from the Nagy government. But, in Hungary, as earlier in East Germany, there was no American assistance because there could be none. The Atlantic Alliance was in complete disarray in the midst of Washington's bitter opposition to the Anglo-French intervention in the Suez. America was in the midst of a presidential campaign and Dulles' paramount objective was to keep both crises down at least until after the elections. In early September, reviewing the then explosive situation in the Middle East, Dulles candidly acknowledged to Emmet Hughes that his main concern was to gain time: "Every day that goes by without some outbreak," said Dulles, "is a gain, and I just keep trying to buy that day. I don't know anything to do but to keep improvising." [44] By October 1956, Dulles himself had begun his bout with cancer and he followed much of the Hungarian revolution from his hospital bed. Said Robert Murphy, then a high official in the State Department, Dulles "like everybody else in the department, was terribly distressed." Yet, no one "had whatever imagination it took to discover another solution. We were just boxed." [45] Emmet Hughes' irritated comment about the position of the State Department during the Suez crisis provided another indication of how complete was the policy vacuum at the State

Department: "The damn trouble is that we don't have a policy in this crisis, and you *can't* try to use a speech as a substitute." [46]

Dulles' second major pronouncement concerned "brinksmanship."

> You have to take chances for peace, just as you must take chances in war. Some say that we were brought to the verge of war. Of course we were brought to the verge of war. The ability to get to the verge without getting into the war is the necessary art. If you cannot master it, you inevitably get into war. If you try to run away from it, if you are scared to go to the brink, you are lost . . . we walked to the brink and we looked it in the face. We took strong action.[47]

Dulles' pronouncement coincided well with his personal philosophy. A pessimist in his general understanding of international relations, the secretary of state was fond of observing that wars had occurred on the average three times every five years since 1480. The introductory sentence of one of his major pieces of writing, *War or Peace,* stated: "War is probable . . . not inevitable . . . not imminent." [48] The probability of war was particularly high in an international system shaken up by the forces of atheistic communism. A relaxation of tension was therefore not necessarily a good thing. "We dare not relax because the moment of relaxation is the moment of peril." [49] It was the moment of peril because, in Dulles' view, it would be unavoidably succeeded by a reappearance of the threat of war against which the nation always had to be prepared. In *War, Peace and Change* he had written: "The creation of a vast armament in itself calls for a condition between war and peace. Mass emotion on a substantial scale is a prerequisite. The willingness to sacrifice must be engendered. A sense of peril from abroad must be cultivated." [50] From Dulles' viewpoint, maintaining international tension was the only way through which essentially satisfied and nonmilitaristic nations could be induced to reverse their usual and normal desire for consumer goods in favor of defense expenditures aimed at keeping America ahead of the power competition. Without some evident menace from the Soviet bloc America's will to maintain its unity and strength might weaken, so Dulles continued to couple his previously quoted announcements of an imminence of Soviet collapse with an exaggerated estimate of their military capabilities.[51]

In practice, brinksmanship consisted of making one's views and policies so ambiguously open to the most extreme assumptions that the enemy would be deterred from taking any action at all. In May 1953, America went to the brink of "a bigger war" when it hinted in New Delhi about its plan to carry the Korean War across the Yalu River into Manchuria.[52] In April 1954, the same strategy was used to aid the French in Dien Bien Phu and to raise more fears in the communist camp over what American reaction might be should the forthcoming negotiations in Geneva fail to bring a satisfactory truce in Indochina.[53] In January 1955, and again in the fall of 1958, Dulles attempted to deter Peking from attacking the off-shore islands of Quemoy and Matsu by brandishing the possibility of committing American forces to their defense.[54] To this effect, the White House secured passage by the senate of the so-called Formosa Resolution, whereby the president was empowered "to include the securing and protecting of such related positions and territories of that area now in friendly hands and the taking of such other measures as he judges to be required or appropriate in ensuring the defense of Formosa and the Pescadores."

In all of these instances, American diplomacy waved the big stick even if it did not mean to use it. There were rumors of an impending use of nuclear weapons against China in 1953; conventional, if not nuclear, forces were gathered for use in Indochina in 1954;* a personal commitment of the American president to Chiang was allegedly made in 1955; units of the Seventh Fleet convoyed nationalist ships supplying Quemoy and Matsu in 1958.[55] In all these instances, too, war was either avoided or ended, and "satisfactory" outcomes were obtained: in Korea where a truce was finally secured in July 1953, after two full years of negotiations; in Indochina where Vietnam was divided

---

* According to John Beale the United States aircraft carriers, *Boxer* and *Philippine Sea,* had atomic weapons aboard and were ready to "strike at staging areas where the Chinese communists grouped the forces they were pouring in behind the Vietminh (*John Foster Dulles,* [New York, 1959], p. 207).

on the 17th parallel, one degree south of the French initial request and three degrees north of Ho Chi Minh's first demand; and in the Taiwan Straits where the communist Chinese were kept at bay. Thus one might possibly argue, as Robert Goold Adams does in his biography of Dulles, that "it was no bad thing for the people in the Kremlin to have that nasty ultimate doubt at the backs of their minds, that some idiot in Washington might not after all loose off an atomic bomb, if Russia went too far." [56] But in pursuing this juggling act of brinksmanship, Dulles also had to conceal the full truth from America's allies who became the most consistent critics of America's and Dulles' apparent intransigeance.

The military policy of the Eisenhower administration was shaped around the so-called doctrine of massive retaliation. Dulles' reasoning was that what was militarily required of small nations on the Soviet and Chinese periphery were indigenous forces strong enough to defeat indirect aggression and to hold off external attack long enough to uncover the aggression while preventing a fait accompli. But once aggression had been uncovered, America could use its great strategic reserve "to retaliate, instantly, by means and at places of [its] own choosing." This capability in turn was expected to restrain Soviet adventurism.[57] In other words, America would display its growing retaliatory power to deter communist aggression, but the forward positions would be sustained by the forward countries themselves. America's participation in local and limited defense operations would be confined essentially to air and sea power to which might be added small but highly mobile and efficient ground units.

Such a strategy relied heavily on Dulles' favorite objective: to keep a potential enemy guessing about the action that the United States might take in a circumstance. But in presenting his strategy Dulles suffered from the image he had built for himself when endorsing such other policies as "liberation" or "brinksmanship." Massive retaliation gave the impression that America looked upon the possibility of war, even nuclear war, with equanimity. Yet, plainly the Eisenhower administration did not systematically condone the overwhelming use of nuclear weapons in any situation against any adversary at any time. Massive retaliation, Dulles wrote in an article for *Foreign Affairs* published in April 1954, "does not mean turning every local war into a world war. It does not mean that if there is a communist attack somewhere in Asia, atom or hydrogen bombs will necessarily be dropped on the great industries of China or Russia." [58] Massive retaliation merely stressed the extreme strategic option open to America in its selection of retaliatory tools, an option that would be neither "necessarily" selected nor "necessarily" ruled out. Retaliation would still be launched on a selective basis. But the important thing, as Dulles saw it, was that the would-be aggressor would now know in advance that he was exposing far more than only those forces that he chose to use for his aggression. Thus aware that he would lose "something" more than he could win, the aggressor would be deterred. [59]

As Bernard Brodie, a leading analyst of nuclear strategy put it, massive retaliation attempted to answer a wish for total solution that suited well the historical mood of the American people, particularly during Asian crises in Korea, Indochina, and Taiwan. [60] It was also a possible answer to the Republican approach to the economics of national strategy. As a result of the Korean War defense expenditures had grown from $14.3 billion and 5 per cent of the gross national product in 1950, to $49.3 billion and 13.5 per cent of the gross national product in 1953. Anxious to reduce such excessive defense budgets, the Republican administration reasoned that more development of, and reliance upon, new weapons could free America from the burden of developing more conventional armament and maintaining ever larger ground forces in innumerable bases abroad.

In a limited sense, massive retaliation was a negative weapon that did little more than continue the former policy of containment. Only major aggression could reasonably establish its credibility. Yet, understood "as-if-it-meant-what-it-said," massive retaliation stirred many misgivings and fears against the recklessness that it implied. The allies wanted to know the meaning of such words as "instantly," "means," and "our" in Dulles' warning of a retaliation launched "instantly with means of our choosing." More specifically, they wanted to know what would actually happen if the threat failed, i.e., if the Soviets refused to be deterred by it. Was a middle way left between inaction and nuclear holocaust? Which weapons would be used in reprisal, where, and when? Would nuclear weapons have been used in order to meet the communist threat in Greece and in Turkey? Whose basic decision would it be to use such weapons? What would be the level of intraallied cooperation in implementing a decision that might sanction the annihilation of those nations in the defense of which massive retaliation was being exerted in the first place?

An Assessment

From a more general perspective, during the Dulles years several pronouncements were made to stimulate the idea that there had been a significant change in America's foreign policy. Besides liberation, brinksmanship, and massive retaliation, other claims attempted to fulfill the same objective. So, to those who felt that Chiang had been betrayed and that he was still the best weapon available against communism in Asia, Dulles promised the eventual unleashing of the nationalist forces against the Peking government. The practical value of unleashing Chiang's 350,000-man army against a regime whose military capabilities had, however briefly, stalemated America in the Korean War was never explained. Would America intervene against Mao if Chiang's attack failed, or would it go to war against Moscow if Chiang succeeded and Moscow decided to help its faltering ally? Finally, for those who felt that American policy in Western Europe had been too conciliatory and that Western European states were not doing their fair share of participation, Dulles threatened Europe with an "agonizing reappraisal of the basic United States policy."

Yet, for all of these efforts, little was drastically new in American policy. The endorsement of high moral principles is a cardinal rule of national policy. "A free society," Dean Acheson observed in 1951, "can call upon profound resources among its people in behalf of a righteous cause." [61] And he too had unequivocally pledged: "We can see no moral compromise with the contrary thesis of international communism." [62] Brinksmanship had been used several times by the Truman administration;

during the Iran crisis, the American president sent an ultimatum to the Kremlin.[63] Even the threat of massive retaliation could be regarded as a new name for an old policy: in case of "open aggression" by enemy armies, nations traditionally attempted "to strike back where it hurts, by means of [their] own choosing." But that choice had also been traditionally limited by circumstances — as it had been in Korea. In his inimitable style, Eisenhower himself discarded the notion that massive retaliation was a revolutionary strategy. "To call it revolutionary," the president stated in one of his news conferences, "or to act like it is something that just suddenly dropped down on us like a cloud from heaven is just not true." [64] As to such other theoretical pronouncements as the "unleashing" of Chiang's forces, these pronouncements too hinted at a bellicosity which had been in effect during the previous Democratic administration when Chiang's harassment of China's mainland had been approved no less actively than it would be during the Republican administration. Having publicly "unleashed" Chiang Kai-shek (as the newspapers put it, although the Eisenhower administration never used the phrase) the administration secretly exacted a pledge from Chiang to restrain him from any offensive action without prior American consent.

In short, Dulles' "new" policies were essentially old policies presented within a theological package that was consistent with America's philosophy of international relations. Although Dulles hardly initiated any policy of lasting importance, his rhetoric confirmed and strengthened the serious doubts that America's allies had about American objectives and policies. Within one week of his inauguration America had warned Western Europe with "a little rethinking of [its] . . . policy in relation to Western Europe." But as his stay in the State Department unfolded, Western Europe's own policies in relation to the United States undertook "a little rethinking." Domestic interferences in favor of Chancellor Adenauer and against Prime Ministers Anthony Eden and Pierre Mendès-France raised furor in Germany, Great Britain, and France respectively. After the Suez crisis, the threat of being left alone played no small part in convincing France to accelerate the development of its own nuclear force.

At the very least, the Dulles policies prevented any more

territory from falling to a communist takeover, and this was accomplished without America getting involved in a war. Yet, the problems awaiting America in the sixties had their most serious roots in the missed opportunities of the fifties: the overall rejection of Moscow's peace initiative of 1953–1955, the persistent refusal to deal with China after Korea, the stubborn rejection of nonalignment as "an immoral and shortsighted conception," the falling into pactomania, the refusal to hold the free elections in Vietnam, the ambivalent Middle East policy over Suez and Lebanon, and the clumsy handling of European allies within the Atlantic Alliance, to cite but a few.

One year after the collapse of the Hungarian revolution, Dulles warned against an American illusion of omnipotence: "We are not omnipotent. . . . Our power and policy are but a significant factor in the world . . . in combination with other factors we are able to influence importantly the course of events. But we cannot deal in absolutes." [65] Yet, when a new Democratic administration took over in Washington, in January 1961, the illusion was at its peak, and the problems associated with it were begging uneasy solutions.

6

The End
of Alliances?

The Nature of Alliances

However helpful it may be, a "sense of community" is not sufficient to bring nations together within an alliance. Alliances are formed primarily against, and only occasionally or secondarily for, someone or something.[1] In periods of highest tension, when the external threat can be easily identified, the unity of a given alliance is most evident. Then, divisive national concerns can be conveniently submerged and overshadowed, at least temporarily, by the main conflict. Clearly enough, in such periods of international crisis the alliance is decisively directed by the dominant power. The alliance becomes "troubled" when the crisis recedes and a sustained period of relative order increases the confidence of the weaker states whose interests become, once again, more strictly national.

The rewards that nations may gain from alliance participation relate to security and, particularly for smaller states, to domestic stability and international status. Linked to security is international stability. In debating its entry into the Atlantic Alliance, France, for instance, raised two security questions. First, would the new alignment affect its alliance with Russia, which was an essential part of the old French *politique de sécurité* against Germany? Second, would the new alignment further freeze the division of Europe, thereby enhancing the likelihood of a confrontation within the international system? At a domestic level, the alliance helped create an effective coalition of non-communist forces in the French Assembly as the "American party" remained a governing coalition force throughout most of the Fourth Republic. Finally, France saw in the alliance the means of recovering, at the least cost, Great Power status. But as these rewards diminished, France's endorsement of alliance policies diminished too.

Neither the perception of national advantages nor the perception of the external threat needs be at all times identical between allies. As mentioned, they converge under conditions of maximum external stress. Differences between America and some of its partners in 1949 were muted in the fifties when each new meeting seemed to reflect the same accord that had been reached so many times before. Yet, beneath this apparent consensus, questions of vital national concern remained unanswered: they re-emerged in the sixties when the Franco-American relationship at best became one of least common disagreement.

The perception of the costs of an alliance is quite complex. As an alliance usually includes numerous escape clauses, this cost may simply be what the member states want it to be at any given time. Alliances are what alliances do and their commitments are more explicitly defined only when the time for action comes. The growth of the commitment, however, may imperceptibly preempt the escape clause. Dean Acheson's pledge in 1949 that an attack upon Western Europe would not necessarily imply America's military action was somewhat irrelevant when American support and combat units stationed in the NATO area amounted to several hundred thousand men. A nation must always relate, and often reappraise, the cost of its participation to the benefits gained through such participation.

In comparing costs and benefits achieved through alliance membership, nations obey two fundamental objectives. On the one hand, while seeking to maximize its own gains, each partner attempts to minimize the cost of alignment. On the other hand, the cost of alignment must remain less than the benefit, thereby providing for a marginal utility of membership that establishes the preferability of alignment over independent action.

Undoubtedly, the smaller allies are particularly eager to gain the security benefit, and the larger allies are particularly eager to share the burdens. To the smaller ally, the assistance provided is never enough and the "taxation" sought is always excessive. If the marginal utility of the alliance is more essential to the junior partner than it is to the senior partner, then the latter's threat of withdrawal can be effectively issued to bring the junior partner back in line. Otherwise, the senior partner confronts its own dilemma over whether or not such reappraisal is indeed possible. In the early fifties, the preservation of the Atlantic Alliance was still regarded as vital to Western Europe's security. Dependent as it was on American power, the alliance could not survive an American withdrawal, so that Washington's occasional threat of an "agonizing reappraisal," if and when taken seriously, could have a corrective effect on the policies of some Western European allies. But such a threat carried less weight in the sixties when disagreement from its allies was met by America with a resigned willingness to "agree to disagree."

In short, alliances need to be evaluated periodically according to their relevance, their desirability, and their effectiveness. One of the foremost experts on NATO, Alistair Buchan, has summarized this need particularly well:

> Alliances are means to an end, whether it be primarily to increase the security of a group of sovereign states in the face of a common adversary, or to increase the diplomatic pressure which they can bring upon him, or share the economic cost and the political risk with either objective. But the international system is an environment in which the fears and goals of nation states, whether they be allies or adversaries, do not remain constant; con-

sequently, alliances — especially those embracing large states or a large group of states — have rarely lasted for a long span of time.[2]

By the end of the sixties, American foreign policy faced the question of whether the time for alliances in general, and the Atlantic Alliance in particular, had come to an end.

Change and Security in Europe

The Atlantic Alliance may have become less relevant when the dominant threat around which it developed lost much of its urgency and credibility, and a détente began between the United States and the Soviet Union. Actually, whether there was détente between the two superpowers was itself debatable. During the early years of the Khrushchev regime Soviet foreign policy appeared to lose much of the caution it had displayed under Stalin, and rocket-rattling became an obsession with the Soviet leader, not only over some areas in Asia, Latin America, and the Middle East but in Europe as well. In November 1958 Moscow warned the West that unless an agreement for the reunification and demilitarization of Berlin was reached within six months, its half of the city would be turned over to the East Germans and a treaty signed with the Ulbricht government. In practice, this six-month ultimatum was to last approximately four years. But during the period, East-West tensions reached the danger level, particularly in the summer of 1961, when, following President Kennedy's meeting with Khrushchev in Vienna, the American secretary of defense ordered a worldwide alert of United States forces.

In retrospect, it seems that Moscow was engaged at the time in a dangerous juggling act that related only in part to Europe. It attempted to devise a policy of coexistence that would diminish the risks of nuclear war. But its conflict with Peking, by making unseemly an interest in collaborating with the United States, increased Soviet inhibitions against a détente that might have signified an open break with China. These two contradictory courses converged in Germany by way of the question of nuclear weapons. Sometime around 1957, the Soviets had agreed to provide Peking with atomic know-how and a sample atomic bomb.[3] But Khrushchev feared that such a Soviet offer, if and when implemented, would be paralleled in the West by similar American action toward West Germany. The end result of this sudden proliferation of nuclear weapons to China and West Germany would impair Moscow's alleged goal of peaceful coexistence. More importantly too, this offer would occur when Moscow's strategic capabilities were themselves dangerously limited. For although unknown to the West at the time (the United States fear of a "missile gap" reached its peak during the presidential campaign of 1960), Khrushchev's display of a rapidly expanding Soviet strategic power from 1957 to 1961 was but a bold exercise in strategic bluffing.[4] Moscow's promise to China was promptly withdrawn in 1959, and, in 1961, Khrushchev explicitly referred to his objective of arranging atom-free zones, first in Europe and in the Far East.[5] By that time, however, it was hardly credible that the Soviets could in any way control Chinese nuclear armament and satisfy a deal that would have exchanged the denuclearization of China for that of Germany. By that time too responsible American officials had begun to recognize that no missile gap existed after all and that the United States continued to enjoy a strategic superiority.[6]

Détente between the two superpowers became more easily recognizable in the aftermath of the Cuban missile crisis, in October 1962, when the world leaped to the brink of disaster. Militarily, the Soviet efforts to install some forty medium-range and intermediate-range ballistic missile launchers in Cuba probably aimed at restoring strategic parity between Moscow and Washington. Short of ICBMs, Russia was simply attempting to move its existing short-range (1,100 to 2,200 miles) missiles closer to continental United States. Politically, the Soviet efforts, if successful, would have represented an ideological victory over Peking, which by then was in open confrontation with Moscow for obtaining the allegiance of worldwide communist parties and for sponsoring wars of national liberation. Such a victory was particularly needed in view of the collapse of Khrushchev's Berlin offensive. In fact, Soviet nuclear bases in Cuba might have been, as the Soviet premier saw it, the decisive argument in enforcing his 1958 ultimatum over Berlin. Finally, economically, this short-cut to strategic parity would have been conveniently achieved at little expenditure for a Soviet economy hampered by lagging growth and pressured by increasing demands for more goods of consumption. The French Kremlinologist Michel Tatu has presented an astute overall description of what might have happened if the Cuban coup had succeeded:

> At the beginning of November most of the missiles shipped to Cuba would presumably have become operational. With this formidable weapon levelled at the heart of America and with the added prestige that accrues to the bolder player, Khrushchev could have faced Kennedy with something approaching triumph. . . . He would then have tried to bargain, primarily on Berlin and perhaps also on the American bases system as a whole, not only in Turkey. Even if he had not obtained anything by this means, he would at least have retained the strategic benefit of his advanced base and the prestige of the man who had scored a crucial point. It is certain therefore that, while the last week in October was a hot one, without it there would have been an even longer and hotter winter.[7]

Under the circumstances, the Soviet maneuver was intolerable to American security. That American bases were located at the periphery of the Soviet Union as well did not justify that the United States would have to tolerate a similar insecurity in a spirit of fairness. In effect, the Cuban missile crisis provided a clear example of massive retaliation in action as President Kennedy warned Moscow of what would happen should these missiles be launched from Cuba: "It shall be the policy of this nation to regard any missile launched from Cuba against any nation in the Western Hemisphere as an attack by the Soviet Union on the United States, requiring a full retaliatory response upon the Soviet Union." [8]

It is not necessary here to go into the details of the thirteen-day crisis of October 1962.[9] With the Soviet missiles evacuated from Cuba, a mood of sober reflection appeared to provide Soviet-American détente with some momentum. "Prudence, peace, and the world's security have won," stated the Soviet premier in December 1962.[10] President Kennedy found the analysis sufficiently believable in the midst of a series of arrangements that included the signing of the test ban treaty, the establishment of a "hot line" that would facilitate direct communications between Moscow and Washington in time of crisis, and adherence to a United Nations resolution banning nuclear weapons from outer space. To Kennedy it seemed that the problem of European security had now been satisfactorily solved. "The whole debate about an atomic force in Europe," he told Spaak of Belgium in 1963, "is really useless, because Berlin is secure and Europe as a whole is well protected. What really matters at this point is the rest of the world." [11] Relaxation of tensions between the two superstates reflected their apparent acceptance of each other's preponderance within their respective spheres of influence, and though these spheres could and would still be probed in such peripheral areas as the Middle East or Southeast Asia, they were well drawn in Europe as, in effect, they had been for over twenty years. In September 1968, the Soviet invasion of Czechoslovakia might have revived East-West tensions. But the crisis soon faded away and hardly any serious call for American intervention was made in America or abroad. Even President Johnson's belated guarantee of Yugoslavia's and Rumania's territorial integrity were sufficiently ambiguous to make its fulfillment doubtful.[12] In January 1969, in his Inaugural Address President Nixon hopefully spoke of the era of conciliation that had succeeded the past era of confrontation.[13]

Throughout the decade, however, America continued to reason that granted such a stalemate, and even granted the Kremlin's willingness to discuss the modalities of this stalemate, it was more urgent than ever to preserve the cohesion of the Atlantic Alliance when negotiations might be about to begin. America had lingering doubts that, possibly based on intended deception, détente was no more than Moscow's application of the old technique of dividing to better conquer. Obviously discord within the Atlantic Alliance created opportunities that Soviet diplomacy might exploit for political advantages. Such discord might even be increased by the Soviets if they abandoned their threatening posture. They could then achieve peacefully what hostile behavior had failed to secure. To this extent, de Gaulle, who became rapidly the symbol of whatever opposition to American policies there was from within the alliance, was Moscow's Trojan Horse.

Yet, such opposition, which was far broader than a Washington-Paris rift, only represented a fundamental change of direction for the alliance. In 1949 and thereafter, earlier conflicts had stemmed from the problems of best defining and implementing Atlantic security (what was to be done, how, and why?) [14] During 1962 to 1965, these divisions were part of a conflict that, taking security at least partly for granted, centered on the means of best defining, promoting, and stabilizing détente between the West and the East (who was going to do it, how, and why?). Begun as a debate over ends and means (what was the function of the alliance and how was it going to be fulfilled?), the Atlantic debate had become one of identity (who was going to fulfill such a function and how?). As the sixties unfolded, the Atlantic Alliance found itself more endangered, in Stanley Hoffman's words, "by the pursuit of the same objective by allies each of which [was] trying to control events than by the pursuit of different objectives by allies that avoid[ed] challenging one another," as had occasionally happened.[15]

Europe as a potential negotiator — or national poles of power in Europe eager to enter the forthcoming talks as equals — reflected the changed distribution of power within the Atlantic area. As we have seen, during the postwar period Western European states had sought and secured American assistance to face their internal problems, solve their colonial disputes, promote their economic recovery, and ensure their security against external aggression. In the early sixties, however, the six European states that had found economic unity through the Common Market developed together into superpower stature. By 1962 the European Economic Community produced almost as much steel as the United States; it was the world's second largest producer of automobiles, first in world imports, second in world exports. And the economies of the whole area grew over twice as fast as that of the United States. Not only economically revived, but also colonially disengaged, politically stabilized, and with no serious security apprehension, Europeans doubted the need of the alliance. Was it in Europe's interest, they asked, to remain in an alliance no longer related specifically to Europe's needs? To this question America applied the same reasoning that Europe had formerly used: the interest of a nation is conceived within the larger framework of its responsibilities. Consider, for example, the statement made by George Ball, then an undersecretary of state, in 1964: "We Americans have few national interests — in the narrow sense — outside our own territory but we have assumed vast world responsibility. . . . The willingness to accept world responsibility — as distinct from the preservation of national interests — is, in our observation and experience, not universal among the NATO membership." [16] Ironically enough, this argument was somewhat reminiscent of that employed by the British and the French in defense of their own empires when they distinguished between their national interest on the one hand, and the "white man's burden" and a *"mission civilisatrice,"* respectively.

Inasmuch as it indicated Western Europe's recovery, Atlantic polycentrism fulfilled America's primary objective in Europe. Yet, this recovery continued to be highly unstable as it was reached within the context of a tacit acceptance of the existing status quo, and without the formal resolution of problems that had plagued the European continent since the end of World War II. These problems were complicated by several factors. As an alliance of status quo countries, the Atlantic Alliance was ill equipped to face the demands for change made by one of its principal members, West Germany. Clearly, the preservation of Europe's status quo was of least immediate risk to Washington. A new European system would open a Pandora's box that might provide more or less security, depending on which elements were strengthened and which elements were weakened. A weakening of the superpowers' military presence in Europe enhanced the formation of an all-European security system, yet also strengthened the interventionist capability of the superpower closest to Europe, the Soviet Union. [17] Within that system itself, Germany's reunification would have to be debated soon. To keep Germany divided would soothe the misgivings of both Europes worried by the consequences of putting back together two of the ten biggest industrial entities in the world. Yet, the paradox of reuniting East and West Europe on the backs of a divided East and West Germany would make the new system largely dependent on West

Germany's potential shift of priorities, away from security, obtained with Washington's blessings, and toward reunification, sought in Moscow.

However convenient, particularly in view of other problems America faced in Vietnam and at home, the preservation of the status quo could not be permanent. Such a status quo rested on the precarious strategic balance achieved by both superpowers (a balance that had compelled their recognition of the status quo in the first place) and the awkward division of Germany. To stabilize the former might be an easier task for American diplomacy than to officialize the latter. That the European status quo was merely a reprieve before further entente or renewed dispute was perhaps best indicated by imagining a Europe twenty years later still plagued with a divided Berlin, still "protected" by the presence of over 300,000 United States troops, and still divided, more or less ideologically, into the Atlantic Alliance and the Warsaw Pact. Clearly, the projection had an element of absurdity that pointed to change as the unavoidable development of the seventies, but poorly described the specific modalities of such change.

Thus, Europe's status quo helped take security for granted; paradoxically, taking security for granted raised requests for changes that might preempt that security. Assuming the unavoidability and desirability of changes in Europe, the major question became one of identity: were such negotiations going to be conducted by nation states, by a European Europe, or by the respective superpower-sponsored alliances?

Massive Retaliation, Flexible Response, and NATO

One of the questions raised in the sixties was whether or not the Atlantic Alliance, as it had been conceived twenty years earlier, could satisfy the renewed search for national independence and national identity. Another question, however, raised doubts about the credibility of that alliance. The end of American nuclear monopoly, plus technological revolutions in nuclear weapons and their means of delivery, had opened a new perspective to the global search for national — as distinct from regional — security. It was possible to rely on nuclear weapons as an instrument of policy as long as American superiority in such weapons was unchallenged. But when such superiority disappeared and the threat of retaliation was balanced with a Soviet counterthreat of similar reprisal, both Europe *and* America asked whether any nation could and should risk destruction for the sake of another nation. And, assuming that America was willing to risk its cities for the defense of Western European cities, was such a commitment credible to partners *and* potential enemies alike?

The question did not permit an easy answer. In June 1963, during his German tour, President Kennedy forcefully stated: "The United States will risk its cities to defend yours because we need your freedom to defend ours." [18] Yet, four years earlier, Christian Herter, then an undersecretary of state, had emphasized: "I can't conceive of the President of the United States involving us in an all-out nuclear war unless the facts showed clearly that we are in danger of devastation ourselves, or that actual moves have been made toward devastating ourselves." [19] The logical conclusion, that of incertitude, was drawn by de Gaulle as he stated, early in 1963: "No one in the world, particularly no one in America, can say if, or where, or when, or how, or to what extent, American nuclear weapons would be used to defend Europe." [20]

In a general vein, the survival of alliances in the nuclear age has depended on a fundamental reform of their structures. But such reforms apparently went in contradictory directions. For one, national commitments, if they were to be credible, needed to be made within a much tighter framework. Such "integration" did not have to be structural, and the "engagement" of a given nation could simply take forms that, in certain situations, preempted its options. This attitude was known, to use Thomas Schelling's phrase, as being "rationally irrational." An irrational policy might be credible to the other side if cloaked in a rational mantle — for example, by making automatic, through one device or another, nuclear retaliation against an aggressor. At the same time, alliances needed to be disintegrated precisely because of the irrationality of the commitment. In practice, the Munich syndrome was finally terminated when the alternative to appeasement moved dangerously close to mutual annihilation: peace was divisible because destruction might be otherwise indivisible. A nation was not going to commit itself to destruction — not merely to the potential loss of human lives or territory as in the past — so that another nation might live. In short, aggression would be met by force — but only up to a point.

Implicit in such a dilemma was the distinction between deterrence and defense. Some argued that by toughening its terms, deterrence would be made more effective. According to this reasoning, massive retaliation had eliminated the risk of limited wars; in the latter stage of the war in Vietnam, many thought of Dulles' strategy with regret. The question, however, was to determine whether it was preferable to live under the choking shadow of nuclear war or to face the occasional pressure of limited conflicts. That Vietnam was a bad limited war did not necessarily mean that all limited wars were bad. Those in the United States and in Europe who argued for a tougher deterrence posture were indeed asking for the irrational to be rationalized into a national policy. They wanted to paralyze the other side with fear. Part of the rationale behind the French *force de frappe* was that contradictory deterrence positions within the alliance (massive retaliation for Paris, flexible response for Washington) would add further doubt to the enemy's calculations.[21] It was assumed, of course, that a rationally irrational policy would not be met with complete irrationality. Yet, what if irrationality did prevail on the other side as well? What if deterrence failed? Then, could the question of defense remain a centralized, multinational question, or would it become instead everyone for himself? To make deterrence possible, Washington needed to pledge its national body to the nuclear defense of Europe. But to make defense possible, it was Europe that might need to give its continental body so that Atlantica might survive a nonnuclear war: rational on one side of the Atlantic, irrational on the other. The 1958 "missile gap" between the United States and the Soviet Union had been transformed, under the Kennedy administration, into a "deterrence gap" between the United States and Europe.

This general uncertainty as to whether or not American strategic forces would be used for the defense of Europe was further enhanced when the Kennedy administration adopted the so-called strategy of flexible response, which was widely regarded in Europe as an effort by Washington to avoid committing to use those weapons to which American territory was most vulnerable.[22]

Flexible response rested on two essential premises. The first was that deterrence might not always work, and that more attention needed to be given to defense. Related to this premise was the belief that a thermonuclear war was manageable provided that the tools required for such management had been carefully examined and cautiously gathered prior to its outbreak. The second premise was, therefore, that a thermonuclear war could be kept limited, depending, among other factors, on the targets selected by the opponents. By concentrating on military targets ("counterstrike capability") America would reduce the other side's damaging capability. At the same time, it would provide the other side with incentives to confine its own strike to military targets as well, thus further increasing the limitation of damages. A counter-city capability could still be kept in reserve as part of a deterrent force operating during the war itself.[23]

To make the strategy meaningful, it was clearly necessary to develop a nuclear capability with a high level of survivability, penetrability, and control against and after a Soviet preemptive first strike. "I should think," argued Assistant Secretary of Defense Paul Nitze in December, 1961, "the most important persuader is to be found in Western nuclear capabilities, their survivability against anything his [Khrushchev's] force can do, their penetration capabilities against defenses, their responsiveness to responsible control, and their accuracy, number and power." [24] The deterrent function of this second strike capability would be fulfilled by maintaining, in McNamara's words, "a highly reliable ability to inflict an unacceptable degree of damage upon any single aggressor, or combination of aggressors, at any time during the course of a strategic nuclear exchange, even after our absorbing a surprise first strike." [25] Of course, the actual workability of a second strike that would distinguish between civilian and military targets was ultimately related to the aggressor's ability to control its own first strike: "In talking about nuclear war," McNamara recognized, "the Soviet leaders always say that they would strike at the entire complex of our military power including government and production centers, meaning our cities. If they were to do so, we would . . . have no alternative but to retaliate in kind." But the new doctrine at least gave Moscow the "strongest imaginable incentive to refrain from striking [American] cities." [26]

Yet, the most effective way of limiting a nuclear war was obviously by avoiding it altogether. Accordingly, McNamara attempted to raise the nuclear threshold and to widen the area of conventional warfare by emphasizing the role that nonnuclear capabilities played in the implementation of America's overall strategy. The American secretary of defense assumed that a wider range of practical alternatives was required to face the new challenges that the Kremlin seemed to be planning. "Unless the Free World has sufficient forces organized and equipped to deal with these challenges at what appears to be the highest appropriate levels of conflict," stated McNamara in February 1962, "we could be put into difficult situations by the communists. In such situations we could lose by default; or we could lose by limiting our response to what appears to be the highest appropriate level — but a level at which we may be inferior; or we could resort to thermonuclear war — the level at which we are superior — but at a cost which could be out of proportion to the issues and dangers involved." [27]

In short, America needed to be able "to respond promptly to limited aggressions, possibly in more than one place at the same time" in order both "to deter them and to prevent them from spreading into larger conflicts." [28] Nonnuclear capabilities, within NATO and elsewhere, grew into major importance for the Kennedy-Johnson administration. Under a formula devised by former Secretary of State Dean Acheson, the European allies were asked to provide the larger part of thirty active and thirty reserve divisions for Central Europe, instead of the sixteen active divisions and scattering of reserves which NATO had available at the time.[29]

McNamara's endorsements of noncivilian targets and nonnuclear weapons attempted to institutionalize the old NATO theory of a pause between each step on the escalation ladder. Escalation from conventional to nuclear war, and from nuclear exchange to nuclear holocaust, would thus remain gradual, and the chances of avoiding it would be accordingly increased. For, whereas massive retaliation had left very little choice following that pause, flexible response left every possibility open: the use of nuclear weapons was postponed but not canceled, military targets were preferred to civilian targets but without precluding them. In sum, McNamara would have indeed liked to keep a war in Europe nonnuclear, or at least to reduce the damage of any nuclear engagement and so preserve as much as possible of the continental United States. Still, such aims were explicitly made secondary to the aim of not losing, as it was indicated that Washington would not accept a loss of territory or any similar defeat. "In the event of a major aggression that could not be repulsed by conventional weapons," emphasized Kennedy, America would "take whatever action with whatever weapons . . . appropriate." [30]

Ultimately, massive retaliation was a policy of minimum deterrence calling for minimum involvement in world affairs inasmuch as the situations where the use of such a retaliation would be acceptable were by definition strictly limited. Flexible response, on the other hand, was a policy of maximum deterrence, because by making retaliation as minimal as possible, it permitted maximum involvement in world affairs. Ironically, it was a strategy in the style of McNamara that made America's continued involvement in world affairs both possible and credible. Military forces, theorized McNamara, must be able "to respond, with discrimination and speed, to any problem, at any spot on the globe at any moment's notice." [31] Yet, it was interpreted widely in Europe as a first step toward the American withdrawal from such an involvement.

That the European allies would have been generally dissatisfied with the McNamara doctrine was not surprising. Obviously enough, what seemed "controlled" on one side of the Atlantic did not look quite the same on the other side. Conventional or nuclear, a war waged in Europe would be "limited" only from a non-European viewpoint. But would any strategy ever gain Europe's favor? If the Soviet Union's nuclear capabilities were overlooked, and the devastating nature of a thermonuclear war ignored, Europeans regarded the military status quo as satisfactory and continued to decrease their defense expenditures. If, on the other hand, Soviet capabilities were "realistically" estimated and the horrors of nuclear war properly emphasized, Europeans might well be constrained to develop their own nuclear forces to ensure a security for which, they thought, America would not fight. If Soviet conventional (nonnuclear) capabilities were conceded to be large, Europeans argued that their contribution in the field of conventional weapons would be useless in shifting the balance. If these capabilities were thought to be small, Europeans might argue that any contribution of theirs was unnecessary.

In the fifties, Europe had found massive retaliation highly dangerous because it implied the potential escalation of any armed confrontation in Europe into a total nuclear war. In the sixties, Europe found flexible response dangerous as well because it might encourage Soviet aggression in Western Europe through the implied reduction in the scope of America's retaliation, hence increasing its acceptability. Europeans, who charged both Moscow and Washington with the intention of confining a war over Europe in Europe, would have liked to see such a war confined to American and Soviet territories. In the age of massive retaliation, American territory was the first target of the Soviet missiles. With flexible response, this was no longer true. The European allies implicitly complained that the McNamara strategy was making the United States more secure at the expense of Europe. Yet, the inescapable fact was indeed that Europe remained more insecure than America by definition — the obvious implication of Europe's geographical location. Situated between both superpowers, Europe held the same position as Poland had held in the past, located between two of the great powers of the time (Russia and Prussia). Europe represented both a stake of the conflict and its battleground, and ultimately a war between the two superpowers might remain "limited" to Europe while their own territory would be totally spared. "Who can say," asked de Gaulle at his apocalyptic best, "that if the occasion arises . . . [the Soviet Union and the United States], while each deciding not to launch its missiles at the main enemy so that it should itself be spared, will not crush the others. It is possible to imagine that in some awful day Western Europe should be wiped out from Moscow and Central Europe from Washington." [32] No one could say, to be sure. Yet, Western Europe's reluctance to be wiped out by Moscow, possibly for the sake of Washington, could only be matched by Washington's own reluctance to be wiped out from Moscow, possibly for the sake of Western Europe.

America and the French Nuclear Force

By the mid-sixties, in the words of Henry Kissinger, the Atlantic Alliance had become a "troubled partnership." [33] New polycentric forces, attributable to the relaxation of tensions within the global system and the transformation in the distribution of power within the alliance, made the preservation of American hegemony increasingly difficult. But a solution of national independence, based as it would have to be on intrinsic military inferiority, was no solution at all while any multinational cooperation short of genuine integration still remained inadequate.

Regrettably enough, American opposition to the French *force de frappe* grew in intensity as the force grew in size. For a long time, de Gaulle assumed that he needed to build the foundation of France's nuclear force before the American government could provide him with the nuclear aid that France needed. In 1959, he was still speaking of his force as "whether we manufacture it or buy it." [34] But Washington's opposition was, at least in part, the consequence of its defense policy. McNamara's strategy implied a high level of centralization, and, most specifically, the indivisibility of a general nuclear war target system: how, for example, could the French, value-centered strategy be reconciled to the American, force-centered strategy? From the viewpoint of the alliance as a whole, Washington argued that the French force would be essentially useless, as American nuclear resources were admittedly sufficient. Of course, the viewpoint of the alliance was precisely what the French force was supposed to bypass, as the French were less interested in the adequacy of the American arsenal than it was with its availability. Washington also remained fairly distressed by the trigger effect that an independent nuclear force, such as France's, might have. Exactly how the trigger might work was never fully stated, yet somehow a small nuclear power could, out of desperation, trigger the two superpowers into a nuclear conflict that they would otherwise have wanted to avoid.

Too much of such a risk, warned Washington, might necessitate reappraising America's commitment to Europe. Finally, a further source of potential harm was related to the Soviet reaction. As it happened, Moscow never expressed much concern over France's nuclear force. Understood as a source of dissension within the Atlantic Alliance, it was even somewhat welcomed. But what would be the reaction of the Soviets if the Germans were to follow the French example? And by reviving nationalistic tendencies were not the French promoting such a possibility?

By and large, from the viewpoint of Washington, America's opposition to France's nuclear force was amply justified on the grounds that such a force was unduly expensive, strategically dangerous, lacking in credibility, and militarily useless. Coming before France's, Great Britain's effort to build and operate its own deterrent system had been a losing struggle against the periodical obsolescence of strategic equipment, against the ever larger costs of such equipment, and against the insurmountable problems of maintaining elementary requirements of deterrent credibility, survivability, and penetrability. Yet, once the creation of such a national nuclear force had become irreversible, a continued opposition to it could only serve to accentuate the differences between the two countries, and a better American strategy might have been to try to manage such a force (as they did Great Britain's), not to defeat it. The arguments used by Washington lacked, to say the least, a minimum amount of empathy. To argue that the acquisition of nuclear weapons was a waste of financial resources while insisting that such resources ought to be spent by the allies to strengthen further their non-nuclear forces and to improve the quality and staying power of these forces was not much of an argument from the viewpoint of Europe. The American policy, one must suspect, was somehow affected by a strong dose of mistrust for Paris and vice versa. This mistrust had been a substantial aspect of American policy toward Europe, and French policy toward America, for a long time after World War II. Washington's policy was also affected by its misunderstanding of the French political scene; Washington continued to deal with the Fifth Republic as if it merely symbolized the personal wishes of General de Gaulle, exclusive of any relationship between him and the French people. Yet, it was clear to many that the French president followed a policy essentially in line with French tradition in such matters. The nuclear policy of France was undoubtedly initiated by the Fourth Republic.[35] It merely reached adolescence under the Gaullist regime and began to mature under his successor.

The MLF and the Problem of Nuclear Control

Unwilling to acknowledge national nuclear forces, Washington was nevertheless aware of Europe's fears. It devised schemes that might at least provide the Europeans with the illusion, if not the fact, of sharing the control and management of an integrated strategic nuclear force. The best-known outcome of this search was the MLF, a projected multilateral force of twenty-five surface ships, each armed with eight Polaris A-3 missiles with a range of 2,000 miles or more.[36] The ships and missiles were to be operated by crews of several nationalities and the decisions to be reached unanimously by the "major" participants, those nations whose financial contribution would reach at least 10 per cent of the overall cost.

The directions that the MLF was expected to take were those of Bonn and Paris. As seen by Washington, the MLF would preempt Germany's impending request for such weapons by providing it with a sense of participation in a common nuclear venture. In practice, however, the idea of MLF came dangerously close to promoting rather than ending such desires, particularly because it implicitly framed the prospect of a nuclear Germany with an American endorsement of West Germany's access to nuclear weapons. At the same time, the MLF was expected to isolate France in Europe by forcing West Germany into an unwanted choice between Washington and Paris. The Soviets could offer reunification to Germany; Paris could offer its sponsorship of the German overtures in Eastern Europe; Washington now thought that it too had something to offer — a share in the control of nuclear weapons. In fact, Bonn's endorsement of the MLF went far toward preempting the Franco-German Treaty of Friendship that de Gaulle and Chancellor Adenauer signed in January 1963. But in return it further embittered the French who continued to regard the American offer as being essentially anti-French.[37]

Awkward in its objectives, the MLF was also inadequate in the scope of its sharing procedure. The need for a unanimous vote gave each participating member a de facto right of veto. But, though a veto from Washington would have left Europe completely impotent, because the MLF represented all of Europe's nuclear resources, a veto from the Europeans would have left Washington just as free to take any unilateral action it deemed necessary as the MLF capabilities represented an insignificant amount of the overall American strategic forces. Occasionally, some American officials, including Secretary of State Dean Rusk and Undersecretary George Ball, hinted that ultimately Washington might relinquish its veto, but neither the timing nor the modalities of this eventuality were ever discussed in detail. And, it was President Kennedy's own evaluation, as reported by Arthur Schlesinger, that "so long as the United States retained its veto (and he [Kennedy] never mentioned renunciation as a possibility . . .) the MLF was something of a fake. . . . He could not see why Europeans would be interested in making enormous contributions toward a force over which they had no real control." [38] No wonder, then, that Europeans generally ignored the American offer, and that the idea of MLF died during the Johnson administration. West Germany expressed real interest, despite Moscow's and Paris' explicit warnings against German participation in such nuclear partnership. Greece and Turkey too accepted the American scheme in principle, as did Italy. But even such acceptances were often conditional, and the feasibility of these nations manning ships multilaterally was never tested.

However imperfect it might have been, the MLF at least sought a solution to the problem of nuclear control within NATO. The problems it encountered were problems that any such search for consultation automatically raised, namely, problems of membership, status, and substance.

When speaking of consultation, it was first necessary to determine who was entitled to participate in the consultation. The MLF implied that the best criterion to adopt was one of financial responsibility. Such a criterion made possible a large number of participants at least so long as MLF costs remained relatively limited. In his September memorandum, in 1958, de Gaulle had suggested, on the other hand, that consultation be confined to three members only, who also happened to be the three permanent Atlantic members of the United Nations Security Council, as well as the only three nuclear members of the alliance.[39] Whether or not either the American or French criteria displayed any realism was debatable, because it was as meaningless to endow the smaller states in Europe with a voice equal to that of Washington as it was to assume that some of the larger states (like Germany or Italy) would long tolerate an exclusive *ménage à trois* between Washington, London, and Paris.

Could all those participating in the consultation be treated as equal regardless of the issue under discussion? One suggestion was that the status of each participant would depend on the interest it had in a given issue. North Africa, Cuba, and Nigeria, to cite but three areas of the world, were regions where France, the United States, and Great Britain obviously had determining interests, respectively. Yet, such a division of diplomatic labor entailed recognizing spheres of influence within the noncommunist world itself, as a matter of fact if not of principle. Furthermore, what distribution could be devised for more crucial issues such as dealing with the communist world, using nuclear weapons, or even for such an area as the Middle East? And would such a distribution of alliance interests imply the extension of the alliance to the whole world?

All such schemes for strengthening the alliance attempted to adjust intraalliance relationships to a transformed political and strategic international situation. But any scheme for making consultation effective was undermined by the potential conflict of national interests between the United States and Europe, and, within Europe, between European states. In an alliance of independent and sovereign states, consultation does not lead to consensus as it does in domestic politics because there is no way for the alliance to induce the minority to follow the wishes of the majority. If a state becomes dissatisfied with the way an alliance works it can always withdraw from it when it feels that the advantages gained from such a withdrawal will outweigh the disadvantages. In an alliance of independent states, consultation indeed presupposes a specific consensus so that, on each specific issue, the consultation may be reduced to the procedure of implementing that consensus.[40]

But consultation could also be promoted through increased integration of America and Europe. This was essentially the idea behind President John F. Kennedy's Grand Design, as expressed in his so-called Declaration of Interdependence of July 4, 1962.

> As the American effort for interdependence now approaches a successful close, a great new effort for interdependence is transforming the world around us. And the spirit of that new effort is the same spirit which gave birth to the American constitution . . . [But] the first order of business is for our European friends to go forward in forming the more perfect union which will someday make this partnership possible.[41]

A formal Atlantic community would depend upon the prior formation of a formal European community.

However grandiose a vision, Kennedy's Grand Design had several shortcomings. First, it called for a very specific Europe: an integrated, supranational Europe born out of the same spirit that had given birth to the union of the American thirteen colonies. But there was hardly any evidence that such a Europe was wanted by the Europeans themselves. The view in Washington seemed to be that if there was as yet no unified Europe, it was because of France's opposition; that indeed Europe had been on the verge of political integration when this was defeated by de Gaulle's singlehanded veto of Great Britain's entry into the Common Market in January 1963. Yet, the evidence indicated that at no time during the Fourth Republic had there been in France a majority in favor of European integration conceived along supranational lines. Indeed, throughout the fifties, French support for European integration, outside of a small group of "maximalists" dedicated to integration, had been the outcome of external pressures understood as security threats, and "Europe" itself was conceived as the best available means to cope with these pressures.[42] The European Coal and Steel Community had been linked to French inability to promote the International Ruhr Authority; the European Defense Community had been related to France's inability to prevent the rearmament of Germany; and the European Economic Community had been very much influenced by the fear of isolation that followed the Suez crisis and Khrushchev's ultimatum to Paris and London. Besides, to believe that the entry of Great Britain into the Common Market would strengthen the forces of supranationality was not entirely logical as the London government carried with it a well-established tradition of opposition to the very idea of supranationality, as displayed in previous years by its positions on various schemes of unification.

Granted a united, supranational Europe, including Great Britain, a Europe that would be speaking with one voice only, would this condition alone make the Atlantic partnership possible? And, above all, would it make it workable? All that a united Europe would mean really was that several nationalisms had been displaced by a larger one, a European nationalism that might raise a far more formidable obstacle to Washington's wishes. The problems inherent in reconciling interests between Washington and Europe, whenever Europe spoke with one voice, were well shown during the protracted discussions on the reduction of tariffs — the so-called Kennedy round.

Finally, the Atlantic partnership would still have to face the two related questions of timing and content: when would the partnership be set up and what would be shared between the partners? To the question when, the answer was that Europe first needed to become a power comparable to America in resources and in political organization. This prospect was obviously a very long-term one, particularly if it related, among other factors, to nuclear resources. Furthermore, this question could only be answered by the United States, as it remained clearly up to the senior partner to decide when the junior partner would be allowed to join the organization. It would also be up to the senior partner to decide what kind of junior partner was acceptable. According to George Ball, a Europe with a will to share its resources would make sharing effective. But as to *what* America would share the answer was, to say the least, dubious. Now and then there were vague hints about giving the European partner authority to fire nuclear missiles without preliminary authorization from Washington, but these were always when-and-if hints. According to George Ball, again, "*If* Europe were sufficiently far advanced toward political unity, we could hopefully look forward to an effective and integrated Atlantic defense founded on a true nuclear partnership. But this is not the case today nor is it likely to be for some time." [43]

Clearly the fact of sharing could not be simply related to the conception of a future admittedly regarded as unlikely for some time. Just as in the fifties the Europeans sought a partnership based on a desire to share American resources, Washington was now seeking a partnership based on a desire to see the Europeans share American burdens. For only then were the terms of the partnership made explicit: a contribution by Europe to the American balance of payments problem, a share of the cost of the war in Vietnam, or even a military endorsement of Washington's objectives there, an increased contribution to the cause of foreign aid — this participation made Europe a true partner.

The End of Alliances?

The Atlantic debate showed that, short of a resurgence of the Soviet threat to the Atlantic area, or for that matter of any other identifiable threat, the good old days of undisputed American hegemony were by and large over. This end was indeed heartening because it indicated that the basic purpose of post–World War II American foreign policy — security for Western Europe from armed aggression — had, at least for the time being, been fulfilled. But the search for true Atlantic partnership was still a thing of the future, which, if not utopian, was much too distant to be acepted as an immediate and workable policy.

Although consultation and debate are always nice ways of comparing differences and exchanging impressions, these differences will not be eliminated by such consultations, however friendly they may be. Even so, America could not easily endorse an ally's effort to solve by itself, without consultation, its own defense problems: this could then be construed as an invitation to other countries, including Germany, to join the nuclear club.

In the sixties, American policies in Europe were generally deficient, less for their intent than for their form. The Atlantic Alliance could not be replaced, as General de Gaulle wanted it, by a classical alliance where each member was theoretically free to use its weapons as it saw fit and then to rely on automatic support from its allies. The technological revolution of the past twenty-five years, the fantastic scale of destruction implicit in any armed conflict, had made a return to a classical balance of power game undesirable. Not that a big power was now unable to protect a smaller power. It could do so provided that the smaller power accepted its strategic subordination to the bigger power and never attempted to force its hand — in other words, provided that the smaller power was willing to relinquish part of its national authority on such essential matters as defense.

But could a nation reasonably accept such a responsibility? The answer was clearly positive only as long as there was no need to meet it. Vietnam, for example, had shown, among many other things, how difficult it was for America to fight a nonnuclear war for someone else. Could one conceive of fighting a *nuclear* war for someone else? Could Washington ever decide that the salvation of Europe lay in the latter's nuclear destruction, and should it ever decide so itself? Or should such a decision, and its subsequent justification, remain eminently national both in the way it was reached and implemented?

These were questions that could not be answered formally. Those who argued for the obsolescence of alliances were also arguing for the obsolescence of warfare. Surely if it was true that alliances were now potentially, if not actually, obsolete because of the nature of war, then it was equaly true that the unacceptable level of destruction that nuclear warfare entailed made war itself obsolete — no longer the continuation of politics by other means but now indeed the termination of politics by total means. But yet, was not war deterred precisely because of such alliances? Would the end of alliances imply the end of the relative security that had prevailed in Europe over the past twenty-five years?

In practice, of course, neither war nor alliances were ended. Only circumstances had changed and because of these changes the Atlantic Alliance now needed some repairs. That these repairs still remained ambiguous reflected the ambiguity of international changes. Only when the direction of these changes could be more firmly determined and their effect more adequately measured would it be posible for United States policymakers to reappraise and ultimately even reverse America's commitments in Europe.

7

The End
of Security?

The Essence of Insecurity

"Security," wrote Robert McNamara shortly after he left the Pentagon, "depends upon assuming a worst plausible case, and having the ability to cope with it." [1] The size and urgency of the "worst plausible case" is, however, difficult to determine. Following Moscow's launching of the Sputnik satellites in October and November 1957, intelligence estimates placed Soviet missile production at a new high, with more than 200 Soviet intercontinental ballistic missiles in place by 1962 at the latest, and perhaps as early as 1960.[2] Given the calculations at the time that 125 to 175 such missiles would be sufficient to preempt all the strategic air bases (SAC) in North America whereas Soviet medium-range missiles already available preempted SAC bases overseas, the panicked conclusion was reached by the Eisenhower administration that America's deterring capacity was obsolete.[3] An accelerated development, deployment, and erection of delivery vehicles was therefore ordered, resulting in deployable liquid-fueled Atlas missiles, submarine-launched Polaris missiles, and, under Eisenhower's successor, deployable solid-fueled Minuteman missiles.

The estimate of an ongoing Soviet build-up was maintained by the Kennedy administration. "Since we could not be certain of Soviet intentions," wrote its secretary of defense, "we had to insure against [it] . . . by undertaking a major build up of our own . . . forces." [4] The Soviet leadership, however, did not increase its strategic forces as significantly as Washington expected it to, and, in February 1962, Senator Stuart Symington, Chairman of the Armed Forces Committee, revealed that intelligence estimates of Soviet missile strength had been revised down to 3.5 per cent of their estimated size in December 1959.[5] Yet, unaffected by these more moderate evaluations, America's strategic build-up continued. By the mid-sixties, the United States held a numerical superiority over the Soviet Union, in reliable, accurate, and effective warheads, both greater than it had originally planned and more than it required.[6]

Moscow's strategic standstill is still puzzling to most observers.[7] Possibly, Khrushchev fell into the practice of studied deception after he witnessed Western miscalculations of the number of deployed Soviet ICBM's. Given the limited technological life of many of these delivery vehicles, Khrushchev may have reasoned that his strategic bluffing would safely outlast the first or second generation of ICBM's and that Moscow could conveniently catch up at a later date. In the meantime, many expenditures would be saved at a time when the Soviet economy was under considerable strain. Finally, Khrushchev may have simply come to believe in the implausibility of an American first strike. This last factor, coupled with the further assumption that losses "acceptable" to the West were lesser than those "acceptable" to the Soviets, might have lessened Moscow's security requirements.

Regardless of Khrushchev's reasoning, America's growing strategic lead could not indefinitely leave unaffected the Soviet Union's own nuclear plans: ultimately, they too defined their security according to their ability to face a worst plausible case.

Still in the words of McNamara, "Soviet strategic planners un-doubtedly reasoned that if our build up were to continue at its accelerated pace, we might conceivably reach in time a credible first-strike capability against the Soviet Union." [8] Four options were then opened to the Soviet leaders.[9] First, they could con-tinue to bluff and to claim strategic superiority regardless of Western disclaimers. Second, they could seek short-cuts to nu-clear parity. Third, they could accept temporary strategic inferi-ority and seek détente. Fourth, they could resume the arms race until they regained at least strategic parity. All of these options were exercised by the Soviet leaders in the sixties, often in com-bination with one another. Moscow undertook its own massive strategic build-up, in part at least, as a response to America's own build-up, undertaken, in part at least, as a response to a perceived Soviet build-up. The search for security had led to still more insecurity.

Such behavior is nothing but traditional behavior in inter-national relations, and, in assuming the worst, nations have re-peatedly helped pave the way for the worst. In August 1945, the United States had atomic resources that its major adversary on the international scene lacked. Instinctively, it based its national security on such weapons. "America's security," wrote President Truman in his *Memoirs*, "and the security of the free world de-pend to a large degree on our leadership in the field of nuclear energy." [10] Loose in the wrong hands, nuclear weapons would spell disaster for both America and the rest of the world, and it increasingly appeared to America that, in the words of Secretary James Forrestal, "[it] could exercise a trusteeship over the atomic bomb on behalf of the United Nations and agree that we would limit its manufacture for use on such missions as the United Na-tions should designate." [11]

This adoption of a policy of nuclear supremacy did not go unchallenged; throughout the latter half of 1945 and 1946, the higher echelons of the Truman administration were involved in a major debate over national versus international control of the atom. To many, including Secretary of War Henry Stimson, the atomic bomb had revolutionized international relations in a way that made reliance on traditional notions of national security dangerous if not obsolete. Different approaches to the search for security needed to be followed, and other methods adopted including the demilitarization and the denationalization of the new technology. Consequently, in September 1945, Stimson, about to retire from government services, urged that direct arrangements with Russia be worked out by the United States (and England) to control the production and use of the atom. Stimson further recommended that work on the improvement or manufacture of the bomb be ended provided the Russians agreed to do likewise. He finally suggested that existing American bombs be impounded with the proviso that they would never be used without common approval of the three governments.[12]

Stimson's proposal was not based on any exaggerated and idealistic vision of Soviet willingness to cooperate. At Potsdam he had expressed much misgiving about Moscow's policies and, upon his return, the aging secretary remained unable to shake the spectre of Soviet oppression that he had vividly witnessed during the conference.[13] Nonetheless, he believed that the good faith of the Kremlin had to be tested once more. Truly, problems between the two countries were considerable; but they were, in Stimson's words, dominated by the atomic bomb. Properly handled, the bomb would be an effective means of assuring continued Soviet cooperation. Aggressively displayed it would be a dangerous tool of confrontation. And Stimson warned: "If we fail to approach them [the Russians] now and merely continue to negotiate with them having this weapon rather ostentatiously on our hip, their suspicion and their distrust of our purposes and motives will increase." [14]

In contrast to Stimson, there was a growing feeling in many American quarters that America's nuclear monopoly represented the surest way of bringing about the long-awaited Pax Americana. The bomb, Secretary of State James Byrnes argued, had placed America "in a position to dictate [its] terms" to the rest of the world.[15] At Yalta, at Potsdam, Stalin had spoken the language of power. The language of power would now be spoken to him, and Byrnes strongly advocated that America preserve and strengthen its nuclear supremacy. "We must use our best efforts," advocated the secretary of state, "to develop better bombs and more of them." [16] When informed by Robert Oppenheimer of the possibilities of a more terrible weapon in a thermonuclear reaction, Byrnes enthusiastically requested that "he and the rest of the gang should pursue their work full force." [17]

Seen in retrospect, both Stimson and Byrnes displayed the same belief in the absoluteness of the policies they advocated. To Stimson, multinational control of the manufacture and use of the atomic bomb would make of the Soviets faithful allies because they would become irreversibly convinced of America's good will; to Byrnes brandishing the bomb would make the Soviets docile followers as they would naturally respect America's atomic supremacy. But Stimson and Byrnes also based their views on the widespread and realistic assumption that America's atomic monopoly would not last long — no more than "from seven to ten years" — so that if any action were to be taken in either direction (conciliation or showdown), such action needed to be taken at once.[18]

At first glance, the proposal made at the United Nations by the United States on June 14, 1946 — a proposal subsequently known as the Baruch Plan — indicated that Truman was after all following, at least partly, the Stimson recommendation of presenting the atomic bomb as part of an international heritage. The plan provided for an international agency that would own and control all nuclear energy facilities and the necessary raw materials. After such international control had been established, America's production of nuclear weapons would be ended, existing stockpiles destroyed, and information concerning nuclear technology made available to all.[19]

From a Soviet viewpoint, the Baruch proposal failed to take into account some of the inevitable requirements of political realism. First, while this system of international ownership and regulatory control was being created and tested in transitional stages, the United States was to be allowed to continue to manufacture and stockpile atomic weapons. By postponing the American sacrifice until the Soviet sacrifice should have been made, the proposal was therefore based on the assumption that Moscow was prepared to grant Washington the confidence that Washington was unprepared to grant Moscow. The Soviets had reason to ask what would then prevent Washington from reneging on its commitment once Moscow had been made incapable of reaching atomic parity. Moscow's refusal to take the first step matched

Washington's own refusal to do the same. To Molotov, who warned on November 7, 1945: "We will have atomic energy and many other things too," [20] Truman replied exactly seven months later: "We should not under any circumstances throw away our gun until we are sure the rest of the world can't arm against us." [21] Both statesmen proved true to their word.

Second, even if America did not renege on its pledge to stop its production, destroy its stocks and submit to the same supervisory inspection as other members of the accord, a state of nuclear inequality would still remain intrinsic to the new system. For, under the Baruch Plan, the United States would preserve a nuclear know-how far more sophisticated (despite any future exchange of information) than that of a Soviet Union pledged, like other states, to abandon nuclear arms research and testing. In denying the Russians a try at atomic parity, the Baruch Plan was naturally unacceptable. Third, beyond Moscow's problematic perception of America's good faith were the problems raised by the formation of the projected international agency. Given the voting distribution at the United Nations, Baruch's required abandonment of the veto power would leave the Kremlin in a semipermanent minority. In the words of one of the Soviet leaders, Moscow would then be dominated by "a majority on whose benevolent attitude . . . the Soviet people cannot count." [22] Conversely, being itself in a semipermanent majority, the United States would be in a position to control the development of both the military and the industrial uses of nuclear energy within the Soviet Union. As any violation of the agreement was expected to be met with "immediate, swift and sure punishment," the Soviet Union would possibly be at the mercy of measures taken against Moscow by a majority largely directed from Washington.*

It was not America's stand alone that caused and fed the atomic arms race already in the making. However imperfect it might have been, the Baruch Plan entailed important and generous concessions and real risks for the United States, not the least

---

* In *Present at the Creation* (New York, 1969), Dean Acheson wrote that such a provision "could be interpreted in Moscow only as an attempt to turn the United Nations into an alliance to support a United States threat of war against the USSR unless it ceased its efforts" to develop nuclear weapons (p. 155).

being America's proposed abandonment of one of its major instruments for balancing the superior manpower of the Soviet
Union. Further concessions would have encountered strong opposition from the Congress.[23] As it was already, American policymakers could rightly assume that the Baruch offer alone was a
first step toward quieting Soviet fears, a step that needed now
to be matched with Soviet concessions rather than with Soviet
requests for further American concessions. Instead, Moscow's
counterproposal at first consisted of calling for the destruction
of atomic stockpiles, whether in a finished or semifinished condition and prior to the elaboration of measures, systems, and organization of control in using atomic energy. This proposal
would have called for a unilateral destruction of the American
advantage, and the Soviet plan also attempted to postpone the
Soviet sacrifice until the execution of the American sacrifice.

In October 1946, Washington's rejection of Soviet concessions on international inspections and the elimination of the
veto rule on day-to-day inspections symbolized the end of searching for new ways to settle international disputes. No part of
their proposal, the American negotiators indicated, was open to
discussion: it would either be accepted in toto, or it would be
abandoned in toto. Its abandonment confirmed Stimson's earlier
forecast: a nuclear arms race of unparalleled magnitude between
the two national giants. "As long as an international agreement
for the control of atomic energy could not be reached," concluded President Truman, "our country had to be ahead of any
possible competitor." [24]

With the Soviets adopting the same line, this mutual search
for nuclear superiority created, after twenty-five years of nuclear
diplomacy, mutual insecurity. In early 1970, the American strategic arsenal included over 1,000 intercontinental ballistic missiles, over 650 submarine-launched missiles, and more than 650
long-range B-52's. Assuming that each missile carried one bomb
and each plane four bombs, America had approximately 4,200
strategic nuclear weapons, plus several thousand more "tactical"
warheads (some of them up to five times more powerful than
the Hiroshima bomb) located within range of the Soviet Union.

But by 1970 the Soviet Union too had developed an arsenal
of staggering dimensions. It was estimated that the Russians pos-

sessed over 1,200 intercontinental missiles, over 300 submarine-launched missiles, and aproximately 150 long-range bombers, plus numerous intermediate-range missiles and planes that could be used against targets in Europe. Although the Soviets probably had fewer nuclear warheads (approximately 1,800), their destructive capability was roughly identical because the Soviet bombs were generally of greater yield and the American population was more concentrated in urban areas.* Shortly after taking office, President Nixon drew the implicit conclusion: "Although every instinct motivates me to provide the American people with complete protection against a major nuclear attack," the American president stated on March 14, 1969, "it is not now within our power to do so." [25] Earlier, in November 1947, America's first secretary of defense, James Forrestal, had testified: "We are dealing with a deadly force *and nothing less than 100 per cent security will do.*" [26]

The Dispersion of Nuclear Weapons

American objection to nuclear proliferation dated from the Truman administration, and it remained essentially unchanged after the Soviets broke the American monopoly in August 1949. But as other nations reached nuclear status, the threat of an uncontrolled proliferation of nuclear powers increased in a way that aroused the concern of the Soviet Union as well and led both superpowers into combining their efforts to deny access to nuclear weaponry to other nations.

Such combined action was especially understandable in view of the diminished difficulties that a nation might face in seeking

---

* These figures might be more meaningful with the following illustrations. In early 1970 America could deliver, with its biggest planes and missiles alone, more than 40 nuclear warheads for each Soviet city with a population of 100,000 or more. According to official United States and United Nations sources, 200 nuclear bombs in the low megaton range, targeted on industrial centers in the United States or in the Soviet Union, would kill directly at least one-third of the population and destroy two-thirds of the industrial capacity of either nation. The question was if American and Soviet armaments were exchanged, would it make any difference to either country?

nuclear standing. By 1965, few if any scientific secrets concerning earlier bomb designs were left. A dozen nonnuclear countries were easily capable of producing enough plutonium 239 for at least one bomb a year.[27] Furthermore, nuclear technology and experience were spreading ever faster, and the list of potential candidates for nuclear status was thus growing. Delivery systems remained a major technological constraint but the requirements of such systems changed from place to place, depending on the defense sophistication and geographic location of hypothetical adversaries. Ultimately, a power might even attempt to acquire nuclear weapons without any obvious means of delivery and resort to various forms of nuclear terrorism. The economics of nuclear armament and that of their means of delivery continued to raise a major obstacle to nuclear proliferation, especially as frequent technological turnovers required the endless pursuit of costly research and development programs on top of the manufacturing costs proper. Altogether, it was estimated that a modest nuclear force with its own modest means of delivery could not be devised by states with a gross national product of less than $10 billion. But this limit still left quite a few candidates. In the words of a notable observer of international affairs, the world might have survived "the winter of the cold war merely to launch [itself] into a spring thicket of new uncertainties."[28]

Why these states would choose to base their defense on such weapons varied from one state or region to another. At least three theories were entertained on this score. A first theory held that a small nuclear power might effectively deter aggression if it could knowingly inflict on enemy targets greater damage than what a potential aggressor might regard as acceptable. Aggression would be deterred even if it could not possibly be defeated on the field, or even if the homeland of the aggressor could not be totally devastated. Such a theory transformed nuclear weapons into a magic equalizer that would automatically preserve a "balance of terror" between all states.[29] As all states did not have the same "value" within the international system, all national nuclear forces did not need to have the same destructive capabilities, and one small nuclear force might thus "equal" a much larger one in deterrent effect.

A second theory held that a small nuclear force could be

used to trigger the forces of the superstate within a given alliance.[30] The stability of deterrence would be increased because national nuclear forces would possibly solidify the interests of a given alliance by threatening a potential aggressor with a multinational retaliation set in motion by a chain reaction of national considerations. Underlying such a theory was the assumption that the terms of a policy of deterrence were as high as the terms of its highest bidder, even if the main share of the deterrent itself was in the possession of the lowest bidder. It was not so much the actual credibility of the dominant power's commitment that was being strengthened, but its *perceived* credibility. Furthermore, a national nuclear force, independently targeted, could neutralize objectives that, although vital to the smaller state, might not have been hit in the first volley of the superstate's retaliation.

Third, it was argued that a small power might seek nuclear weapons in order to face regional problems that the superstates, either because of their nuclear stalemate or because of a lack of national interest, might be incapable or unwilling to solve. Such a theory of "hegemony of terror" would therefore make the nonnuclear state seek nuclear weapons not against either superstate, but in order to secure a regional gain vis-à-vis states that were deprived of any such forces. "To possess atomic weapons," emphasized de Gaulle, an active proponent of national nuclear forces, "is for a country to be in a position to reduce relentlessly a nation which does not possess any." [31] And, in another instance, the then French president reminded his listeners that, in the nuclear age, "the life of any [nonnuclear] nation is . . . absolutely at the mercy of whomever possesses [nuclear] weapons." [32]

In the sixties, American policy remained staunchly opposed to any such reasoning, attempting to prevent a further dispersion of nuclear weapons. As previously indicated, much of American opposition was voiced against France. But beyond France, America more generally attempted to prevent or postpone the entry of other states into the nuclear "club." "I am haunted," President Kennedy confided to one of his aides in March 1963, "by the feeling that by 1970, unless we are successful, there may be ten nuclear powers instead of four, and by 1975, fifteen or twenty. . . . I regard this as the greatest possible danger." [33] The fact is that each theory advanced to defend the national acquisition of nuclear weapons appeared to raise more questions than it answered. "A credible deterrent," pointedly observed Secretary McNamara, "cannot be based on an incredible act." [34] Would the potential aggressor ever take at face value a retaliatory threat that equated a crippling strike with a deadly strike, or a threat that would be based on the suicidal option of igniting nuclear escalation? If such a force were to be devised on the assumption that it would not have to face a major adversary independently, could it be realistically assumed that the other superpower would indeed become automatically a part of the nuclear chain reaction? To devise a limited and yet effective second strike capability would involve baffling qualitative problems. Whereas nuclear weapons might be a quantitative equalizer, a huge technological gap still made the invulnerability and the penetrability of such a second strike difficult to achieve.

Undoubtedly, America's opposition to nuclear dispersion was a sound policy. A small nuclear force could not deter alone, nor oppose alone, a major nuclear power. Nor could it actively coerce a nonnuclear nation without taking an unacceptable risk of retaliation from at least one of the two superpowers. But then, the bomb could be sought by a small state for no specific purpose, as a long-range strategic resource. Unrelated to any specific threat, nuclear status would eventually enable a given nation to cope on its own with the uncertainties of history. This eventuality was part of a great power syndrome that other great powers of the past found as difficult to manage as America and Russia did now.

In attempting to prevent the proliferation of nuclear weapons, the two superpowers found an area of common interest as both states endorsed the major features of the systemic rationale against proliferation. First, proliferation would increase the probability of their eventual use through a variety of unforeseeable contingencies: technical or human failure, leading to the accidental launching of a missile; possible mistakes in tracing the origin of a nuclear attack, leading to an inappropriate response against the wrong enemy; the possibility that domestic political vicissitudes within a new nuclear state might leave such weapons in irresponsible hands, with all the consequences that such a development would entail. Second, proliferation would increase the risk of preventive wars. Such preventive wars might be started by one superstate to prevent the acquisition of nuclear weapons by a nation regarded as intrinsically hostile — a pre-emptive first strike by the Soviet Union against West Germany (despite and against America's protection of West Germany) or a strike by the United States against China at a level of its nuclear development (despite and against a hypothetical Soviet protection of China). Or, preventive wars might be started by one small power to avoid asymmetric dispersion to another small power within the conflict figuration of one area: in Asia between India, Pakistan, and Afganistan, or in the Middle East between Israel and the Arab states. In any and all of these instances, both the United States and the Soviet Union — the "warring brothers" as Raymond Aron called them [35] — despite themselves, might wage a nuclear war of which they would be the first victims. Third, proliferation would accelerate still further the arms race between America and the Soviet Union as each state might become militarily compelled to revise its strategy according to the requirements for a $(n + 1)$ strike. By 1970, the Soviets were seemingly moving toward a third strike capability with America finding it naturally difficult to differentiate between a second strike aimed at the United States and its allies and a third strike aimed at China. Similarly, America was anxious to have enough warheads available to maintain deterrence of the Soviet Union after absorption of, and retaliation against, a hypothetical Chinese nuclear attack.

Preventing Nuclear Proliferation

The management of nuclear proliferation was pursued both unilaterally and multilaterally. On its own America slowly and informally endorsed nuclear guarantees that would be extended to nonnuclear states. In October 1964, President Johnson declared, shortly after the first Chinese thermonuclear explosion: "Nations that do not seek nuclear weapons can be sure that if they need United States support against the threat of nuclear blackmail, they will have it." [36] This pledge was endorsed by President Nixon who stated, through the so-called Nixon Doctrine, that America would "provide a shield if a nuclear power threatens the freedom of a nation allied wtih us, or of a nation whose survival we consider vital to our own security and the security of the [Asian] region as a whole." [37]

Yet, these stated intentions left major questions unanswered. What kind of support would be provided — nuclear or nonnuclear? When would it be provided — before or after an attack had actually taken place? Would the guarantee apply in the case of a nonnuclear attack launched by a new nuclear power against a nonnuclear state? Upon whose command would a hypothetical retaliatory nuclear strike be decided? How would the question of credibility be solved, particularly when possible reciprocity in the measure of retaliation was involved? To be credible, the guarantee would have to be very explicitly stated and its fulfillment made practically automatic — thus leading to an unprecedented commitment whose passage in the senate was highly doubtful. But even if accepted at face value, an American nuclear guarantee would dangerously provide the guaranteed state with a blank check that might be drawn on American resources to promote a more aggressive foreign policy. An American nuclear guarantee might exacerbate rather than limit and moderate international tensions. Finally, assuming both the credibility and the feasibility of a superpower's nuclear guarantee, where would that leave the *other* superpower?

A multinational approach to nuclear proliferation was adopted in July 1968 when sixty-two nations signed the Treaty on the Non-Proliferation of Nuclear Weapons, as proposed at the twenty-second session of the United Nations General Assembly. Essentially, the treaty attempted to cope with proliferation by exacting two pledges. Each nuclear state pledged not to transfer to any other state nuclear devices or control over such devices directly or indirectly, nor to provide any direct or indirect assistance, encouragement, or inducement in that direction. Each nonnuclear state undertook not to manufacture or to acquire nuclear weapons or other nuclear explosive devices. Although additional provisions of the treaty attempted to establish basic safeguards to verify the fulfillment of its obligations and to prevent the diversion of nuclear energy from peaceful use, no enforcing agency was foreseen that might bring to reason the nonnuclear and nuclear states that refused to sign the treaty (for example, France and China by 1970). Moreover, the treaty explicitly recognized each signatory's "right to withdraw from the Treaty if it decides that extraordinary events . . . have jeopardized the supreme interest of its country." This right of withdrawal merely involved three-month notice.

Essentially the treaty against the proliferation of nuclear weapons formalized the mutual concern of the United States and Soviet Union over the spread of nuclear weapons.* Clearly, in order to be effective, such a treaty required no less than a Soviet-American condominium. Only then could control and enforcement be practically worked out. Even if one was to assume that such a condominium was politically feasible, it still raised many more questions than it could answer. What was the moral authority upon which such a condominium would be based? What was its political feasibility at a time when polycentric forces at the periphery of each bloc seemed to be eroding each bloc? Would not polycentric resistance to the continued hegemony of the two superpowers ultimately prove more damaging to international order than the very dispersion that the condominium aimed at avoiding?

The quest for nuclear cooperation between the two superpowers seemed, however, to be farfetched. It had been sought previously, via a test ban treaty, when public concern with the risks of fall-out (an early version of nuclear ecology) had given the whole issue a propagandistic value that made an agreement all the more difficult to achieve. In March 1958, following a protracted test series, Moscow had announced that it would cease testing if other powers would also abstain. Five months later, Washington announced that it would also abstain following completion of its own series of tests, by October 31. Despite new Soviet tests in October, an informal moratorium was achieved

---

* The treaty became operative in 1970 when the United States, the Soviet Union, and forty other nations ratified it.

and respected by both superpowers until August 30, 1961, when the Soviet Union publicly announced its resumption of atmospheric tests.

After the Cuban crisis of October 1962, a mutual and conscious interest in controlling nuclear weapons was explicitly revived. "It seems to me," Khrushchev wrote Kennedy in December 1962, "that the time has come now to put an end once and for all to nuclear tests." [38] Signed in August, the Test Ban Treaty was a partial agreement that covered only tests that did not require excessive, on-the-site control — in the atmosphere, in outer space, and underwater.

The American president hoped to maintain the momentum generated by the treaty, which, at least for a moment, seemed to be opening a whole new range of international possibilities. Nuclear weapons, as Stimson had predicted, had dominated Russo-American relations. If an agreement could be reached in the nuclear field, other agreements might be reached elsewhere, and, in July 1963, the Kremlin described some of these possibilities: a nonaggression pact between NATO and the Warsaw Pact, the reduction of military presence in East and West Germany, more extensive arms control in the nonnuclear field, including cutting defense budgets (informally adopted by the two superpowers in 1965) and control procedures to prevent surprise attacks.[39] But with the death of Kennedy and the escalation of America's intervention in Vietnam the focus of American policy shifted away from thermonuclear accommodation toward guerrilla confrontation.

By 1970 both America and the Soviet Union seemed to be moving in two contrary directions at once. One, exemplified by SALT (Strategic Arms Limitation Talks), which opened in Vienna in April 1970, sought to reinforce the policy of at least limited cooperation that had begun with the adoption of the Test Ban Treaty. The other, exemplified by the ballistic missile defense (ABM) issue, involved significant movement toward confrontation — a movement particularly destabilizing in view of the new technological revolution that was rapidly introducing such new weapons as the Multiple Independently Targeted Reentry Vehicles (MIRV), Fractional Orbital Ballistic Systems (FOBS), and other orbital weapons, together with an extraordinary improvement in missile accuracy as it was spectacularly displayed in each superstate's space program.[40]

ABM Deployment

In the mid-fifties, the development of ballistic missiles ushered in a new phase in the nuclear arms race as the timetable for devastation was reduced from a dozen hours to a mere thirty minutes. At that time America engaged in large-scale research and development on antiballistic missiles that might provide some means of defense against the new technology.

The ABM issue unfolded discreetly within the limits of America's military establishment as each branch of the defense hierarchy attempted to gain control of the new system. In 1955, the Army initiated studies on a point-defense system. With a range of about 300 miles the system was intended to intercept incoming warheads at an altitude below 50 miles. At about the same time, the Air Force initiated studies on an area-defense system capable of intercepting warheads above the atmosphere at altitudes between 300 and 500 miles. The army gained victory in January 1958 when Secretary of Defense Neil McElroy selected the so-called Nike-Zeus system and ordered the Air Force to discontinue its own development work, pending the completion of Nike-Zeus "as a matter of urgency." Through 1958 army officials urged approval of immediate production and follow-up deployment during fiscal year 1960. It was estimated that the whole system could be operational in 1964, if the requested approval was granted. But because he was nearing the end of his term, President Eisenhower decided to leave the final decision on the matter to his sucessor.

When the Kennedy administration took over, the emphasis changed radically. The new administration in Washington found that there was in fact no "missile gap," as the Democrats had charged during the campaign. They found instead that America's tactical and conventional military capabilities were suffering because of a protracted period of near neglect. For example, in early 1961, the new administration considered a long-standing proposal calling for an allied occupation of the southern pan-handle of Laos and the Vientiane area between the two great bends of the Mekong. The plan called for 60,000 men — many more than America could muster at the time: the Eisenhower-Dulles "New Look" had sacrificed ground forces in favor of air power, and so many ground troops could not be sent to Laos without using troops stationed in Europe, at a time when the situation over Berlin had become even more tense.[41]

The Kennedy administration also "discovered" that American strategic retaliatory forces, although numerically strong unlike what had previously been assumed, remained dangerously vulnerable to a surprise thermonuclear attack. At critical moments in the sixties, America might not have had the power to deter Soviet aggression.[42] This new position contradicted the previous hypothesis widely shared up to the mid-fifties, that nuclear deterrence was automatic and that a carefully planned surprise attack could be checkmated almost effortlessly.

Considering the strategic forces available to the United States, and considering the number of missiles necessary to achieve a high probability of destroying them, it was now argued that America did not have the second strike capability that would assure the aggressor of unacceptable damages, even after the absorption of a preemptive first strike. In a highly influential book on thermonuclear war, Herman Kahn, one of the leading authorities in the field, described how an

> inarticulate Russian general could force the following con-clusion on a group of hostile, skeptical, and busy civilians, whether they wanted to believe them or not . . . that [in the hypothetical case of a surprise Soviet-coordinated attack on United States and allied overseas bases] there would be a reason-able chance that the Soviet Union would get away scot free; that there would be a good chance that they would suffer very little damage; and that there would be no chance at all that they would suffer as much damage as they suffered in World War II.[43]

Consequently, the Kennedy administration decided first to accelerate preparations for the special requirements of limited conventional wars, and second, to enhance the survivability of

America's second strike capability by hardening, dispersing, and increasing its strategic retaliatory forces. Production decision on an antiballistic missile system was postponed, but research work was continued. Shorty thereafter, the Nike-Zeus system was transformed into the so-called Nike-X, an area-defense system designed to defend the fifty-two largest United States cities against a massive nuclear attack by the Soviet Union.[44] Finally, in September 1967, Secretary McNamara abandoned his former opposition (which he was later to resume toward the Nixon-proposed ABM system) and announced his decision to deploy a "thin" ABM system, the Sentinel, which would attempt to protect the United States population against a Chinese attack that might become a practical possibility by the mid-seventies.[45] McNamara's decision was confirmed in March 1969 when President Nixon announced his own endorsement of what was now called the Safeguard System, a system slightly different from the Sentinel.[46]

Four objections were raised against Safeguard: the system would not work; it was too expensive; it did not meet any real threat at the time of its development; and it would accelerate the arms race with the Soviet Union.[47]

Past experience with such defensive systems had been particularly negative. Earlier, the Atlas missile had gone from an expected reliability of 80 per cent to an achieved reliability of only 4 per cent.[48] The practical difficulties that ABM would have to encounter were emphasized by the opposition and explained away by the supporters of the administration. Included were, for example, the problems of adequate testing given the practical impossibility of simulating an environment characterized by multiple nuclear explosions in space and in the atmosphere. Possible countermeasures to ABM were also emphasized, the implication being that even if ABM could work it could also be easily bypassed: the radars used to track the incoming missile could be jammed or destroyed by an enemy missile, as could be the computer used to feed the required information to the radar and the defensive missiles; or the computer might be overwhelmed with an infinite amount of decoy objects; or detection by the radars might be avoided by lowering the trajectory of the incoming missile. In effect, feasibility itself depended on the efficiency expected from the system. Clearly, a 100 per cent efficiency was not feasible. A lesser performance might be feasible; at the very least it would undoubtedly complicate the attacker's job, exact a price from the offensive, and possibly reduce casualties.

The problem of cost was twofold. On the one hand, the cost-exchange ratio of defensive against offensive missiles was in favor of the offensive, and the enemy's development of an effective penetration capability could be achieved for a fraction of the ABM system cost. Here, too, the exact ratio depended on the effectiveness required and the reliability of the defense system itself. The second issue, whether or not America could afford the expenditures involved, took a grim view of the administration's estimates. Already by early 1970 the cost of the full twelve-site Safeguard program had increased by $1.6 million to $11.9 million, and David Packard, a deputy secretary of defense, admitted that some continuing cost growth might be experienced.[49] Those opposed to the system pointed to the high-cost unreliability of complex weapon systems and charged that the initial cost would be merely a down payment on a larger system that would continue to grow irreversibly. But those in favor of the system emphasized its relative cheapness: for less than 26 per cent of America's total investment ($46 billion) on its strategic forces from fiscal year 1965 to fiscal year 1970, Safeguard would preserve the viability of the system in new circumstances.[56]

The threat that required an immediate deployment of ABM was also the subject of considerable debate. Progressively, the official justification of ABM moved away from the Soviet Union and toward China. In early 1970, ABM became an "area defense" against a Chinese missile attack, and it was regarded by President Nixon as "absolutely essential" and "virtually infallible." [51] Official estimates suggested that China could have a force of 15 to 75 land-based intercontinental missiles by 1975. In the event of a full-scale clash, it was assumed that a force of 25 Chinese ICBM's would kill up to 23 million Americans. But an ABM system, the Nixon administration argued, would reduce casualties to 1 million or less.[52] This system, in turn, would strengthen the credibility of America's commitment to the security of Asian states, a commitment that, because of the protection extended to

America by ABM, would survive China's acquisition of long-range nuclear capabilities.

The End of Security?

That a crossroad might have been reached was illustrated by the scope of technological improvements already being implemented or devised. By 1970, both superpowers were equipping their missiles with new, multiple, independently targeted reentry vehicles (MIRV), which had an important destabilizing influence given their potential use as "hard target killers." The American Minuteman-1 was being replaced by a Minuteman-3 missile, which mounted a three-part warhead of the MIRV type. Plans called for substituting 500 Minuteman-3 missiles, each with three 200-kiloton warheads, for the same number of single warhead missiles. The Soviet Union, on the other hand, was preparing a three-part multiple warhead for its SS9 missiles. It was estimated that such missiles would have a capability to throw three- to five-megaton warheads in a triangular pattern of sufficient accuracy to compromise the whole United States land-based ICBM system. With over 280 SS9s available or under construction in early 1970, the Soviet Union was regarded by Secretary of Defense Melvin Laird as possibly devising a first strike capability based on the hard target potential of its SS9s.

Beside and beyond ABM, America was also safeguarding its second strike capability by considerably increasing its sea-based strategic resources against which MIRV technology would have lesser effect. The first Poseidon missiles were being installed in place of Polaris missiles. Each Poseidon would be capable of throwing up to 14 warheads, each from 40 to 50 kilotons, with a single booster, and it was estimated that 31 submarines would be equipped by 1974 or 1975 to carry 16 Poseidons instead of 16 single warhead Polaris missiles.

These developments alone might have been sufficient to test critically the stability of the balance of terror by increasing the relative attraction of a first strike surprise attack. On the basis of existing planning, both America and the Soviet Union reportedly were working toward a 300 per cent increase of their nuclear warheads between 1970 and 1975. Yet, the catalogue of nightmares went ever further. In the making was also the so-called Underwater Long-range Missile System (ULMS), a possible successor to the Polaris submarine that would carry up to 20 missiles having a range of 6,000 to 8,000 miles. On the Soviet side, the SS9 was reported to have a growth potential to accommodate as many as 20 separate warheads of Minuteman power.

Finally, America's effort to deploy the ABM system was itself an indication that its supremacy in the field of nuclear weapons had come to an end. Minutemen and SAC bombers were now plainly vulnerable, as were the cities and the people of the United States. Either superpower might have the capacity to devise, as Secretary Laird perceived it, a first strike capability that would possibly expose the other to nuclear blackmail. But did either superpower also have the intention of doing so? A massive attack, prepared and implemented in cold blood, would not destroy a sufficient proportion of the adversary's thermonuclear system for the aggressor to escape retaliation. Yet, it might preempt the will of ordering the retaliation as the aggressor's own second strike would probably be a countercity strike of horrible proportions.

The problem was one of almost sanity versus insanity; but where did sanity end and where did insanity begin? To some, it might appear that the losses of tens of millions of lives and tens of great cities were not "unacceptable" damage. But to others, in the words of McGeorge Bundy, a former adviser to Presidents Kennedy and Johnson, "in the real world of political leaders — whether [in America] or in the Soviet Union — a decision that would bring even one hydrogen bomb on one city of one's own country would be recognized in advance as a catastrophic blunder; ten bombs on ten cities would be a disaster beyond history; and a hundred bombs on a hundred cities are unthinkable." [53] But was not such an assumption as McGeorge Bundy's itself insane? Granted that launching a thermonuclear first strike could only be the work of a madman, ought not the United States devise some protection against it? Throughout history many madmen had indeed attempted to rule the world at a price that sane men would have safely regarded as unacceptable.

In 1970 the answers to such questions remained elusive. Would nuclear weapons terminate wars or would they bring a deadly end to hope? And what was the best policy that America (and other great and not-so-great powers) could follow to assure its own survival and that of mankind: to assume the worst by equating capability with intention, or to assume at least the better by supposing that the latter would help contain the former? One is reminded of Alice's encounter with the White Knight who wanted to be prepared for every contingency.

> "I was wondering what the mouse-trap was for," said Alice. "It isn't very likely that there would be any mice on the horse's back." "Not very likely, perhaps," said the Knight, "but if they *do* come, I don't choose to have them running all about." "You see," he went on after a pause, "it's as well to be provided for *everything*. That's the reason the horse has all those anklets round his feet." "But what are they for?" Alice asked in a tone of great curiosity. "To guard against the bites of sharks," the Knight replied, "it's an invention of my own." [54]

8

The End
of Illusions?

The Heritage

Since 1940, America's enemy in Indochina has been a changing and elusive one. During the months that preceded and followed Pearl Harbor, the enemy was Japan, as Indochina provided the setting for the first application of an American change of attitude toward Japan — from a policy of "restraint and patience" to one of "firmness." [1] Later, toward the end of the Pacific war, the main enemy became colonialism, as President Roosevelt supported Indochina's movement toward independence from France. And later still, with the outbreak of the cold war, the enemy became international communism.*

---

* The growth of America's involvement in Indochina brings to mind a little song quoted, in another context, by one of my colleagues, Professor David Wilkinson. The song narrates the misfortunes of "an old lady/who

Like Korea, Indochina did not engage primary American interest solely on its own merits. Indeed, its intrinsic value to America was little; it was hardly ever a region of major military or industrial importance. True, Indochina represented a valuable source of rice, corn, coal, rubber, and minerals, particularly before it entered three decades of uninterrupted warfare. But even so, Indochina was peripheral to American interests; and, as George Kennan observed in 1966, no decisive developments of the international situation would have been determined in normal circumstances by what happened in that area of the world.[2] Yet, between 1940 and 1970 circumstances never appeared to be normal and United States policy toward the Indochinese peninsula reflected America's concern with Japan and China as Asian powers, with France and Great Britain as allies and colonial powers, and with the Soviet Union as the leader of the communist bloc.

The specific tenets of American policy were placed within the larger framework of a domino theory, periodically adjusted to the enemy involved. In 1940 America assumed that should Japan succeed in consolidating its control of Indochina, Tokyo would next attempt to seize Thailand and continue to press further southward in the Philippines, Malaya, and the East Indies.[3] Nevertheless, this assumption did not immediately commit America to the area: after the fall of France in June 1940, Roosevelt still refused to provide the French governor in Indochina with the aid that the latter had requested to resist Japanese demands. But following the dangerous enlargement of Tokyo's "Greater East Asia Co-Prosperity Sphere," Indochina became, in the words of the late Bernard Fall, "the watershed that separated peace from war in the Pacific." [4] Understood as a test of America's determination to contain Japanese expansion in the Pacific, Indochina deserved more attention from Washington. The American government, Secretary Cordell Hull argued, could not "sit perfectly quiet and be cheerful and agreeable, but static, while

---

swallowed a fly/and I don't know why/Perhaps she'll die." But determined not to die this old lady swallows a spider to catch the fly, then a rat to catch the spider, and a cat to catch the rat, and so forth, until this remarkable, determined, and courageous escalation of countermeasures is ended with "I know an old lady/who swallowed a horse/she died, of course."

most of Asia is 'Manchuriazed.' " [5] On the very day when Tokyo struck at Pearl Harbor, accommodation in Indochina was still being sought on the basis of the so-called Hull note, which, by-passing the French, had proposed that Indochina's neutrality be guaranteed by America, Great Britain, China, Japan, the Dutch government in exile, and Thailand — with all six countries to be given equal treatment in trade and commerce with Indochina.[6]

In 1945, with Japan about to be defeated, President Roosevelt regarded Indochina as a test case of America's determination to end colonialism. The colonial system, believed Roosevelt, "means war. . . . Americans would [not] be dying in the Pacific . . . if it had not been for the short-sighted greed of the French and British and the Dutch. Shall we allow them to do it . . . all over again?" [7] In a new variation of the domino theory, Roosevelt contended that "India, Burma . . . Indochina, and Indonesia — they're all interrelated. If one gets freedom, the others will get ideas. That's why Winston is so anxious to keep de Gaulle in his corner. De Gaulle isn't any more interested in seeing a colonial empire disappear than Churchill is." [8]

By the end of World War II, America's policy in Indochina aimed at preventing the French from returning as the effective colonial overlord in the area. As recorded by his son Elliot, the American president "felt that the French would have no right, after the war, to simply walk back into Indochina and reclaim [it] . . . for no reason other than that it had been their colony." [9] "The case of Indochina," stated Roosevelt on another occasion, "is perfectly clear. France has milked it for one hundred years. The people of Indochina are entitled to something better than that." [10] The case was all the more convincing as French policy from 1940 onward had been to preserve nominal control of Indochina at whatever cost, regardless of the effects that French concessions to Japan might have upon American interests in Asia. At first officially outlined at the interallied level in March 1943, the French were to be replaced by an international trusteeship made up of three commissioners — an American, a Chinese, and a Briton.[11] This trusteeship was later enlarged, in its conceptual form, to include as many as two Indochinese, a Russian, a Frenchman, and a Filipino.[12] With the support of the Soviet Union and China, America foresaw complete independence for the Indochinese states – an independence to be achieved, however, after a length of time that was never clearly specified. In line with such a policy, the American war department refused military assistance to the de Gaulle government when, in March 1945, Tokyo broke its modus vivendi with France, swiftly deposed the French administration, disarmed the French garrison, imprisoned French citizens, and created an independent puppet state with Bao Dai as its Emperor.[13] Only after the last organized French units had been destroyed by the Japanese forces did Admiral Leahy obtain the president's permission to release American aircraft for support missions in Indochina.[14]

Meanwhile there had been organized in Indochina a national-front organization – the Vietminh – under the leadership of one Nguyen Ai-Quee, later to be known as Ho Chi Minh.[15] Although largely dominated by the Indochinese communist party, the Vietminh attempted to unite all Indochinese groups in a total struggle against Japanese miltarism and French imperialism. Within a few weeks of Japan's defeat, the Vietminh succeeded in seizing power and, on September 2, 1945, after the abdication of Bao Dai, a Republic of Vietnam was formally proclaimed with Ho Chi Minh as its president. The small official American delegation present on the scene hailed the "liberators of the Vietnamese people" who were urged to break all links with France. American support of Ho's new government was also informally promised, a promise that was soon denied by Secretary of State James Byrnes who, eager to preserve Paris' support in the growing confrontation with the Soviet Union in Europe, officially disclaimed any American opposition to a French return to Indochina.[16]

Vietnam, however, was already divided. As a result of the Potsdam agreements, Chinese troops had occupied the country north of the 16th parallel, and Great Britain south, for the stated purpose of disarming the Japanese and repatriating allied prisoners of war. In the south, the British governor was under strict orders from London to stay aloof from local politics. Nevertheless, he undertook on his own to restore the authority of France by arming the French soldiers. In so doing, and in a move that MacArthur described as "the most ignoble kind of betrayal," he used Japanese troops against the Vietminh in the fighting that accompanied the latter's expulsion from Saigon.[17] In the North, the Chinese opposed French efforts to reestablish their former rule over the Indochinese states. But though politically sympathetic to Vietnamese aspirations, the Chinese behaved like conquering armies: they seized what they thought they needed, and they thought they needed everything.

In March 1946, with Japan out of Indochina, the British and Chinese forces prepared to leave Vietnam. At the same time the French and the Vietminh signed a treaty that recognized Vietnam as a "free state with its own government, parliament, army and finances," but as a "part of the Indochinese Federation and the French Union." [18] In theory, the agreement of March 1946 was expected to be a preliminary step toward a larger accord that would grant the Indochinese states full independence. In practice, such an agreement gave the French military entry into the north thereby providing the means to undo the concessions that they had just granted — should they so decide. By avoiding an immediate military confrontation, the Vietminh too gained the time it needed to organize its resistance to French reconquest — should this prove necessary. The accord of March 1946 merely signified that the French and the Vietminh were now left alone to settle their differences in a sanguinary war that was officially begun in December 1946.[19] When it ended on July 21, 1954, the war (*la salle guerre*, as it came to be called in France) had cost the French Union forces 92,000 dead or missing, and 72,000 wounded.[20] The Vietminh's casualties ran perhaps three times as high, with countless Vietnamese civilians (estimated by some at 250,000) killed during the fighting.[21]

The American Commitment Takes Shape

As problems with the Soviet Union multiplied following the end of the Pacific war, America's need to foster unity with the European allies also grew. Following his advisers' recommendations, President Truman urged that every effort be made to assist France, morally as well as physically, to regain its status and its strength.[22] Clearly this suggestion included Indochina, whose loss, it was now feared, would be the last blow that might bring

France to its knees. The loss of Indochina would further kill any chance that a pro-American government might have to last in France against the combined opposition of the Gaullists and the communists, as both could be counted on to channel French resentment into a new wave of anti-Americanism.

In 1949, communist successes in China strengthened the French case for increased American support. In January 1950, the recognition of Ho Chi Minh's government by the two communist giants prompted Secretary of State Acheson to dismiss the nationalist claims of Ho Chi Minh, whom Acheson now described as the "mortal enemy of native independence in Indochina."[23] Consequently, America changed the status of the Vietnamese people, though French-ruled, to that of a "free people" resisting "subversion by armed minorities or by outside pressure." [24] Soon thereafter, on February 7, 1950, in a move that completed America's *volte face*, Washington officially recognized Vietnam and each of the two other Associated States of Laos and Cambodia as independent entities within the French Union. Somewhat like Korea, Vietnam had become a theatre of the cold war, with Moscow backing up one faction and Washington supporting the other.

In June 1950, the outbreak of the Korean War seemed to prove the French contention that the conflict in Indochina was "the same war against the same enemy, for the same cause and at the same price of the same sacrifices." [25] To American policymakers, the contention that the free world's determination to resist aggression was being equally tested everywhere appeared plausible. Upon the recommendation of his secretary of state, one of President Truman's first decisions after the attack in Korea was that military aid to the French in Indochina be substantially increased.[26] After Roosevelt and before Eisenhower, the American president was also defining his own domino theory: "We were seeing a pattern in Indochina and Tibet timed to coincide with the attack on Korea, a challenge to the western world. . . . The Chinese communists were Russian satellites. . . . After Korea, it would be Indochina, then Hong Kong, then Malaya." [27]

The theory was hardly disputed at the time and no effort was made to define more specifically America's interests and objectives in Indochina proper. With circumstances less normal than

ever, French and American policy in Indochina became hope-
lessly confused. The French could no longer make war without
American assistance. But with American assistance they could no
longer make peace, as such assistance was predicated on the assumption that the French would not quit. "After seven years of
conflict," reflected General Henry Navarre, the last French
commander in chief in Indochina, "we had reached a complete
imbroglio; from the plain soldier to the commander-in-chief no
one knew why we were fighting." [28] But just as Paris was uncertain whether it was fighting to maintain a colony or to promote
the independence of a noncommunist state, Washington, too,
proved unable to define its objective: to help France or to replace it, to "save" Indochina from communism or from colonialism? And to those few critics who were already pointing to the
danger that American policy in Indochina might displace French
responsibilities and escalate into armed intervention, Secretary of
State Dean Acheson simply replied: "I decided . . . that having
put our hand to the plow, we would not look back." [29] Unknown
to all and never to be declared — thus had begun America's
informal entry into a war that by mid-1971 had cost America
45,000 dead and missing.

The First Vietnam Crisis

As allied commander of NATO, General Eisenhower had
recommended American assistance in the Indochinese war in
order to leave the French with the resources they needed to
maintain their role in Europe.[30] Seen from the perspective of
NATO, such support also strengthened the alliance between Paris
and Washington by reducing France's suspicions of American
aims and motives in the area.[31] As president, Eisenhower implemented and escalated the policy of assistance that had been
inaugurated by his predecessor. This aid had already reached
significant proportions. Estimates in mid-1954 placed the total
value of American military supplies sent to Indochina since 1946
at $2 billion, approximately 15 per cent of the total cost of the
Marshall Plan. In April 1954, the United States announced that
its aid to Indochina for the forthcoming fiscal year would run

to $1.1 billion, as compared to the $150 million that had been granted for fiscal year 1950.[32] Altogether, America accounted for 40 per cent of the total war cost between 1951 and 1954, 60 per cent after September 1953 when an additional $385 million grant was received by the French, and 78 per cent by mid-1954 when efforts were being made to liberate the besieged camp of Dien Bien Phu.[33]

Early in 1954 financial assistance alone was no longer sufficient and American military intervention was seriously discussed. Up to that time, the French government, jealous of its prerogatives on the field and still distrustful of United States intentions, had opposed American participation in the war proper. What contributed to a change of mind was Dien Bien Phu, a remote French outpost that had been established on the northwestern boundary of Vietnam in November 1953 as a barrier against any further Vietminh offensive against Laos.[34] With the 15,000 men of the fortress dangerously threatened by General Giap's superior Vietminh forces, the government of Prime Minister Joseph Laniel attempted to secure an American intervention that would save the embattled camp, stabilize the French position in Laos, and permit a favorable settlement of the negotiations scheduled to open in Geneva that coming spring.

On March 20, a mission headed by General Paul Ely, the French chief of staff, arrived in Washington to elicit American reaction to France's need for additional assistance. In effect, America's commitment to the defense of Indochina had steadily escalated throughout 1953. With increased determination after the Korean War, America warned China that a further deterioration of the situation in Indochina would have "great consequences which might not be confined to Indochina."[35] In 1954, some had even described Dulles' well-publicized January 12 speech on massive retaliation as one prompted by the desire to preempt a mounting communist offensive in that region.[36] From the American side, apparently unsolicited by the French mission, came a more ambitious offer. Partly in line with President Eisenhower's instruction to put at France's disposal all means to save Dien Bien Phu (under attack since March 13) and partly on his own initiative, Admiral Radford, then chairman of the Joint Chiefs of Staff, offered for consideration by Paris an American air raid against the perimeter of the fortress that would be carried out with 200 planes from the Philippines and the Seventh Fleet.[37] Atomic weapons were reportedly available for the contingency of a large-scale Chinese retaliation.[38] Targets in China were even selected, "reasonably related to the area," later said Dulles, although no "great population centers like Shanghai, Peking or Canton." [39]

But Paris' belated approval of the Radford proposal (April 4) came only after a meeting at the State Department (April 3) where a group of leading congressmen refused to endorse military intervention at this time.[40] Instead, the congressmen urged the Eisenhower administration to act within an international coalition that would specifically include Great Britain. Cognizant of the congressional request, Eisenhower intervened personally with British Prime Minister Winston Churchill to secure immediate and united action in Indochina. "I believe," the American president wrote Churchill, "that the best way to put teeth in this concept [of united action] . . . is through the establishment of a new, ad hoc grouping or coalition composed of nations which had a vital concern in the checking of communist expansion in the area. I have in mind, in addition to our two countries, France, the Associated States, Australia, New Zealand, Thailand, and the Philippines." [41] But Great Britain remained firmly committed to a negotiated settlement through the Geneva Conference and, in the interim, adamantly opposed any action that might undermine its success.

In effect, Dulles was neither interested in the immediate problem of Dien Bien Phu, nor in preparing for negotiations with the communists. Instead, he was interested in pursuing the war to a victorious conclusion, and to this effect he was willing to offer American intervention providing he was given commitments by America's allies, including a pledge that France itself would not "withdraw from the battle until it is won" and assurances of complete independence for the Associated States of Laos, Cambodia and Vietnam.[42] From within, the position of the Eisenhower administration was singularly complicated by its contradictory domestic commitments. On the one hand, Eisenhower's early settlement of the war in Korea, as promised during the 1952 campaign, had gained him the enviable reputation of peacemaker, a reputation he was reluctant to sacrifice on the altar of another unpopular war in Asia. On the other hand, the Eisenhower administration had pledged an end to communist gains in Asia and elsewhere and it feared that a refusal to intervene would open it up to the same charges that the Republicans had previously used against the Democrats.

To improve the case for intervention, the stakes in Vietnam were increased by reviving the old domino theory. In his press conference of April 7, Eisenhower reflected on the effect that the communization of one country would have on the others. If one state fell to communism, Eisenhower said, its neighbors would do likewise in a chain reaction, like a row of falling dominoes, and the fall of Indochina would therefore lead to the fall of Burma, Thailand, Malaya, and Indonesia. India would then be hemmed in by communism, and Australia, New Zealand, the Philippines, Formosa, and Japan would all be dangerously threatened. Eisenhower concluded that upon the outcome of the struggle in Indochina could be said to rest the destiny of mankind.[43]

Yet in May, following the fall of Dien Bien Phu, both Eisenhower and his secretary tacitly retreated from this doomsday outlook and flatly stated that retention of Indochina was not essential for the defense of Southeast Asia.[44] Unwilling to condone the "loss" of North Vietnam, the American government at the same time refused to participate officially at the Geneva Conference and to join in its final declaration. Thus the stage was set for later violations by both parties of whatever accords might be concluded at the conference table.

1954: The Geneva Conference

The Geneva Conference convened with the Western allies badly divided. After Dien Bien Phu, France no longer had the will to fight; Great Britain had never wanted to fight; and America would not fight if the others did not also fight. Yet, on the whole, the outcome of the conference was quite favorable to the Western allies, "the best," as Undersecretary of State General Walter Bedell Smith declared upon returning from Geneva, "which we could have possibly obtained under the circumstances." [45] Ho Chi Minh was himself under pressure to bring the war to an end. From without, the communist leader was being pressured by his allies. In the middle of the conference, the Soviet Union appeared specifically anxious to help the new French government of Pierre Mendès-France on the eve of a decisive vote on the status of the European Defense Community; China, whose participation alone represented a major diplomatic victory, was not inclined to enter another war with the West less than a year after the conclusion of the Korean conflict. More generally, both Moscow and Peking wanted to experiment further with the new, more flexible line of policy that had followed Stalin's death. But Ho Chi Minh was also pressured by the Western allies. From Washington came the ever present threat of military intervention, a threat likely to be revived if the conference did not succeed; from Paris French Premier Mendès-France, who had given himself one month to obtain an agreement, was using the threat of his own resignation as an effective lever against Vietminh recalcitrance; his failure could only result in a new government (probably headed by Mendès-France's arch enemy, George Bidault) bent on continuing the war, and even escalating it through the use of conscripts. [46] From within, but unknown to France and its allies, Ho Chi Minh's forces were nearing exhaustion; losses at Dien Bien Phu had been considerable, with casualties reaching an estimated 18,000, including 8,000 deaths; and the lassitude of a war-weary Vietnamese population made guerrilla operations difficult to continue. [47]

Under such circumstances, the communists made substantial concessions to the West. They abandoned several provinces that had always shown allegiance to the Vietminh and they accepted that elections throughout Vietnam should be held as late as two years after the end of the fighting. But the very principle of national elections made such concessions temporary only, as it was widely assumed at the time that Ho's electoral victory was certain.

With regard to Vietnam proper the Geneva Conference produced two main accords. The first of these accords, a bilateral endorsement of a ceasefire, signified the end of military hostilities between the French Union forces and the Vietminh. The 17th parallel was recognized as a "provisional military demarcation line" on either side of which the forces of the two parties were to be regrouped. Vietnam was to be neutralized: all foreign troops and bases were banned from the country, north and south, and both zones were forbidden to adhere to any military alliance. An international commission composed of representatives from Canada, Poland, and India, was set up to supervise and control the implementation of the ceasefire agreement and the organization of the general elections. Finally, the agreement also stipulated that any civilian wishing to move from one zone to the other be allowed to do so, freely, before May 18, 1955. (Roughly 900,000 persons moved southward, roughly 150,000 went northward. More important, though, approximately 5,000 to 6,000 elite Vietminh guerrillas stayed in South Vietnam and went underground.) [48]

Elections were further outlined in a second accord, the Final Declaration, which was signed by no one but was endorsed orally by the representatives of France, Great Britain, China, the Soviet Union, Cambodia, Laos, and the Democratic Republic of Vietnam. Paragraphs six and seven of the Declaration were the crucial clauses and deserve full quotation:

> The Conference recognizes that the essential purpose of the agreement relating to Vietnam is to settle military questions with a view to ending hostilities and that the military demarcation line is provisional and should not in any way be interpreted as constituting a political or territorial boundary. The Conference expresses its conviction that the execution of the provisions set out in the present declaration and in the agreement on the cessation of hostilities creates the necessary basis for the achievement in the near future of a political settlement in Vietnam.

> The Conference declares that, so far as Vietnam is concerned, the settlement of political problems, effected on the basis of respect for the principles of independence, unity and territorial integrity, shall permit the Vietnamese people to enjoy the fundamental freedoms, guaranteed by democratic institutions established as a result of free general elections by secret ballot. In order to ensure that sufficient progress in the restoration of peace has been made, and that all the necessary conditions obtained for free expression of the national will, general elections

shall be held in July 1956, under the supervision of an international commission composed of representatives of the Member States of the International Supervisory Commission, referred to in the agreement on the cessation of hostilities. Consultations will be held on this subject between the competent representative authorities of the two zones from July 20, 1955, onwards.

The documents that sanctioned the Geneva Conference formed a not-so-skillful *trompe l'oeil,* which, meant to please everyone, ended up frustrating everyone. The ambiguity and contradictoriness of these documents were great. Provisions were included to protect the freedom of every Vietnamese in deciding in which zone he wished to live. But at the same time, provisions specifically stated that the division of Vietnam would not last more than two years. Could it seriously be assumed that the Vietnamese people, whose attachment to their land and villages was well known, would go through the procedure of moving from one area to the other (with all the potential risks that such a move might entail) for only two years of relative freedom? To be sure, if unification were necessary, then separation was already implicit. In the words of a well-known expert in international law, "the pretense that a single Vietnam was being dealt with was a weird diplomatic evasion." [49]

The legal dilemmas that the Geneva documents raised were also considerable. With Vietnam recognized since July 4 as a "fully independent and sovereign state," how legally valid was a French general's sanction of matters affecting the administrative and political life of Vietnam? In fact, the South Vietnamese delegation not only refused to sign any agreement at all, but it registered a solemn protest against the Geneva accords and reserved its complete freedom of action to guarantee the independence and unity of Vietnam as the authorities in Saigon understood them. Subsequently South Vietnam refused to be held by the promise of elections. In this opposition, the Saigon government headed by Ngo Dinh Diem held one trump card — the support of the United States. Aware that an election in 1956 would in all likelihood spell Ho Chi Minh's victory, the Eisenhower administration condoned Diem's own refusal to hold such elections until the time, in Diem's words, "when all the conditions of freedom are present," that is to say, until the time when North Vietnam would have somehow ceased to be communist and Diem would have become certain of victory.[50] Eisenhower's position was in turn supported by the Democratic opposition in Congress. "I hope," stated then Senator John F. Kennedy in September 1956, that the United States will "never give its approval to the early nationwide elections called for by the Geneva agreement of 1954." [51] American approval was not given, the elections were not held, and the war was soon to resume.

The Creation of SEATO

With the Geneva Conference out of the way, the Eisenhower administration renewed its efforts to form an alliance that would facilitate united action in South and Southeast Asia on behalf of anticommunist elements. Later, in his *Memoirs,* President Eisenhower credited the Indochina war with having awakened London and Paris to the dangers of international communism in Asia and to the desirability of common action to defeat it.[52] However valid Eisenhower's analysis was, the SEATO Pact, which seemingly expressed the allies' awakening, was signed in spite of the Geneva Conference, rather than because of it. Only when London proved willing to heal the breach opened at Geneva between Great Britain and the United States and to sacrifice its plan for reciprocal guarantees in Asia, was Dulles able to conclude, in less than six weeks, the Southeast Asia Defense Treaty. SEATO linked the ANZUS Pact countries (Australia, New Zealand, and the United States) to two of the CENTO members (Great Britain and Pakistan), two Southeast Asian client states of the United States (Thailand and the Philippines), and France. By a protocol approved simultaneously with the treaty, the protection of the contracting parties was also extended to the territories of Cambodia, Laos, and South Vietnam. Obviously, the test for inclusion was not geographical location in Southeast Asia (only the Philippines and Thailand met such a criterion), but rather an explicit anticommunist determination, a test that excluded both India and Indonesia and such usual components of the domino theory as Burma and Malaya. Specifically embodied in the treaty itself was an "understanding" on the part of the United States that its commitment would apply only to communist aggressions; other aggression merely committed the United States to consultation. The American understanding was meant to assure India that Washington was not thereby committed to assisting Pakistan in the case of a conflict between those two countries.

The commitment itself was somewhat ambiguous. Its language was based upon the Monroe Doctrine principle. In paragraph one of Article IV each party recognized that direct aggression against any one of the contracting parties or associated states would endanger its own peace and safety and agreed to meet the common danger in accordance with its constitutional processes. This provision left to the judgment of each country the action to be taken if an armed attack occurred.

Paragraph two of Article IV dealt with subversion and indirect aggression. It provided for immediate consultation by the signatories whenever a threat other than armed attack endangered the area. But there was no commitment to put it down. During the senate hearings on the question, Secretary Dulles emphatically stated: "If there is a revolutionary movement in Vietnam or in Thailand, we would consult together as to what to do about it. . . . But we have no undertaking to put it down; all we have is an undertaking to consult together as to what to do about it." [53]

SEATO differed from NATO in that it applied only against a very specific enemy. Unlike NATO there was no design to build up a defensive force on the continent of Asia that would be sufficient to resist attack by communist armies. "We do not intend to dedicate any major elements of the United States military establishment to form an army of defense in this area. We rely primarily upon the deterrent of our mobile striking power," testified Secretary Dulles, who added that to do otherwise would involve an "overextension of American military power." [54]

As a result of the First Indochinese War, 1946–1954, America assumed in Southeast Asia an interventionist role that it had successively sought to convince the French to abandon, and then to maintain. But what prospects were there that America would be more successful than the French? First of all, whereas the French were colonialists, America was motivated by its traditional anticolonialism. As Eisenhower proudly put it, this tradition was "born in the circumstances of our own national birth in 1775." [55] It was hoped that American policies in Southeast Asia would be pursued in conjunction with, rather than against, nationalism, albeit noncommunist nationalism — the only kind America recognized as legitimate. The solution that would make America successful where others had failed was relatively simple: to find a national leader who could promote from within a total determination to resist communist imperialism. This, at least, was the conclusion reached by Eisenhower and Dulles. Eisenhower wrote,

> I am convinced that the French could not win the war because the internal political situation in Vietnam, weak and confused, badly weakened their military position. I have never talked or corresponded with a person knowledgeable in Indochinese affairs who did not agree that had elections been held as of the time of the fighting, possibly 80 per cent of the population would have voted for the Communist Ho Chi Minh as their leader rather than Chief of State Bao Dai. Indeed, the lack of leadership and drive on the part of Bao Dai was a factor in the feeling prevalent among Vietnamese that they had nothing to fight for. As one Frenchman said to me, "What Vietnam needs is another Syngman Rhee, regardless of all the difficulties that the presence of such a personality would entail." [56]

America thought it had found a true national leader in Ngo Dinh Diem, and at first Diem appeared to succeed in fostering some national support despite methods that made a sympathetic observer describe his regime in late 1956 as a "quasi policy state characterized by arbitrary arrests and imprisonment, strict censorship of the press and the absence of an effective political opposition." [57] But the resurgence of communist-led resistance in the south in the late fifties already presaged the increasing difficulties that Diem and his American sponsors were to have in maintaining the Republic of South Vietnam in the years to come. Indeed, by 1961, all the difficulties the presence of such a personality as Diem entailed were enough to bring America into a second Indochinese war, a war that by 1972 had yet to be resolved.

The Americanization of the War

The Kennedy and Johnson administrations inherited, rather than originated, the guidelines of American policy toward Indochina. Both Democratic presidents acted on the same assumptions that had motivated their predecessors. The first of these assumptions was America's conception of a monolithic communist bloc. Despite the many reports already available on the split between the two communist giants, Washington refused to conceive of it as plausible at all until 1962. The Kennedy administration thought it had found in Southeast Asia the first application of a new Soviet strategy. As outlined by Khrushchev in January 1961, this strategy indicated that, in the coming period, Moscow would rely primarily neither on nuclear nor on conventional but on guerrilla war.[58] Still perceiving the Soviet Union as the implicit enemy in Indochina, the Kennedy administration naturally resurrected the domino theory, which three previous administrations had already shaped to suit their needs. More than four years before he assumed the presidency, Kennedy, who earlier had watched the French policy in Indochina with great skepticism, had in effect strongly endorsed the domino theory. Vietnam, Kennedy had observed in September 1956, "represents the cornerstone of the Free World in Southeast Asia, the keystone to the arch, the finger in the dike. Burma, Thailand, India, Japan, the Philippines, and obviously Laos and Cambodia are among those whose security would be threatened if the red tide of communism overflowed into Vietnam." In short, Kennedy concluded, Vietnam was "a test of American responsibility and determination in Asia," a test that directly involved America's security in any new outbreak of trouble.[59]

The monolithic image of the communist camp and the endorsement of the domino theory were not the only assumptions governing America's policy in Indochina. Also instrumental were pathological fears of a "China on the march," the rigidity of the East Asian establishment at the State Department, still reminiscent of the McCarthy era, the vulnerability of the Democratic party on Asian policy issues since the "loss of China" charges, the lack of substantial American expertise on Vietnam, and the international setbacks occurred in the Kennedy administration. All of these important environmental factors shaped America's growing military intervention in Vietnam.[60]

In 1954, the end of the Indochinese war had not signified the end of American aid to Vietnam. In fact, during the remaining years of the Eisenhower administration United States economic and military aid to the Diem government had substantially exceeded that given to the French during the war. Furthermore, military "advisers" began to be sent regularly and, by mid-1961, the United States military mission in Vietnam numbered approximately 2,000.[61] Yet, it was not Vietnam but neighboring Laos that, in 1961, posed the most urgent problem to the new Kennedy administration.

Less than twenty-four hours before entering the White House, Kennedy was briefed by the departing president and his cabinet on the impending crisis in Laos.[62] More than $300 million over five years — one of the highest levels of American aid per capita — had failed to transform "neutral" Laos into a Western military outpost. Instead, the pressure that accompanied the aid steadily antagonized neutralist Premier Souvanna Phouma who, in 1958, entered into a political coalition with his half brother, Prince Souphanouvong, leader of the communist Pathet Lao forces that had settled in the two northeastern provinces of Laos where the Geneva accords had specified that the communists were to regroup. By the late fifties, Laos had implicitly become divided between the United States–backed faction of General Phoumi Nosavan and the Pathet Lao, which was receiving large quantities of Sino-Soviet military equipment, despite the 1954 agreements to neutralize the former French colony, but in conjunction with America's own arms shipments to the Phoumi faction.[63] The situation had so deteriorated that, in the waning days of his presidency, Eisenhower felt that America should consider, as a last desperate option, unilateral intervention.[64]

Following some serious military rattling, the Kennedy administration was able to settle the problems with diplomatic rather than military tools. Apparently both sides failed to find in the Laotians those martial virtues that might have warranted a continued build-up toward armed confrontation. United States ambassador to India John Kenneth Galbraith was reported to have told Indian Prime Minister Nehru, "Americans are practical men and did not set military value on the Lao, 'who do not believe in getting killed like the civilized races.'" [65] Moreover, as in April 1954, no ally could be found to support a multilateral military intervention. Finally, the ill fated attempt at invading Cuba, in April 1961, proved instrumental in preventing a repeat performance in Laos. "That operation," narrated presidential adviser Theodore Sorensen, "had been recommended principally by the same set of advisers who favored intervention in Laos. But now the president was far more skeptical of the experts, their reputations, their recommendations, their promises, premises and facts . . ." As the president confided to Sorensen, "Thank God the Bay of Pigs happened when it did . . . otherwise we'd be in Laos by now — and that would be a hundred times worse." [66] In July 1962, following long and difficult negotiations, a coalition government was formed under the sponsorship of thirteen states, including the United States, the Soviet Union, Communist China, and the two Vietnams. It never worked, however, and by 1971 a still implicitly divided Laos continued to await the outcome of the Vietnam war, in between rounds of light combat between the Pathet Lao and the now American-backed Souvana Phouma.

Meanwhile, in South Vietnam the situation had changed from bad to worse. Internal opposition to the Diem regime had reintroduced substantial terrorism as early as mid-1957.[67] Such activities were spearheaded by the Vietminh who had stayed in the South after the 1954 Geneva Conference. In November 1960, a coup led by Diem's own army failed to dislodge him from power. The following month, antigovernment insurgents in the South formed the National Liberation Front (later to be dubbed Vietcong). Although dominated by the communists, the Vietcong, like the Vietminh many years before, included numerous non-communist, nationalist elements. By the end of Kennedy's first year in office, it appeared that the communists had extended their control to approximately four-fifths of the countryside, cutting off some of the major cities, including Saigon, from their hinterland.

The American response to the perceived build-up of the communist forces in the South was a parallel build-up of the Saigon forces. In October 1961, a White House team was sent to Saigon, headed by General Maxwell Taylor, to see what might be done about stabilizing the Diem regime. The Taylor mission recommended sending 8,000 more American troops to end infiltration from the North and to assure Diem of America's readiness to join him in a military showdown with the Vietcong.[68] But to win the civil war from within, the team also recommended that major political reforms be enacted by the Diem government. At first hesitant, Kennedy, whose past performance at the Bay of Pigs and ongoing performance in Laos were rendering him vulnerable to Republican charges of being soft with communism, ordered the proposed build-up: by the time of Kennedy's death, American ground forces in Vietnam amounted to 16,000 men.[69] The letters exchanged between the American and the Vietnamese presidents, like the letters exchanged between Eisenhower and Diem in October 1954, linked the increased American commitment with Diem's pledge of substantial reforms. But though eagerly receiving this increased military assistance, Diem continued to sidetrack the promised reforms.

In November 1963, the collapse of the Diem regime and his assassination signaled the failure of the Eisenhower-Kennedy policy in Vietnam. It was not the Vietcong but the South Vietnamese military, which the United States had so painstakingly built, that overthrew Diem. Thus disappeared the political alternative to Ho Chi Minh on which America had counted for so long a time. But fate did not give the American president the opportunity to recoup his losses by embarking, as he seemingly intended to, on bold new policies in Vietnam. For John F. Kennedy was assassinated three weeks later.[70]

The transition from Kennedy to Johnson provided little opportunity for a major change in Vietnam policy. The main advisers remained the same, and their assumptions remained unchanged. A difference of some import, however, was Johnson's marked inexperience in foreign policy questions — an inexperience that left him considerably dependent on his advisers' recommendations. On two previous occasions in the past, Johnson had played a minor role in the evolution of America's policy in Vietnam. First, in April 1954, as the senate minority leader, he had been a part of the congressional group that had refused to sanction the proposed Radford Plan without prior support of the allies. As vice-president, in May 1961, he had visited Southeast Asia and had returned to urge the president to move America forward promptly in a major effort to help these countries help themselves, not only militarily but politically and economically through much-needed domestic reforms.[70] * Having twice demonstrated a marked reluctance to solutions of force, it was part of Johnson's tragedy to face his first test over Vietnam during a presidential campaign when the flexible military posture established by the McNamara-sponsored reforms allowed him to do what past presidents had been restrained from doing — to send extensive American ground forces to Indochina.

In August 1964, alleged North Vietnamese attacks against American ships in the Gulf of Tonkin caused a sharp increase in American involvement.[71] In Washington, the incident made it possible for the administration to request, and obtain overwhelmingly, passage of the so-called Tonkin Gulf Resolution, whereby the president was empowered by the senate

> to take all necessary measures to repel any armed attack against the forces of the United States . . . to prevent further aggression . . . and to take all necessary steps, including the use of armed forces to assist any member or protocol state of the Southeast Asia Collective Defense Treaty requesting assistance in defense of its freedom.

In Vietnam, the Gulf of Tonkin incident reflected the determination of the Johnson administration to intervene in the war on an unprecedented scale, as soon as domestic conditions might permit — namely, as soon as the elections were over. On February 7, 1965, the Vietcong attack against the American camp of Pleiku

* "In large measure," Vice-President Johnson reported to President Kennedy, "the greatest danger Southeast Asia offers to nations like the U.S. is not the momentary threat of Communism itself, rather that danger stems from hunger, ignorance, poverty and disease." Yet, in the same report, Johnson also indicated a penchant for the domino theory. Failure in Southeast Asia in the battle against communism, he indicated, would signify that "the U.S. inevitably must surrender the Pacific and take up [its] defense on [its] own shores." ("The Pentagon Papers," The *New York Times*, July 1, 1971, p. 4.)

provided the needed opportunity for enforcing a decision that had been taken months before the attack occurred: retaliatory air strikes against North Vietnam were ordered and then continued regularly against an ever increasing list of targets.[72] * At the same time, an accelerated build-up of American ground forces was undertaken: their number reached 267,000 by mid-1966. These two developments transformed a civil war, fought in the South with outside aid by North Vietnam in the manner of a guerrilla war, into a progressively "Americanized" war, waged with American troops doing the bulk of the fighting against an enemy increasingly directed and manned from Hanoi.†

Three years of uninterrupted military and rhetorical escalation followed. American commitment in the area had long since outstripped any reasonable estimation of the importance of the area to America. Extreme ideological arguments were commonly advanced by administration spokesmen to muster support for the war among an increasingly skeptical and restless public. The domino theory was once more reformulated so that the war in Vietnam became the test case for halting communist-inspired wars of national liberation that, if defeated in Vietnam, would never again pose a major threat. Critics of the war argued that local conditions would most certainly cause revolutionary uprisings elsewhere no matter what the outcome of the Vietnam

---

* It had been a continuous official assumption that a major land war in Indochina could be avoided by simply resorting to large-scale bombing. In November 1961, General Taylor had emphasized: "North Vietnam is extremely vulnerable to conventional bombing, a weakness which should be exploited diplomatically in convincing Hanoi to lay off South Vietnam." When the bombing was finally ordered, the Johnson administration confidently predicted that Hanoi would yield after two to six months. ("The Pentagon Papers," The *New York Times*, July 1, 1971, p. 5; June 14, 1971, p. 31.)

† In spite of all the official worry about infiltration into South Vietnam through Laos, a special national intelligence estimate on October 5, 1961, had reported "that 80 to 90 per cent of the estimated 17,000 Vietcong have been locally recruited, and that there was little evidence that the Vietcong relied on external supplies." In February 1963, another such report went on to say that Vietcong recruitment inside South Vietnam was so effective that the war could be continued even without infiltration from the north. ("The Pentagon Papers," The *New York Times*, July 1, 1971, pp. 7–8.)

War.[73] Vietnam was also presented by the Johnson administration as the test of all American commitments throughout the world.[74] But critics asked how America's commitment to defend, say, West Germany — a vigorous, industrial nation with a functioning democracy and with which the United States had a common cultural heritage as well as a common, if troubled, history — could be compared to an ambiguous commitment to defend the government of the Republic of South Vietnam — more and more a military dictatorship in a nation whose culture and history were so different from that of the United States as to make even a common political vocabulary impossible.[75]

Militarily the war in Vietnam could not be won without literally destroying South Vietnam, dislocating further the national fabric of America, alienating the NATO allies who were generally critical of United States actions in Southeast Asia, endangering rapprochement with the Soviet Union, and increasing the chances of armed confrontation with China. But, still more important, the political prerequisites for winning the war were not present in America. Having ballooned to include 540,000 men engaged in the war at a cost of $30 billion per year, the war could no longer be fully justified even with the most extreme rhetorical flourishes. Public dissent reached a new peak early in 1968 when General Taylor, by then the United States ambassador in Saigon, requested an additional troop increase of over 200,000 men. After the presidential primary campaign in New Hampshire, President Johnson decided, on March 31, 1968, to restrict the bombing of North Vietnam in order to clear the way for negotiations to end the war. Disillusioned by the defections of many of those upon whom he had most relied (including Defense Secretary Robert McNamara whose change of heart brought about his replacement by Clark Clifford), embittered by the divisions of his own party where his leadership was challenged at the polls by Senators Eugene McCarthy and Robert F. Kennedy, and most of all stricken by the political failures of his presidency, which had sacrificed an enlightened policy of domestic reform to the spiraling economic and political costs of the war, Johnson made the ultimate gesture of political defeat by removing himself from public life. Though peace negotiations were laboriously organized in Paris, the war went on — difficult to fight in the field, difficult to justify at home, and difficult to end.

The End of Illusions?

This was a difficult time for American policymakers. Events seemed to force them to recognize that the basic premises of their policy in Indochina were generally illusory. First, there was the illusion that the American government had been fighting in Indochina to help the Indochinese acquire or preserve their independence. While ambassador to the French Vichy government, Admiral Leahy had predicted the situation almost correctly when he had said of the forthcoming war in the Pacific: "If Japan is the winner the Japanese will take over French Indochina; if the Allies win, we will take it." [76] Before 1954, the American illusion was to believe that support of the French would satisfy Indochinese claims for independence. After 1954, the illusion was to assume that the Diem government, and the plethora of mini-governments that followed it, up to and including the Thieu-Ky regime, were safeguarding Western democracy in Asia. Anticommunist though they may have been, these governments, just like the Bao Dai government under the Japanese and under the French, were external creations that had little if any support from within the communities over which they ruled. Mostly corrupt, inept, and often ignored, these governments made communism the primary issue because only with that issue did they receive the external support without which they could not survive.*

Second, there was the illusion that should Vietnam (and Indochina) fall, then the rest of Asia would inevitably follow. The

---

* Already in 1961 the reports on Diem that reached the Kennedy administration were reminiscent of the reports on Chiang that, in the late forties, had reached Truman. "He is unable to rally the people in the fight against the Communists," an intelligence appraisal indicated in March 1961, "because of his reliance on virtual one-man rule, his toleration of corruption extending even to his immediate entourage, and his refusal to relax a rigid system of public control." ("The Pentagon Papers," The *New York Times*, July 1, 1971, p. 6.)

"domino theory," as it was used by every American administration since President Roosevelt's, was merely a variation of the
Munich syndrome. In 1954, while discussing the then desperate
situation in Indochina, President Eisenhower had followed the
usual procedure of recalling how the Western democracies had
"failed to halt Hirohito, Mussolini and Hitler by not acting in
unity and in time," thus causing many years of stark tragedy and
desperate peril. "May it not be," asked President Eisenhower
in the same tone President Truman had used before him and his
successors would all use about Vietnam, "that our nations have
learned something from that lesson?" [77] American policymakers
apparently followed the ancient warning to remember history
lest they be doomed to repeat past mistakes. But it was precisely
through the indiscriminate projection of an historical episode that
mistakes were multiplied. Fixed in the past, the enemy was elusive in the present, not only in Southeast Asia, as the ubiquitous
ghost of Hitler was seen in Ho Chi Minh or in a Prince Sihanouk,
but elsewhere and everywhere — in Moscow, Peking, Havana,
and Cairo. Whether or not American interests were at stake
apparently became a moot point. The Munich syndrome, of
which the domino theory was the Asian expression, had clearly
shown that there was but one world and one peace, and with
the communists in power in Moscow only one enemy existed
against which all peace-loving people needed to be protected.

Regardless of its time context, the domino theory was highly
unreasonable.* It granted too much power to China; it granted
too little attention to the unique particularities and requirements
of the states in the area. Although in 1941 Japan did use Indochina as a springboard to take the Philippines, Malaya, and Indonesia, the Japanese thrust was made by sea under covering air

---

* In June 1964, a CIA memorandum submitted to the president forcefully challenged the domino theory. Arguing that so long as the United
States could retain its island bases on Okinawa, Guam, the Philippines,
and Japan, it could wield enough power in Asia to deter China and North
Vietnam from overt military aggression against Southeast Asia, the memorandum emphasized: "With the possible exception of Cambodia, it is likely
that no nation in the area would quickly succumb to Communism as a
result of the fall of Laos and South Vietnam. Furthermore," the memorandum went on, "a continuation of the spread of communism in the area
would not be inexorable." ("The Pentagon Papers," The *New York Times*,
June 13, 1971, p. 39.)

power, both of which Tokyo controlled after Pearl Harbor. But after the end of the war, sea and air power remained strictly in Western hands. If the domino theory was ever applied again in Asia, to a degree yet difficult to appreciate, it could only occur when the dominant Asian power developed sufficient strategic resources to deter American retaliation against its own air control of Asia. In other words, and as President Kennedy belatedly came to believe, the future of China's predominance in Asia had little to do with what America did in Vietnam.[78]

American policy was based on yet a third illusion: the American position in Vietnam, already strong, would grow stronger if more pressure was applied and more risks taken for peace. More arms, more troops, more bombing — with the light at the end of the tunnel always in sight as American forces ever increased and American bombing in North Vietnam extended ever further toward the Chinese border. Elected because he had a "secret plan" for peace President Nixon was the first American president to reduce the size of American military presence in Vietnam. Yet, the American intervention in Cambodia in May 1970, and the subsequent sponsorship of the South Vietnamese foray in Laos the following year, were both exercises in brinksmanship that showed that American policymakers still thought the road to peace lay through more war.*

Still other American illusions about Vietnam had existed. In 1954, the illusion had been that American support of the French in Indochina would get them to accept the European Defense Community in Europe, although France's losses in Asia made it too weak to join EDC in Europe. In 1968, the illusion had been that by waging a war against communism in Vietnam America would strengthen its commitments throughout the world, although physical and psychological losses suffered by America in Vietnam reduced the credibility of those commitments, and the destruction suffered by the Vietnamese themselves reduced, in some of the areas threatened by communist expansion, the desirability of seeing such commitments enforced. American in-

---

* Nixon, however, was still withdrawing American forces from the area. By the end of 1971, these forces amounted to 185,000 men and widespread expectations pointed to a near-total withdrawal for the end of 1972.

sistence on identifying the main enemy as Peking-directed communism helped strengthen the ties between truly nationalist anticommunism, Indochinese communism, and Chinese communism.

But above all, the illusions that were unveiled during the Vietnam War were domestic illusions: the illusion of a superior efficiency that helped America win its wars by quantifying, planning, destroying, and cajoling; the illusion of a superior morality that had made the American flag the flag of mankind but that was now being torn amidst such revelations as the massacre of civilians in South Vietnamese villages; and, finally, the illusion of omnipotence, the illusion that, as D. W. Brogan had written in 1950, "any situation which disrupts or endangers the United States can only exist because some Americans have been fools or knaves" — that the world, in short, would go happily the American way unless some elected or nonelected officials betrayed America's interest and thereby frustrated the world's wishes.[79]

Thus, Vietnam brought to the surface the "one basic fault" that had been previously attributed to one of America's past presidents: the willingness to do anything for people except let them live their own lives. For, what had been concluded of President Woodrow Wilson might well have been concluded of America by the late sixties as a new change of administration was taking place: it "never seemed to understand there's a big difference between trying to save people and trying to help them. With luck you can help 'em. But they always save themselves." [80]

9

The
Continuation
of the Debate

The Nixon Doctrine in Asia

Under the Nixon administration, American commitments abroad remained a fundamental issue in the ongoing reassessment of United States foreign policy. As we have seen, the prolonged military, economic, and human investment in Indochina had intensified and broadened the policy debate of the sixties. The dramatic 1968 campaigns of the late Robert F. Kennedy and of Eugene McCarthy for the Democratic party's presidential nomination helped make the redefining of America's proper role in the world a public pursuit. With isolationism no longer a valid option, the alternatives of limitationism or globalism directed these discussions and served as the guideposts by which the international posture of the Nixon administration would eventually prove to be different from that of previous administrations.

Like Truman's, Nixon's foreign policy was embellished by a doctrine, the distillation of which was provided in a presidential message to Congress, on February 18, 1970. As stated by the president, the central thesis of the doctrine was that America would

> participate in the defense and development of allies and friends, but that it cannot — and will not — conceive *all* the plans, design *all* the programs, execute *all* the decisions and undertake *all* the defense of the free nations of the world. We will help where it makes a real difference and is considered in our interest.[1]

The Nixon Doctrine ostensibly rested on the conviction that the United States had been carrying too much of the burden of maintaining world peace. Part of this burden would now have to be assumed by America's allies: the withdrawal of American troops from Indochina, as well as renewed discussions over the withdrawal of troops from Europe and elsewhere, clearly reflected the immediate implications of the doctrine. Through various programs of Vietnamization, Asianization, and Europeanization, American troops would be ultimately replaced by local forces equipped with American assistance. The resulting new military posture for the United States would also cause a substitution of the "1½ war" strategy for the former "2½ war" principle that had characterized America's conventional posture in the 1960's.*

Such intended reduction of America's role as a military power was expected to follow three major guidelines. First, America would continue to honor all of its treaty commitments.

---

* Nixon's own distinction between the two strategies is as follows:

According to the "2½ war" principle, U.S. forces would be maintained for a three month conventional forward defense of NATO, a defense of Korea or Southeast Asia against a full-scale Chinese attack, and a minor contingency — all simultaneously. . . . Under the "1½ war" strategy we will maintain in peacetime general purpose forces adequate for simultaneously meeting a major Communist attack in either Europe or Asia, assisting allies against non-Chinese threats in Asia, and contending with a contingency elsewhere. (*Department of State Bulletin*, Vol. LXII, March 9, 1970, p. 322.)

Second, America would provide a protective shield if a nuclear power threatened a nation allied with America or a nation whose survival was considered vital to United States security. Third, to nations facing other aggression, namely indirect or nonnuclear aggression, Washington would furnish military and economic assistance when requested, in accordance with its treaty commitments. "But," emphasized President Nixon, America would "look to the nation directly threatened to assume the primary responsibility of providing the manpower for its defense." [2]

When translated into specific terms these guidelines appeared as ambiguous as those that had framed the Truman Doctrine and possibly constituted no less than an extension of that doctrine. Thus the first of these guidelines — that American help would continue to be channeled to all of the allies — obviously introduced no new discrimination or reappraisal. On the contrary, the Nixon Doctrine was a blunt reassertion to "our friends in the world that America's sense of responsibility remains the world's greatest hope for peace." [3] Not only the isolationist option was thereby discarded. For one could agree with the president that America's responsibilities were not limited to the Western Hemisphere and yet propose that these responsibilities could be extended to one area or nation without covering *all* the others. More important was the second guideline, which provided an American guarantee against nuclear aggression in the area. Clearly, Nixon's pledge confirmed and even widened President Johnson's pledge to India in October 1964. By so doing, the Nixon Doctrine implicitly reasserted America's abiding commitment to the military containment of China, the major nuclear threat in the area. With regard to deterrence, China's containment would obviously be achieved by fundamental reliance on nuclear weapons. Such containment would further be enhanced by maintaining, side by side with America's nuclear weapons, large Asian ground armies that would fulfill the initial requirements of self-defense against Chinese aggression.[4] In the seventies, America would thus pursue against China in Asia the same policy that had been tentatively adopted in the fifties against the Soviet Union in Western Europe: deterrence through the threat of massive retaliation, defense through self-reliance. Probably, the same local reluctance to contribute its fair share of conventional resources that had developed in Europe would develop in Asia as well. But more immediately, a dangerous parallel was growing between the aftermath of the Korean War and the Vietnam War: reliance upon nuclear weapons to prevent any such conflict in the future. This was a crucial hypothesis. Granted America's pledge to honor its commitments, granted its pledge to defend other nations from nuclear attack, and granted its efforts to let those nations in the area assume the primary responsibility for their own security — what would America do if those efforts failed? Would it disengage completely and openly admit the failure of its policy, or would it escalate and use its nuclear option? In theory, the Nixon Doctrine might spell self-reliance and disengagement. In practice, however, such a doctrine might under certain circumstances lead to two alternatives only: surrender or nuclear war.

For the new American president, military intervention was justified primarily when a domestic insurgency had shaded into external aggression, and only where and when it made a "decisive" difference and was considered in America's interest. Apart from the unclear and unrealistic problem of defining "external aggression," such a conception of military intervention still left unanswered *when* and *where* America would intervene with military force. It described neither America's interests nor interventionist decisiveness. That the United States did not intend to conceive, design, execute, and implement all the plans, programs, and decisions was nothing new. Now, according to Nixon, future commitments would be considered after a careful appraisal of America's own interests and that of other countries, as well as of America's capacity "to counter those threats at an acceptable risk and cost." [5] Such a valid conviction seemed to recreate a more fundamental equation between objectives sought, means available, and the degree to which the latter might help fulfill the former. Yet, Nixon's statement merely referred to *new* commitments — not to old ones. What about those former commitments whose relevance to present American interests was being disputed? "We are not involved in the world," asserted President Nixon, "because we have commitments; we have commitments because we are involved. Our interests must shape our commitments rather than the other way around." [6] But until the limits of America's involvement and the scope of its interests were more precisely defined, such a principle still left America in the position previously defined by President Truman: unlimited involvement called for unlimited commitments, and if the old commitments were going to be preserved, how would America's interests and involvement be modified?

In Indochina, the involvement was expressed by the American military presence there. Once America had troops in a given area it was in its interest to assure that they were not driven off the field from whatever direction including neighboring areas. Said the president in announcing his decision to send troops to Cambodia: "If we allow American men by the thousands to be killed by an enemy from privileged sanctuaries the credibility of the United States would be destroyed in every area of the world where only the power of the United States deters aggression." [7] With the same reasoning applied by the president to Laos, one could say that involvement in one area of the world, for example Vietnam, created involvement (and hence commitments) in other bordering areas, say Cambodia and Laos. More importantly, one could also ask – if the involvement justified the commitment, what specifically justified the involvement?

The president's view, even as he was enforcing a progressive withdrawal of American ground troops from the area, was still that the United States had entered the war there for a worthy purpose, namely, to allow the South Vietnamese "to decide their own future free of outside interference" and to strengthen "long-term hopes for peace in the world." [8] The former objective – to foster national self-determination without geographical, political, and economic qualification – coincided with President Truman's ambition "to support free peoples who are resisting subjugation by armed minorities or by outside pressure." There was here no promise for a reduction of United States international involvement. On the contrary, the principle was reasserted with renewed fervor. "If," confided President Nixon, "I lived in another country that wanted to be sure and retain its right to self-determination, I would say: 'Thank God that the United States exists at this moment of history.'" [9] Implicit in Nixon's further assertion that America was engaged in a preventive war in Vietnam, "probably the very last one" waged by the United States,[10] was an acceptance of the domino theory according to which communist encroachment in Southeast Asia ultimately imperiled the North American continent. "A just peace in Vietnam," the president stated on June 3, 1970, "is essential, if there is to be a lasting peace in other parts of the world."

But throughout the post–World War II era, the endorsement of the domino theory had been an integral part of the globalist position according to which the major policy objective of the United States must be the worldwide containment of totalitarian forces. President Nixon confirmed suspicion of a globalist bias in an interview with television news commentators on July 1, 1970. In response to a question raised by Howard K. Smith, the president observed:

> If the United States leaves Vietnam in a way that we are humiliated or defeated not simply speaking in what are called jingoistic terms but in very practical terms this will be immensely discouraging to the 300 million people from Japan, clear round to Thailand in free Asia. And even more important, it will be ominously encouraging to the leaders of communist China and the Soviet Union who are supporting the North Vietnamese. It will encourage them in their expansionist policies in other areas.

Such a position in no way reflected, as Nixon had it, a "major shift in United States foreign policy." [11] It was still less a "new philosophy of U.S. foreign policy," [12] and one was called upon to reconcile a stated American unwillingness to shoulder the responsibility of defending Southeast Asia from communist subversion with a remark the president made on July 29, 1969, in Bangkok: "We have been together in the past, we are together at the present and the United States will stand proudly with Thailand against those who might threaten it *from abroad or from within.*" This last qualification was especially important as it preempted further the previous distinction between domestic insurgency and external aggression.

Similarly, the rhetoric employed by the president in explaining his decision to send American troops in Cambodia and to support the South Vietnamese foray in Laos appeared inconsistent with his assertion that the post–World War II era in foreign affairs had passed. In almost every speech since he began withdrawing troops from Vietnam, the president warned the enemy that he would act if the enemy attempted to gain any advantage. Cambodia was a test of America's determination inasmuch as North Vietnam was understood, despite the warnings, to be strengthening its position in the area following Prince Sihanouk's demise. But Cambodia was also an opportunity to remind the Soviet Union, which was then sending advisers and pilots to Egypt, that the American president was still capable of acting swiftly despite any domestic opposition he might encounter. The president stated on April 30, 1970: "If, when the chips are down, the United States acts like a pitiful helpless giant, the forces of totalitarianism and anarchy will threaten free nations and free institutions throughout the world." Such a rationale read ominously like a colloquial revision of the Truman Doctrine: when the chips are down the United States must act like a formidable giant willing to intervene throughout the world to deter aggression by the forces of totalitarianism. The warning was forcefully repeated in the second presidential State of the World message. Should North Vietnam attempt to take advantage of American withdrawal by building up its strength in the South and launching new attacks, the president would "take strong and effective measures to prevent the enemy from jeopardizing [America's] remaining forces." [13]

There too the trend dangerously went in the direction of lowering the nuclear threshold. Granted the sincerity of Nixon's commitment to an orderly withdrawal from the area, it was still feared that by allowing this withdrawal to drag on, too much reliance was placed on Saigon's ability to take over the burden of defending both the area and the remaining American forces, while Washington deterred the communists from launching a new offensive, assuming they could. But should American deterrence fail, and local defense (Vietnamization) collapse, the options opened to Washington were all dangerously unsatisfactory: uninterrupted disengagement with the reluctant admission of failure, renewed escalation of America's participation in the war and heavy casualties, or early recourse ("strong and effective") to tactical nuclear weapons. Granted the complexity of America's withdrawal from the area, the "new" American policy raised such potential risks because the fundamental issues brought forth by the Vietnam War were still being evaded — a reappraisal of America's interests in Asia; a redefinition of the minimum objectives for the fulfillment of which America might be willing to fight, alone or with allies; a reevaluation of military containment of China and an examination of substitute policies; and a revision of the alliances that reflected America's commitment to the containment of China.

The Nixon Doctrine in Europe

In Europe, Nixon's articulation of "partnership" was also presented as one of the new fundamental tenets of America's foreign policy. "Genuine partnership must increasingly characterize the alliance," insisted the American president in the 1970 State of the World Message.[14] Describing a primary international objective of his new administration, Nixon stated, "we have to re-establish the principle and practice of consultation. For too long in the past the United States has lead without listening, talked to our allies instead of *with* them and informed them of new departures instead of deciding with them." [15] As we have seen, partnership and consultation were indisputably valid components of an alliance policy. However, as Henry Kissinger had written before he became the adviser on foreign affairs to the White House, "consultation . . . is far from a panacea. It is least effective when it is most needed: when there exists basic differences of assessment or of interest. It works best in *implementing* a consensus rather than in *creating* it." [16]

In discussing European partnership, the new president casually revealed that "America's contribution will continue to be unique in certain areas, such as in maintaining a nuclear deterrent and a level of involvement sufficient to balance the powerful military position of the U.S.S.R. in Eastern Europe." [17] But it was precisely in those areas that an identity of interests and policies was lacking. And it was because of this "unique" contribution that President Kennedy's and President Johnson's own implementation of partnership had failed. To assert, as Nixon did, that those questions that divided the Atlantic Alliance must be addressed "in full consultation" with America's allies did not much elucidate the questions involved or the ways in which these differences might be resolved. It was an act of faith more than it was a specific policy. Nor could one find much change in an approach that would maintain close consultation "at every stage, not on a take-it-or-leave-it basis but by seeking the advice [of the allies] on the whole range of options we have under consideration." [18] In the two previous decades also, America had made no pretense to react disinterestedly to advice. But it was when such advice did not correspond to national policy objectives that America had become unreceptive and rifts in the partnership had developed. In 1970 when America sent troops to Cambodia, France, among other European powers, felt that Washington's failure to consult its allies on this decision violated the Nixon Doctrine's conception of partnership in the European theater.

"Disagreements must be faced openly and their bases carefully explored. Because our security is inseparable we can afford the most candid exchange of views," still stated Nixon.[19] Undoubtedly, the security of the United States and of Western Europe were interrelated; however, security interests were not identical and means for providing security were not equally appropriate for both areas. Had they been, no strategic debate would have occurred between the two sides of the alliance. In asserting the inseparability of American and Western European security, Nixon assumed a commonality of strategic interest, an assumption that could be expected to be as severely challenged in the future as it had been in the most recent past. If significant American troop withdrawals ever took place with the avowed objective of inducing the European partners to bear a greater burden of Atlantic defense, the result might be instead either a revival of demands for a European nuclear force or the disintegration of the alliance, with European nations seeking separate accommodation with the Soviet Union. As C. L. Sulzberger wrote in early 1970, "the problem of Europeanizing the cold war is as intricate if less emotional than the problem of Vietnamizing the hot war."[20] But here too the fundamental issues went beyond the withdrawal of American forces: a reappraisal of America's interests in Europe; a redefinition of the minimum interests for which America might be willing to fight, alone or with its allies; a reevaluation of the military containment of the Soviet Union and an examination of substitute policies; and a revision of the alliances that reflected America's commitment to the containment of the Soviet Union. The questions were the same as those raised with regard to Asia, and the forthcoming debate would probably evolve around them, beginning (but only beginning) with a belated answer to whether or not American troops would remain in Western Europe, and in what number.*

During the first three years of the Nixon administration, America attempted to modify the manner in which its commitments were to be honored. The United States, however, did not reduce those commitments, nor fundamentally depart from its previous globalist foreign policy. That the president had no intention yet of redefining America's global interest was perhaps best revealed in the answer he made at a May 8, 1970, press conference. It was, said the president, a "moot question" whether the war had been worthwhile: "now that America is there, if . . . we withdraw from Vietnam and allow the enemy to come into Vietnam and massacre the civilians there by the millions, as they would if we do that, let me say that America is finished insofar as the peacemaker in the Asian world is concerned."

The Continuation of the Debate

To analyze, late in 1970, America's articulation and implementation of its foreign policy was a torturous, often baffling experience. The ambiguities that permeated America's international program left the observer, professional or otherwise, per-

---

* In 1971, President Nixon had decided against such a withdrawal "without reciprocal action by our adversaries." Undiminished American presence, the president went on, "provides the sense of security which encourages our [Atlantic] partners' efforts to unite and do more for themselves." (The *New York Times,* February 26, 1971.) The call for reciprocal action still assumed Soviet conventional superiority in Europe; the need for American military presence in Europe to enhance the latter's sense of security still assumed a Soviet military threat and the need to contain it. These assumptions were, as we have seen, strongly debated, as were the continued assumptions that there was a direct relationship between Europe's sense of security and its unification, or between the presence of American troops on the Continent and Europe's willingness to shoulder an equitable share of the costs of defense.

plexed. One day America spoke as if peace was around the corner; the next it acted as if there would never be an end to war and as if the military efforts of the cold war era would have to be endlessly pursued. One day America spoke in the name of national self-determination; the next it acted as if the only form of self-determination it would accept was a full espousal of the American way of life. In one instance America spoke of the sanctity of human life; in another it acted as if final victory would be determined by the successful implementation of its Vietnam "search and destroy" policy. In one instance America impressed the world with its strength and its virtue; in another it made itself hated by some for what it was doing, by the remainder for not doing it more effectively.

There was in all this a curious mixture of three, fundamental human features — irony, tragedy, and absurdity: irony in the status of a nation that unveiled its growing impotence in its hour of greatest strength; tragedy in the behavior of a nation whose indisputable dedication to peace was expressed in policies of brinksmanship and military intervention; and absurdity in the situation of a nation that was transforming its international dreams into a latent domestic nightmare. As John W. Gardner forcefully put it in 1970:

> While each of us pursues his selfish interest and comforts himself by blaming others, the nation disintegrates. . . . Nothing we are doing to help or harm our friends or foe in Southeast Asia can compare to what we are doing to ourselves as a nation. The erosion of spirit that we have experienced is beyond calculation. Weighed against that erosion, any geopolitical advantage in the war must seem as pitifully small.[21]

Entering the seventies, the enemy had become more elusive than ever as one sought the solutions that would reverse an erosion of national spirit that foreign policy had been instrumental in bringing to surface.

But also entering the seventies, the meaning of the Vietnam debate for the future was itself very elusive. That the public generally wanted no more Vietnams was not surprising. They had also wanted no more Koreas many years before they "discovered" Vietnam. To be sure, in another time and at another place another administration might find it more difficult than before to justify another American intervention along the usual lines of self-determination and American security. More difficult but not impossible, and it appeared hazardous to predict how much America's disenchantment with its foreign policy (especially if it was perceived from the Vietnam experience) would survive the war proper. If it did not, then the debate would have probably been held in vain. If it did, then, in 1971, the real Vietnam debate was only beginning.

Yet, the limits of this debate were elusive too. Given America's power there was little room for self-retrenchment: America's participation in world affairs had finally been decided by history. But given the nature of power in the nuclear age, few options were available for radical solutions. Perhaps the "new" diplomacy was no more than an exercise in futile agitation as it lent itself to few lasting penalties and still fewer lasting rewards.

Any withdrawal by a major power such as the United States would be heavy of consequences, obviously difficult to foresee, probably difficult to control. In George Liska's words, "some positive reactions in the domain of self-reliance, are possible; but many more negative repercussions, in the domain of expansion of rivals, and defeatism of friends and dependents, are certain." [22] This area of "negative repercussions" was particularly dangerous, and it would have to be defined with special caution. Assuming, as Liska did, that the vastness of America's imperial commitments had provided the United States for twenty years with a new margin of error, such margin now appeared to have been exhausted by the Vietnam War. For this war had seemingly shown that a war started at the periphery of the empire could actually come and tear the very fabric of national life: would it be that the Vietnam War actually demonstrated that peace could indeed be divisible though *war* had become indivisible inasmuch as, in the future, war abroad might also mean war at home?

When withdrawal was mentioned, it was based upon the extension of regional balances (especially in Europe and in Asia) that would be set to contain the expansive states of the area (especially Russia and China). Western Europe (grouped around Bonn, Paris, London, or any combination of these) and Japan might be delegated a share in America's imperial responsibilities.

Conceived as such, though, America's withdrawal would still be minimal: in Europe as well as in Asia, America's representatives would continue to draw much of their deterring capability from the credibility of America's guarantee to come to the rescue should deterrence fail. Besides, what would happen if both the contained state and the containing state (or states) were to get together in an alliance aimed (directly or not) at America?

A critique of America's foreign policy is at its best when it deals with the past. The analyst can weave a dialogue between himself and recent history, condemn what has failed and, occasionally, praise what has succeeded. Although it can be used as an avenue to direction, criticism can not be used as a substitute for direction because ultimately its guidelines are, when translated into practice, as ambiguous as those they are supposed to replace.

Explicitly or not, the criticism of America's foreign policy made during the Vietnam War raised the same two questions that in one way or another the United States had attempted to resolve throughout its history. First, what were America's vital interests: did they extend to the whole international community or did they end with the Western Hemisphere? Second, assuming a common understanding of these interests, were they actually threatened — how and by whom?

But the Vietnam War added two new questions, both related to the collapse of America's national illusions and, to some extent, the end of the public's innocence. First, assuming that one knew what these interests were, and how and against whom they needed to be safeguarded, could they be preserved at all? The illusion of omnipotence, which had previously made such a question useless to ask, might ultimately give way to a no less dangerous illusion of impotence. Such a growing feeling of impotence had been apparent when, during America's foray into Cambodia, Nixon's announcement was received with an air of déjà vu, and, whether for or against the ensuing demonstrations, much of the general public assumed the worst. The other question that Vietnam helped raise again was that of America's purpose and the ways in which it could be achieved. Gone was the belief that good intentions purified any action that might be undertaken in their name. Dramatically, Senator Gravel, a war

critic from Alaska, deplored the fall of "the greatest representative democracy the world has ever known" into "the swamp [of]
petty war lords, jealous Vietnamese generals, black marketeers
and grand scale dope pushers." [23] "The irony — and to some the
tragedy — " wrote Robert W. Tucker in a more measured manner,
"of America's position today is that at the height of her power
her purpose has become irrelevant to most of the world." [24]

   Increasingly irrelevant because increasingly ill defined, and
it was no less ironical, and tragic, that America's "new" purpose
was best outlined by those who endorsed the war most. To
George Liska, for example, there was no need for national self-
pity. Interpreting the war as a police operation — the first imperial war of the United States fought at the remote frontier of
the empire — Liska warned:

> If the United States come out of the military confrontation in
> Asia and out of the diplomatic confrontation in Europe with a
> sharpened sense of how to differentiate its role and distribute the
> various components of national power in the different areas of
> the world, it will have ascended to the crucial and perhaps last
> step toward the plateau of maturity. It will then have . . . be-
> come a true empire — a strong and salient power with the sense
> of a task exceeding its national limits but not its national re-
> sources . . . the primary power in the relevant world [whose
> task would be] to supervise . . . primarily a nuclear peace,
> even if on the subnuclear level the world order may have to be
> to a large extent an American order.[25]

   Such an inability of the critics to provide answers to the
questions that they themselves raised pointed to the worst in
them — an inability to deal with the future. For when the critique
of the past was completed, a modicum of consensus slowly re-
emerged. Remarkably, many critics and apologists alike ultimately agreed that besides the obvious objective of avoiding
nuclear confrontation, United States policy still must be to maintain a balance of power in Europe and in Asia; that some containment of Russia and China still must be organized (although
there was wide disagreement over the forms such containment
might take); that the Western Hemisphere was still of paramount
importance to the United States; and that America still must
overlook the general evolution of the underdeveloped countries.

In short, the critics, like the apologists, restricted the manner in which change might occur within the international system and precluded some change altogether.

A confusing debate that had stemmed from a confusing war at a confusing time would probably lead to a confusing lesson too. Confusing because of its obvious simplicity, such a lesson told the public that it was high time for America to step down from its pedestal, renounce its self-righteousness, and contain its grandiosity — in short such a lesson taught the public that America as a nation was neither better nor worse than others, troubled friends and elusive enemies alike.

Notes

Chapter One: The Protracted Debate

[1] Raymond Aron, "Reflections on American Diplomacy," *Daedalus* (Fall 1962), p. 719.

[2] Daniel Conway, ed., *The Writings of Thomas Paine* (New York: G. P. Putnam's Sons, 1894–96), Vol. 1, p. 88.

[3] Arnold Wolfers and Lawrence W. Martin, eds., *The Anglo-American Tradition in Foreign Affairs* (New Haven: Yale University Press, 1956), p. 162.

[4] *Ibid.*, p. 161.

[5] Samuel Eliot Morison, et al., *Dissent in Three American Wars* (Cambridge, Mass.: Harvard University Press, 1970), p. 3.

[6] Quoted in Paul A. Varg, *Foreign Policies of the Founding Fathers* (Baltimore: Penguin Books, 1970), p. 160.

[7] From an Address of the Minority of the House of Representatives to their Constituents, 1812. In Dorothy B. Goebel, ed., *American Foreign Policy: A Documentary Survey, 1776–1960,* (New York: Holt, Rinehart and Winston, 1961), p. 52.

[8] Wolfers and Martin, eds., *op. cit.*, p. 162.

9 *Ibid.*, p. 145.

10 Selig Adler, *The Isolationist Impulse* (New York: Macmillian, 1957), p. 14.

11 From a Speech to the House of Representatives, January 19, 1824. In Goebel, ed., *op. cit.,* p. 70.

12 From a Speech to the House of Representatives, January 21, 1824. Cited in Goebel, ed., *op. cit.,* p. 72.

13 Adler, *op. cit.,* p. 15

14 For Clay's statement, see Goebel, ed., *op. cit.,* p. 93.

15 For a development of this theme see Thomas A. Bailey, "America's Emergence as a World Power: The Myth and the Verity," *Pacific Historical Review* (February 1961), pp. 1–16.

16 Quoted in *Ibid.*, p. 12.

17 See Wilson's Address to Congress Asking for Declaration of War, April 2, 1917. Albert Fried, ed., *A Day of Dedication: The Essential Writings and Speeches of Woodrow Wilson* (New York: Macmillian, 1965), pp. 301–10.

18 Wilson's Address on Fourteen Points, Fried, ed., *op. cit.,* p. 321.

19 Quoted in Robert E. Osgood, *Ideals and Self-Interest in America's Foreign Relations* (Chicago: The University of Chicago Press, 1953), p. 260.

20 Message to Congress, April 2, 1917. Fried, ed., *op. cit.,* p. 306.

21 Wilson's Address on Five Points, September 27, 1918. Fried, ed., *op. cit.,* pp. 334–39.

22 See Alexander de Conde, *The American Secretary of State* (New York: Praeger, 1962), pp. 65 ff.

23 Arthur H. Vandenberg, Jr., ed., *The Private Papers of Senator Vandenberg* (Boston: Houghton Mifflin, 1952), p. 10.

24 As quoted by Dean Acheson, Address before the Civic Federation of Dallas, June 13, 1950. *Department of State Bulletin,* Vol. XXII, p. 1038 (hereafter cited as *Bulletin*).

25 Harry S. Truman, *Memoirs* (Garden City, N. Y.: Doubleday, 1955), Vol. 1, p. 97.

26 The *New York Times,* February 26, 1971.

27 See, for instance, J. William Fulbright, *Old Myths and New Realities* (New York: Vintage Books, 1964) and *The Arrogance of Power* (New York: Vintage Books, 1967).

28 The *New York Times,* February 19, 1970.

29 Morison, *op. cit.,* p. 49.

30 See Reinhold Niebuhr, "The Foreign Policy of American Conservatism and Liberalism," in Reinhold Niebuhr, ed., *Christian Realism and Political Problems* (New York: Scribner's, 1953), pp. 58–64.

31 Walter Lippmann, *The Cold War: A Study in U.S. Foreign Policy* (New York: Harper and Row, 1947), pp. 21–3.

32 William Pfaff, "A Case Against Interventionism," in Irving Howe, ed., *A Dissenter's Guide to Foreign Policy* (Garden City, N. Y.: Doubleday, 1968), p. 95.

33 Richard Rovere, *Reflections on United States Policy* (London: Bodley Head, 1968), p. 43.

34 For a complete treatment of this period see Joseph M. Jones, *The*

Fifteen Weeks: An Inside Account of the Genesis of the Marshall Plan (New York: Viking Press, 1955).

35 Acheson's reaction is described, and his words are quoted in Jones, *op. cit.*, pp. 189–96.

36 Cited in Seyom Brown, *The Faces of Power: Constancy and Change in United States Foreign Policy from Truman to Johnson* (New York: Columbia University Press, 1968), p. 7.

37 Robert W. Tucker, *Nation or Empire? The Debate Over American Foreign Policy* (Baltimore: Johns Hopkins Press, 1968), p. 23.

38 Richard M. Pfeffer, ed., *No More Vietnams? The War and the Future of American Foreign Policy* (New York: Harper and Row, 1968), p. 13.

39 See Edmund Stillman and William Pfaff, *Power and Impotence: The Failure of America's Foreign Policy* (New York: Random House, 1966), p. 15.

40 Stanley Hoffmann, *Gulliver's Troubles, or the Setting of American Foreign Policy* (New York: McGraw-Hill, 1968), p. 110.

41 Pfeffer, ed., *op. cit.*, p. 123.

42 Address at Johns Hopkins University, April 7, 1965. *Bulletin*, Vol. LII, pp. 606–10.

43 Address to the Veterans of Foreign Wars, March 12, 1968. *Bulletin*, Vol. LVIII, p. 439.

44 Quoted in Osgood, *op. cit.*, p. 177.

45 Quoted in Stillman and Pfaff, *op. cit.*, p. 6.

46 *Ibid.*, p. 10.

47 Michael Harrington, "American Power in the Twentieth Century," in Howe, ed., *op. cit.*, pp. 9–10.

48 William A. Williams, *The Tragedy of American Diplomacy* (New York: Delta Books, 1961), p. 21.

49 Phrases used by President Kennedy and President Johnson, respectively. Quoted in Richard J. Barnet, *Intervention and Revolution: America's Confrontation with Insurgent Movements Around the World* (New York: World Publishing Company, 1968), p. 11.

50 Sorensen, *Kennedy* (New York: Harper and Row, 1965), p. 563.

51 From Acheson's address to the University of California, Berkeley, March 16, 1950. *Bulletin*, Vol. XXII, p. 477. Some of Acheson's most representative statements have been conveniently compiled by McGeorge Bundy, ed., *The Pattern of Responsibility* (Boston: Houghton Mifflin, 1951).

52 Cited in Williams, *op. cit.*, p. 63.

53 The first statement is quoted by Williams, *op. cit.*, p. 64. The second statement is quoted by Osgood, *op. cit.*, p. 176.

54 Address to the Veterans of Foreign Wars. *Bulletin, op. cit.*

55 The *New York Times*, June 5, 1969.

56 Quoted in Osgood, *op. cit.*, p. 177.

57 Address to the Veterans of Foreign Wars. *Bulletin, op. cit.*

58 Quoted in Samuel Flagg Bemis, *A Diplomatic History of the United States*, 4th Ed. (New York: Holt, Rinehart and Winston, 1955), p. 472.

59 From Acheson's remarks to the National Press Club, January 12, 1950. *Bulletin*, Vol. XXII, p. 114.

60 Michael Harrington, *op. cit.*, p. 23.

[61] Charles Burton Marshall, *The Exercise of Sovereignty* (Baltimore: Johns Hopkins Press, 1965), pp. 47 ff.

[62] See Pfaff, "A Case Against Interventionism," *op. cit.*, p. 95 ff.

Chapter Two: The Politics of Confrontation

[1] Harry S. Truman, *Memoirs* (Garden City, N.Y.: Doubleday, 1955), Vol. 1, p. 246.

[2] Quoted in John L. Snell, *Illusion and Necessity: The Diplomacy of the Global War, 1939–1945* (Boston: Houghton Mifflin, 1963), p. 212.

[3] As quoted by Winston Churchill, *Triumph and Tragedy* (Boston: Houghton Mifflin, 1953), p. 355.

[4] Churchill, *The Hinge of Fate* (Boston: Houghton Mifflin, 1950), p. 935.

[5] Milovan Djilas, *Conversations with Stalin* (New York: Harvest Book, 1962), pp. 73–4.

[6] Churchill, *The Hinge of Fate, op. cit.*, pp. 745 ff.

[7] A. J. P. Taylor, *The Origins of the Second World War* (New York: Premier Books, 1963), pp. 158 ff.

[8] Churchill, *Triumph and Tragedy, op. cit.*, p. 364.

[9] Quoted in Chester Wilmot, *The Struggle for Europe* (London: Collins, 1952), p. 578.

[10] Quoted in Adam B. Ulam, *Expansion and Coexistence: The History of Soviet Foreign Policy* (New York: Praeger, 1968), p. 381.

[11] Truman, *op. cit.*, Vol. 1, p. 91.

[12] Charles de Gaulle, *Mémoires d'Espoir* (Paris: Librairie Plon, 1959), p. 206. See also Truman, *op. cit.*, Vol. 1, pp. 88 ff.

[13] Cited in William N. Neumann, *After Victory: Churchill, Roosevelt, Stalin and the Making of the Peace* (New York: Harper and Row, 1969), p. 90.

[14] Arthur H. Vandenberg, Jr., ed., *The Private Papers of Senator Vandenberg* (Boston: Houghton Mifflin, 1952), p. 175.

[15] Truman, *op. cit.*, Vol. 1, p. 78.

[16] Herbert Feis, *Churchill, Roosevelt and Stalin: The War They Waged and the Peace They Sought* (Princeton, N.J.: Princeton University Press, 1957), pp. 600, 636.

[17] Roosevelt's envoy to Moscow, Harry Hopkins, left Stalin convinced that Russia would not surrender in 1941. "There is unbounded determination to win," he cabled Roosevelt. Cited in Robert Sherwood, *Roosevelt and Hopkins: An Intimate History* (New York: Harper and Row, 1950), pp. 339, 342–3. See also Robert A. Divine, *Roosevelt and World War II* (Baltimore: Penguin Books, 1970), pp. 80–3.

[18] Quoted in D. F. Fleming, *The Cold War and its Origins* (Garden City, N.Y.: Doubleday, 1961), p. 135.

[19] Truman, *op. cit.*, Vol. 1, p. 360.

[20] Quoted in Herbert Feis, *The Atomic Bomb and the End of World War II* (Princeton, N.J.: Princeton University Press, 1966), p. 87. Feis, however, does not believe that Churchill's perception of Truman's mood is justified by the minutes of the Potsdam Conference.

21 Truman, *op. cit.*, Vol. 1, p. 50.

22 *Ibid.*, Vol. 1, p. 71.

23 *Ibid.*, Vol. 2, p. 1.

24 Quoted in Walter LaFeber, *America, Russia and the Cold War* (New York: John Wiley, 1967), p. 62.

25 Robert A. Divine, *op. cit.*, p. 22.

26 See, for example, George Kennan's recollections in his *Memoirs, 1925–1950* (Boston: Atlantic-Little, Brown, 1967), *passim.*

27 William Langer and Everett Gleason, *The Undeclared War, 1940– 1941* (New York: Harper and Row, 1952), pp. 537–38.

28 Truman, *op. cit.*, Vol. 1, p. 477.

29 Gar Alperovitz, *Atomic Diplomacy: Hiroshima and Potsdam* (New York: Vintage Books, 1967), pp. 43, 57.

30 Truman, *op. cit.*, Vol. 2, p. 1.

31 See General Hurley's testimony to the Senate Committees on Armed Services and Foreign Relations. U.S. Senate, *Hearings on the Military Situation in the Far East,* 82nd Congress, 1st Session (1951), pp. 2827–62.

32 *Ibid.*, pp. 2948–3053.

33 Edward Stettinius, *Roosevelt and the Russians: the Yalta Conference* (Garden City, N. Y.: Doubleday, 1949), p. 6.

34 Quoted in Martin Herz, *Beginnings of the Cold War* (New York: McGraw-Hill, 1969), p. 5.

35 U.S. Senate, *Military Situation in the Far East, op. cit.*, p. 58.

36 United States Strategic Bombing Survey, *The Campaigns of the Pacific War* (Washington, D.C.: Government Printing Office, 1946), pp. 323, 331.

37 Walter Millis, ed., *The Forrestal Diaries* (New York: Viking Press, 1951), p. 31.

38 Alperovitz, *op. cit.*, p. 31. This meeting worried both Stimson and Marshall who feared that the Russians might subsequently delay their entry into the Pacific war until, observed Marshall, America "had done all the dirty work." Feis, *The Atomic Bomb, op. cit.*, p. 36.

39 George Kennan, *Russia and the West under Lenin and Stalin* (Boston: Little, Brown, 1960), p. 354.

40 Truman, *op. cit.*, Vol. 1, p. 411.

41 As recalled by Stimson, "even the New Mexico test would not give final proof that any given bomb was certain to explode when dropped from an air plane." Henry Stimson and McGeorge Bundy, *On Active Service in Peace and War* (New York: Harper and Row, 1948), p. 617.

42 Barton J. Bernstein, ed., *The Truman Administration: A Documentary History* (New York: Harper and Row, 1966), p. 8.

43 Truman, *op. cit.*, Vol. 1, p. 412.

44 From the Stimson Diary, August 10, 1945. Quoted in Alperovitz, *op. cit.*, p. 190.

45 Alexis de Tocqueville, *Democracy in America* (New York: Random House, Vintage Books, 1954), Vol. 1, p. 452. Cited in William P. Gerberding, *United States Foreign Policy: Perspective and Analysis* (New York: McGraw-Hill, 1966), p. 98.

46 George Liska, *Imperial America: the International Politics of Primacy* (Baltimore: Johns Hopkins Press, 1967), p. 5.

47 Ulam, *Expansion and Coexistence, op. cit.*, p. 448.

[48] Truman, *op. cit.*, Vol. 1, p. 87.

[49] *Ibid*, p. 421.

[50] Alexander Werth, *Russia at War: 1941–1945*, (New York: E. P. Dutton, 1964), p. 1004.

[51] Kennan, *Memoirs, op. cit.*, p. 241.

[52] Khrushchev's famous and posthumous attack on Stalin was delivered at a closed session of the Twentieth Party Congress in February, 1956. It appears in Robert V. Daniels, ed., *A Documentary History of Communism* (New York: Random House, 1962), Vol. 2, pp. 224–31.

[53] See Winston Churchill's own account of his agreement with Stalin in *Triumph and Tragedy, op. cit.*, pp. 226 ff.

[54] On postwar Eastern Europe, see Hugh Seton-Watson, *The East European Revolution*, 3rd Ed. (New York: Praeger, 1956), pp. 167–230.

[55] Quoted in Louis Halle, *The Cold War as History* (New York: Harper and Row, 1967), p. 53.

[56] Quoted in Gabriel Kolko, *The Politics of War: The World and United States Foreign Policy, 1943–1945* (New York: Random House, 1968), p. 471.

Chapter Three: Expansion and Containment

[1] Quoted in George Ball, *The Discipline of Power* (Boston: Little, Brown, 1968), p. 29.

[2] Louis Halle, *The Cold War as History* (New York: Harper and Row, 1967), p. 112.

[3] Marshall's speech, which served as a springboard for the plan bearing the general's name, was delivered at Harvard University, June 5, 1947. See *Department of State Bulletin* Vol. XVI, pp. 1159–60 (hereafter cited as *Bulletin*).

[4] Harry B. Price, *The Marshall Plan and its Meaning* (Ithaca, N.Y.: New York University Press, 1955), p. 31.

[5] Jacques Fauvet, *La IVème République* (Paris: Presses Fayard, 1960), pp. 32–3.

[6] Quoted in A. W. DePorte, *De Gaulle's Foreign Policy, 1944–1946* (Cambridge, Mass.: Harvard University Press, 1968), p. 80.

[7] Herbert Feis, *Roosevelt, Churchill and Stalin: The War They Waged and The Peace They Sought* (Princeton, N.J.: Princeton University Press, 1957), p. 477.

[8] The Anglo-Russian alliance of 1942 and the Franco-Russian alliance of 1944 were terminated in May 1955, following West Germany's admission into the Atlantic Alliance.

[9] See Simon Serfaty, *France, de Gaulle and Europe* (Baltimore: Johns Hopkins Press, 1968), pp. 27–49.

[10] On November 30, 1950, as the Chinese were launching their offensive in Korea, President Truman emphasized in a press conference that the United States would "take whatever steps are necessary to meet the military situation." He was then asked whether such steps would include the "active consideration of the use of the atomic bomb." "There has always been active consideration of its use," the American president replied. (Tru-

man, *Memoirs* [Garden City, N.Y.: Doubleday, 1955], Vol. 2, p. 419.) In fact the Joint Chiefs of Staff had already recommended against the use of atomic weapons in North Korea.

11 See Alfred Grosser, *La IVème République et sa Politique Extérieure* (Paris: Armand Colin, 1961), p. 221.

12 From Acheson's statement to the Senate Committee on Foreign Relations, August 8, 1949. Cited in Bundy, ed., *The Pattern of Responsibility* (Boston: Houghton Mifflin, 1951), p. 71.

13 Truman, *op. cit.*, Vol. 2, p. 380.

14 From a radio address, March 18, 1949. *Bulletin*, Vol. XX, p. 384.

15 X (George Kennan), "Sources of Soviet Conduct," *Foreign Affairs*, July 1947, pp. 556–82.

16 Kennan, *Memoirs* (Boston: Little, Brown, 1967), p. 358.

17 This is Kennan's own evaluation of his *Foreign Affairs* article. *Ibid.*, p. 359.

18 *Ibid.*, pp. 365–67. See also Joseph H. Jones, *The Fifteen Weeks* (New York: Viking Press, 1955), pp. 385–7.

19 Price, *op. cit.*, p. 88.

20 *Ibid.*, p. 399.

21 Quoted in Halle, *op. cit.*, p. 144.

22 Kennan, *Memoirs*, *op. cit.*, p. 337.

23 As reported in Price, *op. cit.*, p. 26.

24 In January 1948, for example, The *New York Times* ran a feature article entitled, "Kremlin, as usual, comes to the rescue of ERP" (European Recovery Program). Quoted in *ibid.*, p. 60.

25 *Ibid.*, p. 397.

26 Ulam, *Expansion and Coexistence* (New York: Praeger, 1968) p. 439. See also Marshall D. Schulman, *Stalin's Foreign Policy Reappraised* (Cambridge, Mass.: Harvard University Press, 1963).

27 In October 1948, for example, in response to the question: "What would you do if the Red Army occupied Paris?" Maurice Thorez, head of the French communist party, replied with a declaration of all-out support for the Russian army even if it should enter French territory. Schulman, *op. cit.*, p. 58.

28 John C. Campbell, ed., *The U.S. in World Affairs, 1948* (New York: Harper and Row, 1948), pp. 499–500.

29 Robert E. Osgood, *NATO, the Entangling Alliance* (Chicago: Chicago University Press, 1962), p. 23.

30 Lawrence S. Kaplan, ed., *NATO and the Policy of Containment* (Lexington, Mass.: D. C. Heath, 1962), p. 21.

31 From Acheson's radio address, March 18, 1949. *Bulletin*, Vol. XX, p. 387.

32 State Department, *American Foreign Policy, 1950–1955: Basic Documents*, Vol. 1 (General Foreign Policy Series 117), p. 836.

33 *Ibid.*, p. 843.

34 Osgood, *NATO, op. cit.*, p. 50.

35 As Acheson stated in the Senate Hearings on the Atlantic Alliance. See some extracts in Bundy, ed., *op. cit.*, p. 65.

36 See, for example, Acheson's statement to the Senate Foreign Relations Committee, February 8, 1949. Bundy, ed., *op. cit.*, p. 52.

37 Acheson's radio address, March 18, 1949. *Bulletin, op. cit.*, p. 384.

[38] Alexander Werth, *France, 1940–1955* (London: Readers Union, 1957), p. 315.

[39] From Acheson's news conference, December 22, 1950. *Bulletin,* Vol. XXIV, p. 3.

[40] Bundy, ed., *op. cit.,* p. 77.

[41] See Chapter 6, pp. 126–150.

[42] Senate Committee on Foreign Relations, U.S. Senate, *Hearings on the North Atlantic Treaty,* 81st Congress, 1st Session (1949), p. 47.

[43] See Raymond Aron and D. Lerner, eds., *France Defects EDC* (New York: Praeger, 1957).

[44] Richard P. Stebbins, ed., *The U.S. in World Affairs, 1950* (New York: Harper and Row, 1951), p. 269.

[45] Thomas W. Wolfe, *Soviet Power and Europe, 1945–1970* (Baltimore: Johns Hopkins Press, 1970), pp. 34–5.

Chapter Four: The Globalization of Containment

[1] Tang Tsou, *America's Failure in China, 1941–1950* (Chicago: Phoenix Books, 1963), p. 361.

[2] From Acheson's remarks to the National Press Club, January 12, 1950. *Department of State Bulletin,* Vol. XXII, p. 118 (hereafter cited as *Bulletin*).

[3] Truman, *Memoirs* (Garden City, N.Y.: Doubleday, 1955), Vol. 2, p. 61.

[4] See more particularly Acheson's statement before the Senate Committees on Armed Services and Foreign Relations. U.S. Senate, *Hearings on the Military Situation in the Far East,* 82nd Congress, 1st Session (June 4, 1951), pp. 1838–57.

[5] *The China White Paper,* August 1949 (Stanford: Stanford University Press, 1967), p. 311. Originally issued as *United State Relations with China,* Department of State Publication, 1949.

[6] *Ibid.,* p. 315.

[7] For example, Wang Ping-nan, then a CCP press officer in Chungking and later China's ambassador in Warsaw, declared in November 1946: "It's all right for the United States to arm the Kuomintang because as fast as they get it we take it away from them." Quoted in John Melby, *Mandate of Heaven: Record of a Civil War, China 1945–1949* (Toronto: Toronto University Press, 1968), p. 36.

[8] U.S. Senate, *Military Situation in the Far East, op. cit.,* pp. 1838–57.

[9] Truman, *op. cit.,* Vol. 1, pp. 507–9. Tang Tsou, *op. cit.,* pp. 365–6.

[10] On September 13, 1943, for example, in addressing the Kuomintang Central Executive Committee, Chiang said: "We should clearly recognize that the Chinese communist problem is a purely political problem and should be solved by political means." *The China White Paper, op. cit.,* p. 530.

[11] Quoted by Acheson in U.S. Senate, *Military Situation in the Far East, op. cit.,* pp. 1838–57.

[12] *Ibid.*

13 From Ambassador Stuart's report to Secretary Marshall, August 10, 1948. *The China White Paper, op. cit.,* pp. 885–6.

14 Truman, *op. cit.,* Vol. 2, pp. 67–8.

15 Tang Tsou, *op. cit.,* pp. 356–7.

16 *The China White Paper, op. cit.,* p. 886.

17 *Ibid.,* p. xvi.

18 From Acheson's remarks to the National Press Club, January 12, 1950. *Bulletin,* Vol. XXII, p. 115.

19 Truman, *op. cit.,* Vol. 1, pp. 316–7.

20 *Ibid.,* Vol. 1, p. 445. Russian forces reached Korea on August 12 while American forces only landed in Korea by September 8.

21 John W. Spanier, *The Truman-MacArthur Controversy and the Korean War* (Cambridge, Mass.: Harvard University Press, 1959; Norton Library Edition, 1965), p. 16.

22 Acheson, *Present at the Creation* (New York: W. W. Norton, 1969), p. 405.

23 See, for example, Marshall's senate testimony of May 7, 1951. U.S. Senate, *Military Situation in the Far East, op. cit.,* p. 373.

24 On China's motivation in entering the Korean War, see particularly Allen S. Whiting, *China Crosses the Yalu* (New York: Macmillan, 1960).

25 On the earlier phase of the Sino-Soviet split, see Conrad Brandt, *Stalin's Failure in China, 1926–1927* (Cambridge, Mass.: Harvard University Press, 1958).

26 Quoted in Tang Tsou, *op. cit.,* p. 572. See also David Rees, *Korea: The Limited War* (Baltimore: Penguin Books, 1970), p. 107.

27 According, for example, to Allen S. Whiting, *op. cit.,* p. 124.

28 Tang Tsou, *op. cit.,* p. 576.

29 U.S. Senate, *Military Situation in the Far East, op. cit.,* p. 75.

30 Whiting, *op. cit.,* p. 45.

31 Truman, *op. cit.,* Vol. 2, p. 329.

32 Kennan, *Memoirs* (Boston: Little, Brown, 1967), p. 238.

33 Truman, *op. cit.,* Vol. 2, p. 333.

34 *Ibid.,* Vol. 1, p. 289.

35 Rees, *op. cit.,* pp. 32–3.

36 U.S. Senate, *Military Situation in the Far East, op. cit.,* p. 10

37 From his statement to the Senate Committees on Armed Services and Foreign Relations, February 16, 1951. Cited in Bundy, ed., *The Pattern of Responsibility* (Boston: Houghton Mifflin, 1951), p. 93.

38 For an early analysis of Washington's reaction to the outbreak of the Korean War, see Alexander C. George, "American Policy Making and the North Korean Aggression," *World Politics,* January 1955, pp. 209–32.

39 See Whiting, *op. cit.,* pp. 37–8.

40 Quoted in Tang Tsou, *op. cit.,* pp. 557–8.

41 From Acheson's address to the General Assembly of the United Nations, September 20, 1950. *Bulletin,* Vol. XXIII, p. 524.

42 Truman, *op. cit.,* Vol. 2, p. 341.

43 In a television interview on September 10, 1950. *Bulletin,* Vol. XXIII, p. 463.

44 U.S. Senate, *Military Situation in the Far East, op. cit.,* p. 397.

45 See Bernard Brodie's comments on this "odd idea" in *Strategy in the Missile Age* (Princeton, N.J.: Princeton University Press, 1959), p. 319.

46 Spanier, *op. cit.*, p. 28.

47 Quoted in Tang Tsou, *op. cit.*, p. 576. See also Rees, *op. cit.*, pp. 106–7.

48 As indicated by Secretary of Defense Marshall. U.S. Senate, *Military Situation in the Far East*, *op. cit.*, p. 359. See also Truman, *op. cit.*, Vol. 2, pp. 380–2.

49 Truman, *op. cit.*, Vol. 2, p. 343.

50 Besides Spanier, *op. cit.*, see Arthur M. Schlesinger, Jr., and Richard Rovere, *The General and the President* (New York: Farrar, Straus and Giroux, 1951).

51 Truman, *op. cit.*, Vol. 1, p. 210.

52 MacArthur's speech may be found in U.S. Senate, *Military Situation in the Far East*, *op. cit.*, pp. 2553–8.

53 *Ibid.*, p. 207.

54 *Ibid.*, p. 68.

55 *Ibid.*, p. 1720.

56 *Ibid.*, pp. 6, 130.

57 *Ibid.*, p. 9.

58 *Ibid.*, pp. 103 and 29, respectively.

59 *Ibid.*, p. 490.

60 *Ibid.*, p. 732 (from General Bradley's testimony).

61 *Ibid.*, p. 42.

62 Truman, *op. cit.*, Vol. 2, p. 444.

63 *Ibid.*, Vol. 2, p. 449.

64 U.S. Senate, *Military Situation in the Far East*, *op. cit.*, p. 13.

65 *Ibid.*, p. 370 (from Marshall's testimony). For MacArthur's comments see his own *Reminiscences* (New York: McGraw-Hill, 1964), p. 377.

66 As reported by Truman, *op. cit.*, Vol. 2, pp. 351–353.

67 U.S. Senate, *Military Situation in the Far East*, *op. cit.*, p. 100.

68 From remarks made on two occasions in February 1950. Cited in Bundy, ed., *op. cit.*, p. 30.

69 U.S. Senate, *Military Situation in the Far East*, *op. cit.*, p. 263.

70 State Department, *American Foreign Policy, 1950–1955: Basic Documents*, Vol. 1 (General Foreign Policy Series 117), p. 911.

Chapter Five: The Irony of Power

1 Hull poured out his grievances to Breckinridge Long on September 30, 1945. Fred L. Israel, ed., *The War Diary of Breckinridge Long* (Lincoln, Neb.: University of Nebraska Press, 1966), pp. 386–8.

2 Dean Acheson, "The Eclipse of the State Department," *Foreign Affairs* (July 1971), p. 601.

3 Dean Acheson, *Present at the Creation* (New York: W. W. Norton, 1969), p. 213.

4 Truman, *Memoirs* (Garden City, N.Y.: Doubleday, 1955), Vol. 1, p. 551.

5 *Ibid.*, Vol. 1, p. 546.

6 Joseph Kraft, "In Search of Kissinger," *Harper's* (January 1971), p. 54.

7 Quoted in Emmet John Hughes, *The Ordeal of Power: A Political Memoir of the Eisenhower Years* (London: Macmillian, 1963), p. 254.

8 *Ibid.,* p. 157.

9 Quoted in Robert Goold-Adams, *The Time of Power: A Reappraisal of John Foster Dulles* (London: Weidenfield and Nicolson, 1962), p. 264.

10 Sherman Adams, *Firsthand Report: The Story of the Eisenhower Administration* (New York: Harper and Row, 1961), pp. 87–91. Such surveillance, suggests Adams, was maintained by Dulles from his sickbed even when it became apparent that he would never be able to return to his office.

11 *Ibid.,* p. 89.

12 Quoted in John Beale, *John Foster Dulles: 1888–1959* (New York: Harper and Row, 1959), p. 310.

13 *Ibid.,* p. 156, and Hans J. Morgenthau, "John Foster Dulles," in Norman A. Graebner, ed., *An Uncertain Tradition: American Secretaries of State in the Twentieth Century* (New York: McGraw-Hill, 1961), p. 305.

14 Quoted in Ole Holsti, et al., *Enemies in Politics* (Chicago: Rand McNally, 1967), p. 40.

15 Quoted in Michael A. Guhin, "Dulles' Thoughts on International Politics: Myth and Reality," *Orbis* (Fall 1969), pp. 865–90.

16 Dulles, "Security in the Pacific," *Foreign Affairs* (January 1952), p. 183.

17 Dulles, *War, Peace and Change* (London: Macmillan, 1939), p. 47.

18 Quoted by Hughes, *op. cit.,* pp. 208–9.

19 Address of October 15, 1956. The *New York Times,* October 15, 1956.

20 Dulles, *War, Peace and Change, op. cit.,* pp. 266–7.

21 Speech made in New York, January 25, 1954. *Department of State Bulletin,* Vol. XXX, p. 110 (hereafter cited as *Bulletin*).

22 David Heller and Deane Heller, *John Foster Dulles: Soldier of Peace* (New York: Holt, Rinehart and Winston, 1960), p. 41.

23 In a broadcast made in Great Britain, October 23, 1958. *Bulletin,* Vol. XXXIX, p. 734.

24 Hughes, *op. cit.,* p. 109.

25 *Ibid.,* p. 137 (emphasis in the original).

26 News conference, May 15, 1956. *Bulletin,* Vol. XXIV, p. 885.

27 Quoted in Hughes, *op. cit.,* pp. 104–5.

28 Reported by Goold-Adams, *op. cit.,* p. 303.

29 Senate Committee on Foreign Relations, *Hearings* (February 24, 1956), p. 19. Quoted in Holsti, *op. cit.,* p. 65.

30 Quoted in *ibid.,* pp. 66–7.

31 Guhin, *op. cit.,* p. 888.

32 Goold-Adams, *op. cit.,* p. 305.

33 See Richard Rovere, *Senator Joe McCarthy* (New York: Harcourt Brace Jovanovich, 1959).

34 Quoted in Acheson, *Present at the Creation, op. cit.,* p. 365.

35 Louis L. Gerson, *The American Secretaries of State and their Di-*

plomacy: John Foster Dulles (New York: Cooper Square Publishers, 1967), p. 111.

[36] Message of January 21, 1953. *Bulletin,* Vol. XXVIII, p. 170.

[37] Richard P. Stebbins, ed., *The U.S. in World Affairs, 1953* (New York: Harper and Row, 1955), pp. 18–22.

[38] See Dulles' article in *Life,* May 19, 1952.

[39] Stebbins, ed., *op. cit.,* pp. 16–7.

[40] Quoted in Coral Bell, *Negotiations from Strength, op. cit.,* p. 89.

[41] Beale, *op. cit.,* p. 313.

[42] Roscoe Drummond and Gaston Coblentz, *Duel at the Brink: John Foster Dulles' Command of American Power* (Garden City, N.Y.: Doubleday, 1960), p. 88.

[43] See, for example, Paul Kecskemeti, *The Unexpected Revolution* (Stanford: Stanford University Press, 1961) and Raymond L. Garthoff, *Soviet Military Policy: a Historical Analysis* (New York: Praeger, 1966), pp. 155–72.

[44] Hughes, *op. cit.,* p. 178.

[45] Robert Murphy, *Diplomat Among Warriors* (London: Collins, 1964), p. 526.

[46] Hughes, *op. cit.,* p. 217 (emphasis in the original).

[47] James Shepley, "How Dulles Averted War," *Life* (January 16, 1956).

[48] Dulles, *War, Peace and Change, op. cit.,* p. 317.

[49] Quoted in Beale, *op. cit.,* p. 317.

[50] Dulles, *War, Peace and Change, op. cit.,* p. 90.

[51] Andrew Berding, *Dulles on Diplomacy* (Princeton, N.J.: Van Norstrand, 1965), p. 23.

[52] Goold-Adams, *op. cit.,* pp. 74, 102.

[53] See Chapter 8, pp. 180–2.

[54] Tang Tsou, *The Embroilment over Quemoy: Mao, Chiang and Dulles* (Salt Lake City: University of Utah, Institute of International Studies, International Study Paper No. 2, 1959).

[55] Goold-Adams, *op. cit.,* pp. 161, 171, 286.

[56] *Ibid.,* p. 209.

[57] See Dulles' address entitled "The Evolution of Foreign Policy," January 12, 1954. *Bulletin,* Vol. XXX, pp. 107–10.

[58] Dulles, "Policy for Security and Peace," *Foreign Affairs* (April 1954), p. 359.

[59] The "classic" critique of Dulles' massive retaliation position is presented by William W. Kaufmann, *Military Policy and National Security* (Princeton, N.J.: Princeton University Press, 1956), pp. 12–38.

[60] *Strategy in the Missile Age, op. cit.,* pp. 223 ff.

[61] From Acheson's statement to the senate on the relief of General MacArthur, U.S. Senate, *Military Situation in the Far East,* 82nd Congress, 1st Session (June 4, 1951), p. 1720.

[62] Address at the University of California, Berkeley, March 16, 1950. *Bulletin,* Vol. XXXIII, p. 474.

[63] See James L. Payne, *The American Threat: The Fear of War as an Instrument of Foreign Policy* (Chicago: Markham Publishing, 1970), pp. 22 ff.

[64] Quoted in Goold-Adams, *op. cit.,* p. 131.

65 Dulles, "Challenge and Response in United States Policy," *Foreign Affairs* (October, 1957), pp. 25–56.

Chapter Six: The End of Alliances?

1 On this question see George Liska, *Nations in Alliance: The Limits of Interdependence* (Baltimore: Johns Hopkins Press, 1962), Part I.

2 Alistair Buchan, "The Future of NATO," *International Conciliation* (November, 1967), p. 5.

3 Adam Ulam, *Expansion and Coexistence* (New York: Praeger, 1968), p. 634.

4 Thomas W. Wolfe, *Soviet Power and Europe* (Baltimore: Johns Hopkins Press, 1970), p. 85. See also Arnold L. Horelick and Myron Rush, *Strategic Power and Soviet Foreign Policy* (Chicago: The Chicago University Press, 1966).

5 Ulam, *op. cit.*, p. 656.

6 Wolfe, *op. cit.*, p. 86.

7 Michel Tatu, *Power in the Kremlin: From Khrushchev to Kosygin* (New York: Viking Press, 1970), pp. 241–2.

8 The *New York Times,* October 23, 1962.

9 See Elie Abel, *The Missile Crisis* (Philadelphia: Lippincott, 1966) and Robert F. Kennedy, *Thirteen Days: A Memoir of the Cuban Missile Crisis* (New York: W. W. Norton, 1969).

10 Ulam, *op. cit.*, p. 677.

11 Arthur Schlesinger, Jr., *A Thousand Days: John F. Kennedy in the White House* (Boston: Houghton Mifflin, 1965), p. 872.

12 See, for example, Robert L. Pfaltzgraff, Jr., "The Czechoslovak Crisis and The Future of the Atlantic Alliance," *Orbis* (Spring 1969), pp. 210–22.

13 More on Nixon's policy toward the Atlantic Alliance in Chapter 9, pp. 207–9.

14 Pierre Hassner, *Les deux Europes et les deux grands* (Paris: Centre d'Étude de Relations Internationales, Institut des Sciences Politiques, 1966).

15 Stanley Hoffmann, *Gulliver's Troubles* (New York: McGraw-Hill, 1968), p. 410.

16 George Ball, "NATO and World Responsibility," *The Atlantic Community Quarterly* (Summer 1964), p. 215.

17 See, for example, George Kennan, *Russia, the Atom and the West* (London: Oxford University Press, 1958). For a reply to Kennan, see Dean Acheson, "The Ilusion of Disengagement," *Foreign Affairs* (April 1958), p. 371–83.

18 The *New York Times,* June 26, 1963.

19 Hearings on his nomination as secretary of state, Senate Foreign Relations Committee, April 21, 1959, p. 10.

20 News conference of May 15, 1962.

21 For a further discussion of this question, see Chapter 7, pp. 159–66.

22 The main rationale for the new strategy was first delivered publicly by Secretary McNamara at Ann Arbor, Michigan, June 16, 1962. *Bulletin,* Vol. XLVII, pp. 64–9.

23 Address before the Fellows of the American Bar Foundation, Chicago, February 17, 1962.

24 Remarks to the Institute for Strategic Studies, London, December 11, 1961. Quoted in William W. Kaufmann, *The McNamara Strategy* (New York: Harper and Row, 1964), p. 109.

25 Address to editors of United Press International, San Francisco, September 18, 1967. The *New York Times,* September 19, 1967.

26 In McNamara's address at Ann Arbor, Michigan. *Bulletin, op. cit.*

27 Address before the Fellows of the American Bar Foundation, *op. cit.*

28 Quoted in William W. Kaufmann, *Military Policy and National Security* (Princeton, N.J.: Princeton University Press, 1956), p. 59.

29 *Ibid.,* p. 105.

30 Quoted in Seyom Brown, *The Faces of Power* (New York: Columbia University Press, 1968), p. 176.

31 Quoted in Seymour T. Deitchman, *Limited War and American Defense Policy,* 2nd Ed. (Cambridge, Mass.: Massachusetts Institute of Technology, 1969), p. 5.

32 De Gaulle's press conference of November 10, 1962, The *New York Times,* November 11, 1962.

33 Kissinger, *The Troubled Partnership* (New York: McGraw-Hill, 1965).

34 Simon Serfaty, *France, de Gaulle and Europe* (Baltimore: Johns Hopkins Press, 1968), p. 144.

35 See Lawrence Scheinman, *Atomic Energy in France under the Fourth Republic* (Princeton, N.J.: Princeton University Press, 1965).

36 See Kissinger, *The Troubled Partnership, op. cit.,* pp. 129–62. The case for the MLF is concisely presented by Robert E. Osgood, *The Case for the MLF: A Critical Evaluation* (Washington, D.C.: The Washington Center of Foreign Policy Research, 1964).

37 Serfaty, *op. cit.,* p. 128.

38 Arthur Schlesinger, Jr., *op. cit.,* p. 872.

39 De Gaulle, *Mémoires d'Espoir: Le Renouveau, 1958–1962,* Vol. 1 (Paris: Librairie Plon, 1970), pp. 214 ff.

40 Kissinger, *op. cit.,* p. 223–34.

41 John F. Kennedy, "The Goal of an Atlantic Partnership," July 4, 1962. *Bulletin,* Vol. XLVII, pp. 131–3.

42 Serfaty, *op. cit.,* p. 51 ff.

43 George Ball, "U.S. Policy Toward NATO," in Karl Cerny and C. W. Briefs, eds., *NATO in Quest of Cohesion* (New York: Praeger, 1965), p. 18.

Chapter Seven: The End of Security?

1 Robert S. McNamara, *The Essence of Security: Reflections in Office* (New York: Harper and Row, 1968), p. 52.

2 Charles Murphy, "The White House Since Sputnik," *Fortune* (January 1958), pp. 98–101.

[3] George H. Quester, *Nuclear Diplomacy* (New York: Dunellen Company, 1970), p. 160.

[4] McNamara, *op. cit.,* p. 58.

[5] Stuart Symington, "Where the Missile Gap Went," *The Reporter* (February 15, 1962), pp. 21–3.

[6] McNamara, *op. cit.,* p. 57.

[7] Thomas W. Wolfe, *Soviet Power and Europe* (Baltimore: Johns Hopkins Press, 1970), pp. 84 ff.

[8] *Ibid.,* p. 60.

[9] Roman Kolkowicz, et al., *The Soviet Union and Arms Control: A Superpower Dilemma* (Baltimore: Johns Hopkins Press, 1970), p. 29.

[10] Truman, *Memoirs* (Garden City, N.Y.: Doubleday, 1955), Vol. 2, p. 294.

[11] Walter Millis, ed., *The Forrestal Diaries* (New York: Viking Press, 1951), pp. 94–6.

[12] On September 21, at the last cabinet meeting attended by Stimson, the proposal of the secretary of war was supported by acting Secretary of State Dean Acheson, Undersecretary of War Robert Patterson, and Secretary of Commerce Henry Wallace. Opposed to it were notably Secretary of the Treasury Fred Vinson, Attorney General Thomas Clark, and Secretary of the Navy James Forrestal. Truman, *op. cit.,* Vol. 1, pp. 525–7.

[13] Richard G. Hewlett and Oscar E. Anderson, Jr., *The New World: 1939–1946* (University Park, Pa.: Pennsylvania State University Press, 1962), p. 416.

[14] Henry L. Stimson and McGeorge Bundy, *On Active Service in Peace and War* (New York: Harper and Row, 1948), pp. 642–6.

[15] Truman, *op. cit.,* Vol. 1, p. 87.

[16] James Byrnes, *Speaking Frankly* (New York: Harper and Row, 1947), p. 275.

[17] Hewlett and Anderson, *op. cit.,* p. 417.

[18] Byrnes, *op. cit.,* p. 261.

[19] On the Baruch Plan, see Hewlett and Anderson, *op. cit.,* pp. 531–619.

[20] Quoted in Hewlett and Anderson, *op. cit.,* p. 461.

[21] Quoted in Walter Lafeber, *America, Russia and the Cold War* (New York: John Wiley, 1967), p. 35.

[22] Inis L. Claude, Jr., *Swords into Plowshares: The Problems and Progress of International Organization* (New York: Random House, 1959), p. 317.

[23] Quester, *op. cit.,* p. 20.

[24] Truman, *op. cit.,* Vol. 2, p. 306.

[25] The *New York Times,* March 15, 1969.

[26] Quoted in D. F. Fleming, *The Cold War and Its Origins* (Garden City, N.Y.: Doubleday, 1961), p. 487.

[27] Richard Rosecrance, *Problems of Nuclear Proliferation,* Security Studies Project, University of California, Los Angeles (1966), p. 12.

[28] A. Buchan, ed., *A World of Nuclear Powers?* (Englewood Cliffs, N.J.: Prentice-Hall, 1966), p. 9.

[29] See, for example, Pierre Gallois, *The Balance of Terror* (Boston: Houghton Mifflin, 1961).

30 See, for example, André Beaufre, *Deterrence and Strategy* (New York: Praeger, 1965).

31 News conference of July 23, 1964, French Embassy. *Speeches and Press Conferences*, No. 208, p. 7.

32 Speech of September 30, 1963. André Passeron, *De Gaulle Parle, 1962–1966* (Paris: Fayard, 1966), p. 220.

33 Arthur Schlesinger, Jr., *A Thousand Days* (Boston: Houghton Mifflin, 1965), p. 897.

34 Quoted in *ibid.*, p. 853.

35 Raymond Aron, *Peace and War Among Nations* (Garden City, N.Y.: Doubleday, 1966), pp. 441 ff.

36 The *New York Times*, October 19, 1964.

37 See Nixon's "State of the World Message," The *New York Times*, February 19, 1970.

38 Schlesinger, *op. cit.*, p. 895.

39 *Ibid.*, pp. 915–6.

40 MIRV is described as a system of multiple warheads carried by one reentry vehicle (ICBM's, etc.) that can be maneuvered on independent courses to separate targets. Three-warhead Minuteman 3 began to be deployed by the United States in the summer of 1970: the first Poseidon-armed submarine (with each Poseidon missile capable of carrying ten warheads) was deployed in March 1971. FOBS is described as a system involving the delivery of nuclear weapons from low-altitude orbital trajectories. The advantage of FOBS is a more difficult detection thanks to a trajectory that is lower than that of ICBM's. Disadvantages, however, include a smaller payload and poorer accuracy.

41 Roger Hilsman, *To Move a Nation* (Garden City, N.Y.: Doubleday, 1967), p. 128.

42 Albert Wohlstetter, "The Delicate Balance of Terror," *Foreign Affairs* (January 1959), pp. 211–35.

43 Herman Kahn, "The Nature and Feasibility of War and Deterrence," in Walter Hahn and John C. Neff, eds., *American Strategy for the Nuclear Age* (Garden City, N.Y.: Doubleday, 1960), p. 230.

44 See Jerome B. Wiesner, et al., eds., *ABM; An Evaluation of the Decision to Deploy an Antiballistic Missile System* (New York: Signet Broadside, 1969), p. 4.

45 Robert S. McNamara, "The Dynamics of Nuclear Strategy," address delivered in San Francisco, September 18, 1967. *Bulletin*, Vol. LVII, pp. 443–51.

46 The *New York Times*, March 15, 1969.

47 Wiesner, eds., *op. cit.*, p. 3–60.

48 *Ibid.*, p. 14.

49 The *New York Times*, February 25, 1970.

50 Harry G. Gelber, "The Impact of Chinese ICBM's on Strategic Deterrence," *Orbis* (Summer 1969), p. 427.

51 The *New York Times*, February 2, 1970.

52 Gelber, *op. cit.*, p. 411.

53 McGeorge Bundy, "To Cap the Volcano," *Foreign Affairs* (October, 1969), pp. 1–21.

54 Lewis Carroll, *Alice's Adventures in Wonderland and Through the Looking Glass* (New York: Signet, 1960), p. 206.

Chapter Eight: The End of Illusions?

1 Cordell Hull, *Memoirs* (New York: Macmillan, 1948), Vol. 1, p. 904.

2 See George Kennan's testimony to the Senate Committee on Foreign Relations, February 10, 1966. *Vietnam Hearings* (New York: Vintage Books, 1966), p. 108.

3 Sumner Welles, *Seven Decisions that Shaped History* (New York: Harper and Row, 1951), p. 82.

4 Bernard Fall, *The Two Vietnams* (New York: Praeger, 1963), p. 45.

5 Hull, *op. cit.*, Vol. I, p. 913.

6 Fall, *op. cit.*, p. 46.

7 Elliot Roosevelt, *As He Saw It* (New York: Duell, Sloane and Pearce, 1945), pp. 74, 115.

8 *Ibid.*, p. 72.

9 *Ibid.*, p. 165.

10 Hull, *op. cit.*, Vol. II, p. 1597.

11 *Ibid.*, p. 1597. See also General Joseph W. Stilwell, *The Stilwell Papers* (New York: William Sloane, 1948), p. 246.

12 Fall, *op. cit.*, p. 53.

13 Philippe Devillers, *Histoire du Vietnam de 1940 a 1952* (Paris: Éditions du Seuil, 1952), pp. 122–5.

14 Admiral William D. Leahy, *I Was There* (New York: McGraw-Hill, 1950), pp. 338–9.

15 There are several good political biographies of Ho Chi Minh. See, for example, Jean Lacouture, *Ho Chi Minh* (New York: Random House, 1968).

16 Joseph Buttinger, *The Smaller Dragon: A Political History of Vietnam* (New York: Praeger, 1958), p. 231.

17 MacArthur is quoted in George McTurnan Kahin and John W. Lewis, *The United States in Vietnam* (New York: Dell Publishing Company, 1967), p. 24 (revised edition, 1969). This incident is well narrated in Ellen J. Hammer, *The Struggle for Indochina, 1940–1955: Vietnam and the French Experience* (Stanford: Stanford University Press, 1954), pp. 115–9 (paperbound edition, 1966).

18 Buttinger, *op. cit.*, p. 242.

19 On the agreement of March 1946, see Fall, *op. cit.*, pp. 74–7.

20 Richard P. Stebbins, ed., *The United States in World Affairs, 1954* (New York: Harper and Row, 1956), p. 256.

21 Fall, *op. cit.*, p. 129.

22 Truman, *Memoirs* (Garden City, N.Y.: Doubleday, 1955), Vol. 1, p. 15.

23 Hammer, *op. cit.*, pp. 250–1.

24 Buttinger, *op. cit.*, p. 361.

25 In the words of General de Lattre de Tassigny, then commander of the French troops, during an official visit in Washington in September 1950. French Embassy, *Service de Presse et d'Information* (September 20, 1951), p. 2.

26 Dean Acheson, *Present at the Creation* (New York: W. W. Norton, 1969), p. 639.

27 Truman, *op. cit.*, Vol. 2, pp. 381, 399.

28 Philippe Devillers and Jean Lacouture, *La Fin d'une Guerre* (Paris: Éditions du Seuil, 1960), p. 12.

29 Acheson, *op. cit.*, p. 674.

30 Dwight D. Eisenhower, *Mandate for Change, 1953–1956* (Garden City, N.Y.: Doubleday, 1963), p. 336.

31 Truman, *op. cit.*, Vol. 1, p. 15.

32 Stebbins, ed., *op. cit.*, p. 217.

33 Melvin Gurtov, *The First Vietnam Crisis* (New York: Columbia University Press, 1967), p. 32 (paperbound edition, 1968).

34 On Dien Bien Phu see more particularly Bernard Fall, *Hell in a very Small Place: the Siege of Dien Bien Phu* (Philadelphia: Lippincott, 1966). See also Jules Roy, *La Bataille de Dien Bien Phu* (Paris: René Julliard, 1963).

35 In a statement made by Secretary Dulles, September 3, 1953. Quoted in Gurtov, *op. cit.*, p. 32.

36 *Ibid.*, p. 57.

37 Devillers and Lacouture, *op. cit.*, p. 70 ff.

38 Gurtov, *op. cit.*, p. 95. Beale, *John Foster Dulles* (New York: Harper and Row, 1959), p. 207. J. R. Tournoux, *Secrets d'État* (Paris: Librairie Plon, 1960), pp. 462–3. Reliance upon atomic weapons is denied by Eisenhower, *op. cit.*, pp. 344 ff.

39 James Shepley, "How Dulles Averted War," *Life* (January 16, 1956), pp. 70 ff.

40 An account of this meeting is found in Chalmers H. Roberts, "The Day We Didn't Go to War," *The Reporter* (September 14, 1954), pp. 31–5.

41 Eisenhower, *op. cit.*, p. 347.

42 Speech made at Los Angeles, June 11, 1954. *Bulletin*, Vol. XXX, pp. 971–3.

43 Sherman Adams, *Firsthand Report* (New York: Harper and Row, 1961), p. 120 ff.

44 "What we are trying to do," said Dulles on May 11, 1954, "is to create a situation in Southeast Asia where the domino theory will not apply . . . to save all of Southeast Asia if it can be saved; if not to save essential parts of it." Stebbins, ed., *op. cit.*, p. 237.

45 Statement made July 23, 1954. *Ibid.*, p. 255. Following Dulles' departure, General Smith remained in Geneva as an American "observer."

46 See Pierre Rouanet, *Pierre Mendès-France au Pouvior, 1954–1955* (Paris: Robert Laffont, 1965), pp. 107 ff.

47 Stebbins, ed., *op. cit.*, p. 236.

48 *Ibid.*, p. 285.

49 Victor Bator, *Vietnam – a Diplomatic Tragedy* (New York: Oceana, 1965), p. 204.

50 Quoted by William Anderson and Wesley R. Fishel, "The Foreign Policy of Ngo Dinh Diem in Vietnam," in Wesley R. Fishel, ed., *Anatomy of a Conflict* (Ithaca, Ill.: F. E. Peacock, 1968), p. 206.

51 John F. Kennedy, "America's Stake in Vietnam," an address to the American Friends of Vietnam, September, 1956. Anderson and Fishel, *op. cit.*, p. 146.

52 Eisenhower, *op. cit.*, p. 347.

[53] State Department, *American Foreign Policy, 1950–1955: Basic Documents,* Vol. 1 (General Foreign Policy Series 117), p. 936.

[54] *Ibid.,* p. 937.

[55] Eisenhower, *op. cit.,* p. 373.

[56] *Ibid.,* p. 372.

[57] William Henderson, "South Vietnam Finds Itself," *Foreign Affairs* (January 1957), p. 288.

[58] Arthur Schlesinger, *A Thousand Days* (Boston: Houghton Mifflin, 1965), p. 540.

[59] In Kennedy's speech to the American Friends of Vietnam, *op. cit.,* pp. 144–5.

[60] See James C. Thompson, "How Could Vietnam Happen? An Autopsy," *Atlantic Monthly* (April 1968).

[61] Kahin and Lewis, *op. cit.,* p. 185.

[62] On America's problems in Laos, see, for example, Arthur J. Dommen, *Conflict in Laos: the Politics of Neutralization* (New York: Praeger, 1965).

[63] Theodore Sorensen, *Kennedy* (New York: Harper and Row, 1965), p. 644.

[64] Schlesinger, *op. cit.,* p. 163.

[65] *Ibid.,* p. 337.

[66] Sorensen, *op. cit.,* p. 644.

[67] Fall, *op. cit.* pp. 359 ff.

[68] Schlesinger, *op. cit.,* p. 545.

[69] Kahin, *op. cit.,* p. 185.

[70] For a plausible account of Kennedy's change of heart on Vietnam, see Kenneth O'Donnell, "LBJ and the Kennedys," *Life* (August 7, 1970), pp. 44–8.

[71] A penetrating study of the Gulf of Tonkin episode is provided by Joseph C. Goulden, *Truth is the First Casualty: The Gulf of Tonkin Affair — Illusion and Reality* (New York: Rand McNally, 1969).

[72] See Townsend Hoopes, *The Limits of Intervention* (New York: David McKay Company, 1969), p. 28. See also Tom Wicker, *JFK and LBJ: the Influence of Personality upon Politics* (Baltimore: Penguin Books, 1969), pp. 184–209.

[73] See, for instance, Dean Rusk's statement to the Senate Foreign Relations Committee, February 18, 1966. *Vietnam Hearings* (New York: Vintage Books, 1966), pp. 236–7.

[74] *Ibid.,* pp. 247–8.

[75] See, for example, David Mozingo, "Containment in Asia Reconsidered," *World Politics* (April, 1967), pp. 361–78.

[76] Leahy, *op. cit.,* p. 44.

[77] Eisenhower, *op. cit.,* p. 347.

[78] According to the columnist Arthur Krock, quoted in Walter Lafeber, *America, Russia and the Cold War* (New York: John Wiley, 1967), p. 228.

[79] Brogan, "The Illusion of American Omnipotence," *Harper's* (December, 1952).

[80] Quoted in William A. Williams, *The Tragedy of American Diplomacy* (New York: Delta Books, 1961), p. 82–3.

Chapter Nine: The Continuation of the Debate

[1] "U.S. Foreign Policy for the 1970's: A New Strategy for Peace," Report to Congress, February 18, 1970. *Department of State Bulletin*, Vol. LXII, p. 276 (hereafter cited as "State of the World Message").

[2] *Ibid.*, p. 294.

[3] The *New York Times*, April 8, 1971.

[4] See Earl Ravenal, "The Nixon Doctrine and Our Asian Commitments," *Foreign Affairs* (January 1971), pp. 201–17.

[5] "State of the World Message," *op. cit.*, p. 277.

[6] *Ibid.*, p. 276.

[7] The *New York Times*, April 30, 1971.

[8] "State of the World Message," *op. cit.*, pp. 298, 297.

[9] From columnist C. L. Sulzberger's interview with President Nixon, The *New York Times*, March 10, 1971.

[10] *Ibid.*

[11] The *New York Times*, November 4, 1969.

[12] *Ibid.*, March 10, 1971.

[13] *Ibid.*, February 26, 1971.

[14] "State of the World Message," *op. cit.*, p. 283.

[15] *Ibid.*, p. 284.

[16] Henry Kissinger, *The Troubled Partnership* (New York: McGraw-Hill, 1965), p. 225.

[17] "State of the World Message," *op. cit.*, p. 285.

[18] *Ibid.*, p. 286.

[19] *Ibid.*

[20] The *New York Times*, March 22, 1970.

[21] As quoted by columnist James Reston, The *New York Times*, May 17, 1970.

[22] George Liska, *Imperial America* (Baltimore: Johns Hopkins Press, 1967), p. 112.

[23] *Los Angeles Times*, June 30, 1971.

[24] Robert W. Tucker, *Nation or Empire?* (Baltimore: Johns Hopkins Press, 1968), p. 110.

[25] Liska, *op. cit.*, pp. 108–9.

Index